A STAGE FOR DEBATE

GERMAN AND EUROPEAN STUDIES

General Editor: Jennifer L. Jenkins

A Stage for Debate

The Political Significance of Vienna's Burgtheater, 1814–1867

MARTIN WAGNER

UNIVERSITY OF TORONTO PRESS
Toronto Buffalo London

Toronto Buffalo London
utorontopress.com

ISBN 978-1-4875-0955-2 (cloth)
ISBN 978-1-4875-0957-6 (EPUB)
ISBN 978-1-4875-0956-9 (PDF)

German and European Studies

Library and Archives Canada Cataloguing in Publication

Title: A stage for debate : the political significance of Vienna's Burgtheater, 1814–1867 / Martin Wagner.
Names: Wagner, Martin, 1983–, author.
Series: German and European studies ; 49.
Description: Series statement: German and European studies ; 49 | Includes bibliographical references and index.
Identifiers: Canadiana (print) 20230166296 | Canadiana (ebook) 20230166342 | ISBN 9781487509552 (cloth) | ISBN 9781487509576 (EPUB) | ISBN 9781487509569 (PDF)
Subjects: LCSH: Burgtheater (Vienna, Austria) – History – 19th century. | LCSH: Theater – Political aspects – Austria – Vienna – History – 19th century. | LCSH: Theater – Political aspects – Europe – History – 19th century.
Classification: LCC PN2616.V52 W34 2023 | DDC 792.09436/1309034 – dc23

Cover design: John Beadle
Cover image: Rudolf von Alt, "Der Michaels-Platz in Wien," c. 1860. GS_GBS3810, Theatermuseum, Wien.

The German and European Studies series is funded by the DAAD with funds from the German Federal Foreign Office.

DAAD Deutscher Akademischer Austauschdienst
German Academic Exchange Service

We wish to acknowledge the land on which the University of Toronto Press operates. This land is the traditional territory of the Wendat, the Anishnaabeg, the Haudenosaunee, the Métis, and the Mississaugas of the Credit First Nation.

This book has been published with the help of a grant from the Federation for the Humanities and Social Sciences, through the Awards to Scholarly Publications Program, using funds provided by the Social Sciences and Humanities Research Council of Canada.

University of Toronto Press acknowledges the financial support of the Government of Canada, the Canada Council for the Arts, and the Ontario Arts Council, an agency of the Government of Ontario, for its publishing activities.

Canada Council for the Arts
Conseil des Arts du Canada

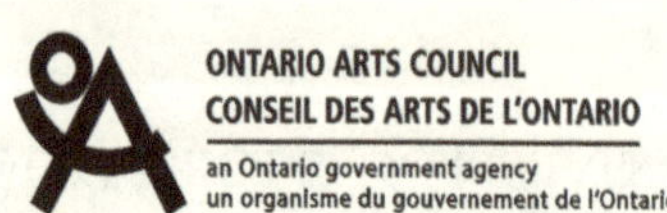

Funded by the Government of Canada
Financé par le gouvernement du Canada

This book is for Moses.

Contents

Illustrations

Acknowledgments

I am grateful for the supportive research environment at the University of Calgary and for everyone who was kind enough to talk with me about this book, especially Benjamin Brückner, Will Stovall, and Jennie Han. I am indebted to Annika Gilgen and Richard Slipp for the excellent research that they contributed. I am thankful, too, to Stephen Shapiro at the University of Toronto Press for his incisive feedback and for helping me along on the road to publication. The two anonymous reviewers of my manuscript provided very detailed and constructive feedback. Part of the work on this book was funded by an Insight Development Grant of the Social Sciences and Humanities Research Council of Canada (Grant Number 430-2017-00401).

A STAGE FOR DEBATE

Introduction: Reassessing the Mid-Nineteenth-Century Burgtheater

This book is about the most important cultural institution of the Austrian Empire, Vienna's court theatre. While its official name has varied over the course of its history, it is usually known as the *Burgtheater* ("palace theatre" or "castle theatre"), after the court residence's name, *Hofburg* (literally, "court castle"). Originally built inside the *Hofburg*, the Burgtheater, was, in the eighteenth century, moved to its own relatively modest building on the Michaelerplatz, next to the *Hofburg* (before moving in 1888 to the pompous neoclassical complex on Vienna's Ringstrasse that it still inhabits today). In the mid–nineteenth century, the Burgtheater was the most prestigious stage in German-speaking Europe, and there were, generally, few theatres elsewhere on the continent that would have been considered serious competition. Berlin's court theatre (Berliner Hoftheater) and Paris's Théâtre-Français would have been the most likely contenders. Writing in 1863, the successful novelist, playwright, and journalist Gustav Freytag deemed the Burgtheater to be the only German-language stage with a significant impact on the productions of other theatres: if a play was successful in the Burgtheater, it was sure to be successful elsewhere as well.[1]

The Burgtheater in Contemporary Scholarship

In the nineteenth century, countless articles and books were published that chronicled all that passed on Vienna's main stage, from the content of newly introduced plays to the private lives of the actors, playwrights, and theatre directors. But theatre historians and literary critics of the twentieth and twenty-first centuries paid, relatively speaking, less attention to this eminent institution, treating the Burgtheater instead mainly as part of larger investigations into Vienna's exceptionally rich and diverse theatre history.[2] This is all the more true for

English-language scholarship, in which German-language theatres have generally received scant attention. This neglect is striking considering how extensively German literature in general has been discussed in the Anglosphere.

It took until 1996 for the first English-language monograph on Viennese theatre history to appear. W.E. Yates's seminal *Theatre in Vienna: A Critical History, 1776–1995* finally acknowledged Vienna's central status as a European city of theatre, comparable in this respect only to Paris or London. In the years since, a few scholars have followed up on Yates's remarkable survey with more detailed investigations into the Burgtheater's history. Dorothea Link focused in *The National Court Theatre in Mozart's Vienna* (1998) on the relatively brief and early period from 1783 to 1792.[3] More recently, in *The Burgtheater and Austrian Identity* (2007), Robert Pyrah turned to the Burgtheater's support of nationalist politics during the First Republic (1918–34) and Austro-Fascism (1934–8). Strikingly, these monographs omit the very period in which the Burgtheater enjoyed its greatest renown as the leading German-language stage, i.e., the mid–nineteenth century.[4] It is this gap, more precisely the period from 1814 to 1867, marked by the four consecutive directorships of Joseph Schreyvogel (in office, 1814–32), Johann Ludwig von Deinhardstein (1832–41), Franz Ignaz von Holbein (1841–9), and Heinrich Laube (1849–67), that the present study seeks to close.[5]

The neglect of the mid-nineteenth-century Burgtheater is even more striking when one turns to recent English-language books on Austrian and Habsburg history more broadly. Here, the Burgtheater often receives little more than a passing mention.[6] The theatre that was established by the enlightened emperor Joseph II in 1776, that attracted generations of emperors as regular visitors (often pleased and sometimes outraged), and that is still alive and well today, is absent from much of the latest English-language scholarship on Habsburg Austria.

In the few German-language accounts that twentieth-century critics have produced of the nineteenth-century Burgtheater, this institution is typically dismissed as either apolitical or hopelessly conservative – in either case, as a stage for good acting, but light entertainment, entirely out of touch with the decisive social and political innovations of the period. The harshest polemic of this type can be found in a book that the former Burgtheater director Gerhard Klingenberg published in 2003 on the history of that stage.[7] In *Das gefesselte Burgtheater* (*The Burgtheater in Chains*), Klingenberg describes the Burgtheater as "a conservative and reactionary theatre that was hostile to literature" ("ein literaturfeindliches Theater des Konservatismus und der Reaktion"; 19).[8] By "conservative," Klingenberg means "the avoidance of socially relevant topics" ("das Meiden gesellschaftlich relevanter Themen"; 19).

The Scope of Political Discourse in the Mid-Nineteenth-Century Burgtheater

The established image of the Burgtheater as a bastion of mindless conservatism is misleading. As I argue in this book, the Burgtheater was a crucial stage for debates on key topics of Austrian liberalism. If we want to understand the range of positions discussed in Austria on the questions of individual liberty, women's role in society, or the meaning of German nationalism, the repertoire of the Burgtheater is a key resource. The core of this book (chs. 4–6) is devoted to a detailed analysis of each of these three topics in order to explore the diversity of positions that the different plays brought to the Burgtheater stage.

Instead of talking about the Burgtheater (or Viennese theatre in general, for that matter), historians of nineteenth-century Austrian liberalism often speak about the coffeehouses, the clubs, and newspapers as important venues for political debate.[9] All these are, to be sure, significant sites for the history of Austrian liberalism. Coffeehouses were important as meeting places, and so were, incidentally, Vienna's beautiful surroundings in which artists, journalists, and intellectuals gathered for long walks and excursions, which sometimes extended over several days. But the importance of coffeehouses and outings in the mountains is not an argument against the significance of the Burgtheater. The main (male) Burgtheater playwrights of the period, notably Franz Grillparzer (1791–1872) and Eduard von Bauernfeld (1802–90), were a part of these clubs, circles, and social activities.[10] They ate, drank, talked, and walked regularly with the leading liberals of the period, both from within Austria and from the German states to the north.[11]

There is no categorical divide between the leading liberal circles and the leading contributors to the Burgtheater – at best there is a continuum, for one would certainly be hard-pressed to find any downright radical voices among the Burgtheater writers and directors. More importantly, throughout the decades, Burgtheater playwrights brought to their stage whatever was possible to produce under the restrictions that the Austrian theatres doubtlessly faced. Indeed, these playwrights tended to err on the side of audacity and where their audacity was not rewarded, they dealt with confrontations with the censors. In other words, self-censorship, albeit important, did not as a rule go so far as to preclude any and all meaningful free speech.[12]

The Burgtheater served as an important platform for contemporary cultural and political debates, but, to be clear, it was not a place for radical voices. In contrast to other European theatres, the Burgtheater also did not become the site of any major unrest. The history of nineteenth-century European and North American theatre includes a number of rather turbulent incidents in which the actions and actors on stage incited violent outbursts.[13] The production of Victor Hugo's *Hernani* at the Théâtre-Français in 1830, which broke with the carefully guarded conventions of French stage practice, caused a clash between liberal critics and conservative defenders of these conventions. Six years later, the outrage over Nikolai Gogol's social-critical comedy *The Government Inspector* (1836) forced, upon its production in St. Petersburg, the author into exile for over a decade. Thirteen years after that, in 1849, the so-called Astor Place Riots in New York saw violent outbursts between the supporters of two leading actors, Edwin Forrest and William Charles Macready, which culminated in the intervention of the army and the death of thirty-one rioters.

One simple fact that these and other incidents have in common is that they did not happen in Vienna and that they certainly did not happen in the Burgtheater. Hugo's *Hernani*, incidentally, was banned in Austria in 1830 ("Komparatistik Wien Zensurdatenbank") and had to wait until 1879 to be performed in the Burgtheater (Rub 101).[14] Gogol's *Government Inspector* had its premiere in the Burgtheater only in 1887 (Rub 305).

Under the restrictions in place in Vienna, not all was possible, and the Burgtheater usually abided by the laws and expectations imposed on it. That being said, there were still important cases in which the censors did let pass a play that subsequently showed its ability to cause affront and controversy. Among the better-known of these moments of controversy is the 1838 production of Grillparzer's only comedy, *Weh dem, der lügt* (*Woe to the Liar*). Much to the indignation of some parts of the audience (and very likely to the great pleasure of others), the play's hero is a witty and irreverent kitchen helper (*Küchenjunge*) (Paoli, *Grillparzer und seine Werke* 44–5). While servant-figures were popular as sidekicks in the period, they did not normally occupy the main role.[15] What is more, at one point in the play, the privilege of nobility is called into question in view of all humanity's descendance from God. At that assertion, the aristocrats in the Burgtheater's audience are reported to have leaned out of their boxes to hiss.[16]

As the example of Grillparzer's *Weh dem, der lügt* shows, plays in the Burgtheater did raise socially and politically relevant questions and received for that very fact strong emotional responses from the audience. This is not to say that Grillparzer's play caused a real scandal to the public just because some of the spectators were hissing. For the most part, Austrians appear to have remembered *Weh dem, der lügt* simply as a mediocre production of a much anticipated and yet largely disappointing comedy by their greatest living playwright.[17] More importantly, audible expressions of displeasure were unusual, but not unheard of in the Burgtheater. Finally, the Burgtheater was, contrary to what the frequent attacks on it as an institution of the aristocracy may suggest, well known for the heterogeneity of its audience in terms of social standing, political affiliations, and literary tastes. In other words, the tensions caused by Grillparzer's play were nothing completely new to the Burgtheater, and because they never exceeded a certain level of emotional intensity or violence, they were not seen as a major disturbance.

To avoid a misunderstanding in this presentation of the Burgtheater as a stage for political debate, it should be stated that there were topics that simply could not be discussed in any form on any of the Viennese stages of the mid–nineteenth century. This applies mostly to the role of the Catholic Church and Christian faith in the empire as well as to the legitimacy of the Habsburg rulers, but, with qualifications, also to sexual morality. In general, the debates were limited by the constraints of Austria's notoriously strict censorship system (which was even stricter for the theatre than for the printed page) and, in the case of the Burgtheater, the direct oversight of the Habsburg family.

It is easy to come by entertaining anecdotes of the censorship system's awkward attempts to cut any and all political allusions out of the performed plays, in the Burgtheater as well as in Vienna's other theatres. Already in the late 1780s, before the introduction of the stricter censorship measures of the following decades, the verse "Long live freedom" ("Es lebe die Freiheit") in Mozart's opera *Don Giovanni* had to be substituted with "Long live jollity" ("Es lebe die Fröhlichkeit") (Rady 221–2). More broadly, the infamous 1795 memorandum of Vienna's long-serving theatre censor Karl Hägelin (in office, 1770–1805), which remained an unofficial reference for Austrian theatre censorship throughout the first half of the nineteenth century, is full of what appear at least by today's standards as almost unbelievably stringent moral and political rules (Bachleitner, *Die literarische Zensur* 244). As Hägelin remarks, it is the responsibility of the censors to ensure that two people who are in love never leave the stage together ("daß nie zwei verliebte Personen miteinander vom Theater abtreten"; Lothar 41). More importantly, no Austrian uniform was allowed to be worn on stage; the words "Enlightenment" ("Aufklärung"), "freedom" ("Freiheit"), or "equality"

("Gleichheit") were not to be uttered; nor could any words be used that signified a church office (42–3).

Despite these and many other restrictions, there was, as the following chapters show, much that *could* be said. More important still, for each topic presented by the playwrights, the rich and diverse repertoire offered a variety of different viewpoints. Whoever frequented the Burgtheater on a regular (that is, weekly or even daily) basis – and these frequent visitors still formed an important part of the audience in the mid-nineteenth century – was confronted with a multitude of different positions. Moreover, looking around themselves in the audience, spectators witnessed a multitude of different reactions to those various opinions presented on stage. The high nobility in the boxes reacted differently from the educated members of the upper middle class seated in the parterre, and these spectators were again different from the occasional visitors in the cheap seats high up in the fourth gallery. Through the production of its heterogenous repertoire for a diverse audience, the Burgtheater incited debate – and itself already performed a debate.

The notion mentioned earlier of the Burgtheater as either a conservative or apolitical stage is not the invention of twentieth-century critics. Already in 1848, the liberal Austrian journalist Siegmund Engländer called the Burgtheater "an institution for the private entertainment of the well-fed aristocracy" ("eine Privatunterhaltungsanstalt einer satten Aristokratie"; Engländer 195). This verdict appears to fit squarely with the kind of dismissal that we know from Klingenberg's 2003 book, *Das gefesselte Burgtheater*. However, as always, context matters. Importantly, in his verdict Engländer referred to the Burgtheater from before the revolution of March 1848, which led to a short period of greater freedom for the theatres in Vienna. Now, after the premiere of Friedrich Hebbel's bourgeois tragedy *Maria Magdalena* in May 1848, with its daring portrayal of middle-class immorality, Engländer thought that the limitations of the old Burgtheater had been overcome. In other words, the harsh attack on the Burgtheater is used as a means to explain the Burgtheater's current greatness (as well as the greatness of Hebbel, whose close companion Engländer became soon afterwards).[18]

Engländer polemically exaggerates the contrast between the Burgtheater before and after 1848. If the Burgtheater was so very quick to respond to the newfound liberties after the temporary abolishment of theatre censorship in March 1848, this was because it had, for decades, fostered a moderate liberal discourse and because it had many liberals among its own ranks. Strikingly, one of the central agents in the abolishment of censorship, Eduard von Bauernfeld, was at the same time the most successful Burgtheater playwright in the years leading up to the revolution. Aristocrats, with their typically more conservative leanings, remained only a (strong) minority in the audience, although heavily over-represented when compared to their overall share of the population. Already at the beginning of the period here under investigation, they constituted only about a third of the entire audience, and their share decreased further over the course of the nineteenth century (Stauss 15). In addition, the Burgtheater was always an important attraction even for its politically progressive critics. When the Young German Karl Gutzkow visited Vienna in 1845, for instance, one of his first walks was to the Burgtheater: "Here was my asylum," Gutzkow writes emphatically, "here I could find myself; here was a kind of home" ("Hier war mein Asyl, hier konnte ich mich sammeln, hier war eine Art Heimath"; Gutzkow 154).

Situating the Mid-Nineteenth Century in the Larger History of the Burgtheater

In the decades before and after the 1848 revolution, the Burgtheater was an important site of debate for Austrian liberals' concerns. While this book focuses on this period, it is useful to recall that the Burgtheater had been in operation for much longer. Exactly when the Burgtheater was founded is a matter of controversy, and the conventionally stated date of 1776 can be used only with some caveats. Already in the mid-seventeenth century, there was a space devoted to theatre within the confines of the Habsburg palace (Yates, *Theatre in Vienna* 5–6). These rooms, however, were transformed into ballrooms in the 1740s (6). Then, in March 1741, the Enlightenment empress Maria Theresia established a theatre next to the Habsburg palace – it was called "Königliches Theater nächst der Burg" ("Royal Theatre Next to the Palace"). This location, which had previously served as a tennis court, remained, through various extensions and renovations, the site of the Burgtheater until the opening of the ostentatious new Burgtheater on the Ringstrasse in 1888 (the same building that is still being used today).

Maria Theresia had no real interest in theatre. She was highly sceptical about the moral value of the stage and was unwilling to devote much funding to the Burgtheater. Indeed, she did not even visit it until February 1742, almost a year after its foundation in the new location (Lothar 7). For the next several decades, the Burgtheater lingered, staging French drama (in the original French) for the high aristocracy as well as popular Viennese comedy for the rest of the population. Financially, the theatre never became really viable. French drama especially had a limited audience. Money began flowing in only in 1759, when the theatre began to function also as a gambling hall, offering faro tables as alternative entertainment during the performances (16). As a cultural institution, the Burgtheater was negligible during this time. When the influential German Enlightenment bookseller and critic Friedrich Nicolai visited Vienna in 1761, he contemptuously noted that Vienna had reached a state of cultural development that Saxony had attained three decades earlier (16).

Matters changed in 1776, when Maria Theresia's son Joseph II established the Burgtheater as a "Nationaltheater nächst der k.k. Burg" ("National Theatre Next to the Royal and Imperial Palace"), and it is this year that is conventionally remembered for the foundation of the Burgtheater. The Enlightenment idea of a *Nationaltheater* is most commonly associated with the short-lived Hamburger Nationaltheater (1767–9), to which Gotthold Ephraim Lessing, another leading figure of the German Enlightenment, had crucially contributed. But it was in Vienna that the *Nationaltheater* became linked to a much bigger and much longer lasting institution.

The idea of *Nationaltheater* continued to reverberate for at least the next century in German theatre discourse, although its meaning and connotations evolved during that period. Gradually, the idea of "national" unification outweighed the idea of Enlightenment education that was originally associated with the term.[19] In the history of the Burgtheater itself, the term "national" remained contested territory. It was given up in 1792 under Joseph II's successor Leopold as part of the reactionary backlash against the revolution in France.[20] More than half a century later, the term "national" was reintroduced during the revolutionary uproar of 1848, but abandoned again in 1852, when Emperor Franz Joseph sought to roll back the achievements of the revolutionaries.

Joseph II took much greater interest in the Burgtheater than did his mother and fostered a more ambitious repertoire. Until Joseph II's death in 1790, the Burgtheater introduced several plays by Shakespeare and Lessing. In 1787, it performed a play by Friedrich Schiller (*Die Verschwörung des Fiesco zu Genua*; Rub 19) and, five years before that, in 1782, it even brought Greek antiquity back on stage with Euripides's *The Trojan Women* (Rub 13). Running only three performances, Euripides's play was not a success, and nothing of the sort was attempted again for a long time. It took until the 1880s before Ancient Greek playwrights were given another chance (and even then, success was very limited). But the performance of the Greeks in 1782 is still noteworthy. Even at the court theatre in Weimar, where Goethe and Schiller had been great advocates of Greek literature, the Greeks were not well represented before the last third of the nineteenth century. In Weimar, Sophocles's

Antigone saw five performances between 1809 and 1813; Euripides was not performed until 1869, and then only in a selection of scenes that Schiller had translated; Aeschylus was first performed in 1882.[21]

The decades after Joseph's II's death, marked first by repressive measures against the influx of revolutionary sentiments from France to Austria and then by the wars against Napoleon, are generally seen as a period of decline for the Burgtheater. With the end of the Napoleonic wars, the Burgtheater flourished again and became the unquestioned leader among German-language theatres, boasting a broad repertoire and a widely admired ensemble. Over the following roughly fifty years, until the end of Heinrich Laube's directorship, the Burgtheater enjoyed the greatest renown in all of its history. During this period, from 1814 to 1867, roughly one thousand new plays were introduced under four different theatre directors (their names are, again, Schreyvogel, Deinhardstein, Holbein, and Laube). Of these leading personalities, especially Joseph Schreyvogel's improvement of the repertoire and his successful hiring of outstanding actors are thought to have helped the Burgtheater attain its high status (even Klingenberg, in his diatribe against the Burgtheater, is forced to make an exception for Schreyvogel). In the 1820s, during the years of Schreyvogel's tenure, the Burgtheater passed Berlin's court theatre as the most prestigious German-language stage (Laube, *Das Burgtheater* 125–6). And while the Burgtheater had less luck with its subsequent two directors (Deinhardstein and Holbein), it was thriving again under Laube's leadership in the 1850s and 1860s.

When Laube was let go in 1867, he was quick to point out the Burgtheater's inevitable decline. The great days of the Burgtheater, he warned, had come to an end. We would probably do well to take Laube's assertions with a grain of salt. After all, Laube did not leave on good terms with the court office overseeing the Burgtheater. Moreover, contrary to Laube's warning, some of his nineteenth-century successors did achieve considerable things during their time in office: Franz von Dingelstedt (1870–81) expanded the repertoire by introducing hitherto neglected plays by the recently deceased Franz Grillparzer and Friedrich Hebbel, alongside naturalist plays by Henrik Ibsen (Klingenberg 65). Some years later, Max Burckhard (1890–8) reached a socially more diverse audience by offering shows at lower entrance fees (75).

Nevertheless, Laube's gloomy statements do resonate with the broader public perception of the Burgtheater around 1870 (Bauernfeld, *Gesammelte Schriften* vol. 12). This was not only the fault of the subsequent directors or even of the court offices, but also of a sense of general decline of Viennese theatre. The 1870s and 1880s were experienced as a period of relative dearth of dramatic talent, and, ultimately, of a decline of literature as the main magnet of talent. As Eduard von Bauernfeld, the Burgtheater's leading comic playwright of the mid–nineteenth century, wistfully writes in his 1873 autobiography: "Nowadays, genius shows itself almost exclusively in the natural sciences" ("Das neue Geniale zeigt sich aber zumeist nur in der Naturwissenschaft"; Bauernfeld, *Gesammelte Schriften* 12: 194).

In hindsight, Laube's and Bauernfeld's pessimism seems, of course, vastly exaggerated. Both in the time around 1900 (with Hugo von Hofmannsthal, Ödön von Horváth, and Arthur Schnitzler), and in the final decades of the twentieth century (with Thomas Bernhard, Peter Handke, and Elfriede Jelinek), Vienna and Austria became once more a crucial centre of theatre, producing many of the most important German-language playwrights. And yet Bauernfeld is right in his assertion that an important form of Viennese theatre disappeared in the late 1860s and early 1870s, when some of the Burgtheater's most renowned playwrights – both Grillparzer and the today largely forgotten Friedrich Halm (1806–71) – were dying. The fact that Austria itself was, after its defeat in the battle against Prussia at Königgrätz in 1866, evidently in decline as well further contributed to this sense of the end of an era. Writing in 1895, at the grave of the important Burgtheater translator Betty Paoli, the Burgtheater actor Josef Lewinsky yearningly looked back at the era of "Alt-Österreich" ("Old Austria"), which he dates from 1806 to 1866 and which he largely associates with the presence of Franz Grillparzer (Lewinsky 6).

The sense of loss that Laube, Bauernfeld, and Lewinsky felt might have been all the more genuine as they were fully aware that the mid-nineteenth-century blossoming whose end they regretted had anyway only been the blossoming of an epigonic age. "We are all epigones" ("Wir sind alle Epigonen"), Bauernfeld sighs in his autobiography (*Gesammelte Schriften* 12: 194). Mid-nineteenth-century Burgtheater playwrights understood that they were working after Goethe and Schiller (and, to a lesser extent, also after Lessing and Kleist). If their drama had any value, it was because it mastered the canon of Weimar classicism (and thereby helped establish that canon) and because it was able to transform this canon into a more digestible form and idiom, relevant to the tastes and concerns of mid-nineteenth-century audiences.

In modern times, we are prone to look down on the epigones, and the oblivion into which many Burgtheater playwrights have fallen is a clear testimony to that dismissal. Bauernfeld himself would surely have realized the limitations of the epigones, but he saw in epigonic art also an important form of preservation. He followed up his sigh that "we are all epigones," with the call: "Let us preserve whatever is possible to preserve" ("Erhalten wir, was zu erhalten möglich ist"; Bauernfeld, *Gesammelte Schriften* 12: 194). As the talented epigones vanished, Goethe and Schiller seemed to go down with them, and the new art that might come to replace them was not yet on the horizon.

The Burgtheater's Political Context

The years between 1814 and 1867 are not only important in Vienna's theatre history, but also in Austria's political history. During these fifty-some years, the Habsburg monarchy held a crucial position as an independent power in the centre of Europe: it was a potent force between France in the west and Russia in the east. To be sure, this was a period of many trials and tribulations, and it was ultimately a period in which this empire slowly but surely disintegrated. And yet the ultimate downfall that would follow this beginning of decline was, even in 1867, still half a century away.

Although the Habsburgs had given up their centuries-long leadership of the Holy Roman Empire in 1806 (which had led to the immediate collapse of that empire), they had successfully re-established their powers as emperors of Austria around the same time. The title Emperor of Austria had been adopted by Franz I in 1804 (who, at that time, was still reigning as Franz II, Emperor of the Holy Roman Empire) in response to Napoleon's coronation as Emperor of France. But it was really only after Napoleon's defeat in 1813 and the re-partitioning of Europe at the Congress of Vienna in the following two years that the Austrian emperor, thanks not least to his top diplomat, Klemens von Metternich, was able to assert his power and regain much of his traditional territories. This power was to last for the rest of Franz's reign (until 1835). Under Franz's two successors, Austria remained a crucial power, although both saw its influence decline. While Ferdinand I (1835–48) could maintain the territorial integrity of the empire, the Hungarian struggle for independence gained momentum during his time on the throne. And when, in 1848, revolution swept across the continent and reached Austria, he was seen as lacking in strength, and he needed to cede the throne to his nephew, Franz Joseph (r. 1848–1916), who became Austria's penultimate emperor.

Franz Joseph, only eighteen years old at the time of his coronation, reigned for two thirds of a century and became thus one of Europe's longest serving monarchs of all time. He is sometimes credited as one of the main reasons why the Habsburg Empire did not collapse even earlier than it did (in 1918). His long and stabilizing presence on the throne notwithstanding, the signs of decline were obvious, and Franz Joseph suffered many defeats during his reign. In 1859, the Habsburgs lost control over Lombardy. In 1866, Franz Joseph's brother Maximilian's brief stint as Emperor of Mexico ended with Maximilian's execution. In that same year, Franz Joseph himself saw his armies lose at Königgrätz a decisive battle against Prussia, whose rise as the decisive German power had become unstoppable. In 1867, Franz Joseph had to give Hungary special status as a semi-independent kingdom. Four years later, in 1871, the Prussian king was with his army in Versailles, and a united German Empire was proclaimed, in which Austria and the Habsburgs played no part.

However, even though in retrospect we are inclined to see much of the nineteenth century as a history of Habsburg decline, the half-century between 1814 and 1867 was, except for the revolutionary year of 1848, still a period of relative stability in which Austrians found themselves, independent from the recently abolished Holy Roman Empire, under the sway of the – more or less – unquestioned rule of the Habsburg family.

Under this relatively stable rule of the Habsburgs, Austrian liberalism struggled to gain power, but eventually succeeded. The initial years after the defeat of Napoleon were relatively quiet years, and it was only after France's revolution of July 1830 that liberals gained ground in Austria and increasingly voiced their frustration over the repressive censorship system and the lack of a constitution. With the revolution of March 1848, both concerns were answered – or at least as much was promised. In truth, censorship was re-established already in 1850, and the constitution that Franz Joseph eventually passed in 1851 kept most power in the hands of the absolute sovereign. The following decades were marked by long waiting and slow progress, until in 1867, Austria received its first modern constitution that deserved that name and that included a comprehensive catalogue of individual liberties alongside the guarantee of freedom of the press.[22] In view of his recent military defeats, Franz Joseph was no longer able to hold on to his position as absolutist ruler.[23]

What this brief survey of Austrian history is meant to show is that while the historical end point of the present study in 1867 is primarily defined by the end of Heinrich Laube's appointment as director of the Burgtheater as well by the death of a generation of defining Burgtheater playwrights, this year also marks the end of a political era in Austria. With the year 1867, the political conditions under which theatre and liberalism operated fundamentally changed.

A Note on Method

This book not only takes a closer look at the mid-nineteenth-century Burgtheater than scholars have done so far, but it also takes a methodologically new route. It supplements traditional theatre studies (that is, the study of institutions and performance practices) with a deeper commitment to the dramatic texts that were performed in the Burgtheater. Through a close textual analysis of many of the most successful dramatic works of the period, I seek to map out the implicit debates that emerged from the Burgtheater repertoire. The essential category that informs this analysis is thus the theatre's repertoire: the collection of texts that a theatre ensemble has at its disposal at a given point. The selection of the repertoire is the product of specific institutional, cultural, and political practices that are the subject of theatre studies, but the repertoire's content reveals its rich meaning only to the patient study of literary criticism.

Studies of the Burgtheater so far have tended to prioritize productions of canonical, intellectually ambitious plays over lighter entertainment and have thus failed to seriously engage a significant portion of the repertoire.[24] Breaking with that pattern, this book provides a detailed assessment of the social and political commentary inherent in the often-dismissed entertainment repertoire, and it reads these plays alongside plays by Shakespeare, Schiller, Goethe, and Grillparzer. Importantly, the conventional disregard for lighter playwrights has also led to a neglect of nineteenth-century female playwrights in Burgtheater studies because the plays by women were almost exclusively in the popular genres. For playwrights like Johanna Franul von Weißenthurn (1772–1847),[25] Amalie von Sachsen (1794–1870), or Charlotte Birch-Pfeiffer (1800–68), writing entertainment was not simply a matter of choice. Instead, their writing in the genres of entertainment was also a product of the narrow limits set on female authorship in the mid–nineteenth century. It is illuminating to study the ways in which these female playwrights productively debated questions of social relevance in their works while conforming, at least in large part, to the generic and normative expectations of the time.[26] And it is especially illuminating to study women's productions alongside those of the popular male playwrights of the period, who often faced similar, albeit not identical, expectations both in terms of moral and political conformity and in terms of the entertainment function of their plays.

While close readings of individual plays feature prominently in my approach, it is especially the comparison between different plays that reveal the extent to which the Burgtheater served to foster debate. In this book, I read repertoire not only as an assembly of independent plays, but as one large text itself with internal repetitions, resonances, and variations. For the Burgtheater's actors as well as for its regular audience members, the repertoire was an ever-present background that influenced the meaning of each individual new production. Plays whose social and political content may appear relatively unremarkable when read in isolation become, through their divergence from other plays in the repertoire, meaningful as contributors to ongoing debates in Viennese and Austrian society. One of the crucial ideas underlying the present study is that the variety between the positions of different plays is a stronger indicator of a theatre's contribution to debate than the radicality of any single play.

The Chapters of This Book

In the first chapter of this book, I present a historically grounded essay on method in which I develop my guiding concept of repertoire as a polyphonous text, building here on Mikhail Bakhtin's notion of polyphony. Bakhtin, of course, developed the concept of polyphony with respect to the modern novel, specifically the novels of Dostoevsky. Yet the concept of polyphony can be usefully applied to the extended corpus of a theatre repertoire. Admittedly, the nineteenth century did not have a clear awareness of the importance of theatre as a space for polyphony. As much as theatre shaped the everyday life of many citizens of the middle and upper classes in the nineteenth century, and as much as theatres of the period were characterized by large and heterogenous repertoires, there were few attempts to think about the significance of theatre in terms beyond the impact of an individual play. What is more, there is also no evidence that those responsible for the repertoire of the Burgtheater intended their stage to be a platform for a debate of diverse standpoints; to the extent that variety was discussed, this was with respect to genre, not the political content of the plays. In other words, for the nineteenth-century Burgtheater, repertoire polyphony is to be understood as a consistent *effect*, but not as the *intended product* of the structures at work in and around that theatre.

Before applying the concept of repertoire polyphony to key discourses of nineteenth-century liberalism in the remaining chapters of this book, the second and third chapters provide an overview of the repertoire of the Burgtheater between 1814 and 1867. In chapter 2, I address fundamental questions concerning the process by which plays were included and retained in the repertoire, and I shed light on the complex distribution of agency across such diverse bodies as theatre directors and actors, the court and the censorship office, the critics, and the audience. In chapter 3, I look at the repertoire itself to analyse important trends in terms of its international scope, its negotiation of genre, and its navigation of the competing demands for entertainment and education.

Each of the remaining three chapters of this book applies the concept of repertoire polyphony to one prominent nineteenth-century social or political debate. Chapter 4 focuses on discussions of freedom and obedience. Chapter 5 is devoted to debates over women's role in society. Chapter 6 explores the discussion of national identity in the Burgtheater. In each case, the emphasis is on the relative range of positions that we see represented in the Burgtheater's repertoire concerning the respective topic. The conclusion, finally, outlines how this present book can serve as a case study for future work in four distinct areas: the broader history of the Burgtheater; the history of Austrian liberalism; a comparative study of European theatre repertoires; and the study of the politics of art.

Each chapter presents its own argument and can be read as an independent essay. That said, the main goal of this monograph is to show the Burgtheater as the stage of rich and varied debates, and just how far this variety reached – and where its limits were – will become much clearer to those who peruse the entire book. What is more, the three topics that constitute the subjects of chapters 4, 5, and 6 are importantly interconnected. The general understanding of freedom and obedience (ch. 4) is reflected in the portrayal of women's agency (ch. 5) and, to some extent, also in the way in which nineteenth-century playwrights thought about the relation between individual and nation (ch. 6). Finally, a reader of the entire book will become better acquainted with the ways in which key playwrights in the Burgtheater's history contributed to a range of important contemporary debates. First and foremost among these playwrights is the liberal Eduard von Bauernfeld, whose works figure prominently in each of the three final chapters of this book. While a fuller reassessment of Bauernfeld's significance for the cultural and political history of nineteenth-century Austria remains long overdue, the present study can nevertheless highlight some central features of Bauernfeld's writing, thought, and political activism.

1 What Makes a Theatre Politically Significant?

In the long nineteenth century, literature enjoyed greater significance in Europe than ever before or after. In German-speaking Europe especially, literacy rates rose to a degree that the majority of the population – and by the end of the century even the vast majority – could read. Printing and paper production equally made advances that allowed the quicker and wider production of texts. Public and private libraries as well as the newly emerging popular genres (detective fiction, the adventure novel, science fiction, etc.) brought literature into more and more households. Even though many people remained excluded from the reading and writing of literary works,[1] literature had become a mass medium in ways that it could not have been in earlier times and in which it has never been again since the rise of the competing media of radio, film, television, and beyond.

While the special status that literature enjoyed in the nineteenth century is well known, it is less often acknowledged just how unusually important drama and theatre were in German lands in the long nineteenth century. This relative neglect of the nineteenth century in the European history of theatre has perhaps to do with the fact that other episodes, including the theatre of Ancient Greece and of Elizabethan England, stand out even more prominently than does the German nineteenth century. In Ancient Greece, theatres had attracted at least (and perhaps not only) the male and free citizens[2] in astonishing numbers: the theatre in Epidaurus held fourteen thousand spectators; the theatre in Ephesus twenty-four thousand (Pfister 42). In Elizabethan London, theatres were not as large as those in Greece – Shakespeare's Globe Theatre accommodated "only" two thousand spectators – but they remained hugely important sites where people from almost all walks of life could gather: men as well as women, and people from the lowest ranks up to the high nobility, leaving excluded only some strict Puritans who shunned stage performances (56).

German and Austrian theatre of the long nineteenth century can compete neither with the size of the Greek amphitheatres nor with the inclusivity of the Elizabethan stage. But if one narrows the perspective from the European continent to the German-speaking countries alone, the nineteenth century does become very important and perhaps without parallel in its sustained productivity and societal reach.[3] In Germany, where, compared to other large European countries, the theatre had long been marginalized to local courts, Latin schools, and wandering troupes, the mid to late eighteenth century brought about tremendous change, effected by the productive collaboration of theatre directors, actors, critics, and writers. In the generations of Friederike Caroline Neuber and Johann Christoph Gottsched, Gotthold Ephraim Lessing and Conrad Ekhof, German drama and theatre were progressing at a higher pace than ever before, and German playwrights were at the forefront of innovation in Europe (Holland and Patterson). They had adopted the new bourgeois tragedy from England as well as the serious comedy from France, while also developing, in the *Sturm und Drang* ("storm and stress"), a distinctly new form of playwriting. While much of this literary innovation belongs to the mid to late eighteenth century, it was the nineteenth century that served to fully canonize the works from Lessing to Goethe, Schiller, and Kleist, and that produced a vast and hugely popular middlebrow literature in imitation of the classics. Additionally, nineteenth century theatre was able to benefit from a number of newly created stages of the late eighteenth century, so that there were now permanent stages on which to perform works by the classics alongside more recent popular drama.

In Vienna, the long nineteenth century of the theatre began in 1776. In this year, Joseph II established the Burgtheater as *Nationaltheater*, and he declared the so-called *Spektakelfreiheit* (literally, "freedom of spectacle"), which allowed the creation of new theatres in and outside Vienna (pending police approval). Until that year, the production of theatrical performances had been the exclusive right of the two court theatres (the Burgtheater as well as the Kärntnertortheater, the latter of which subsequently became the opera house). The newly declared freedom led to the foundation of several commercial theatres in the city that shaped Vienna's theatre history for the nineteenth century in important ways. Most notable among these new foundations were the Theater in der Leopoldstadt (est. 1781), the Theater in der Josefstadt (est. 1790), and the Theater an der Wien (est. 1801). The first two of these theatres were roughly similar to the Burgtheater in size; the Theater an der Wien was noticeably larger. While the Burgtheater could accommodate an audience of about 1,300 people, the Theater in der Josefstadt and Theater in der Leopoldstadt each had room for about one thousand people. The Theater an der Wien fit two thousand people.

These new theatre foundations remained for a long time the only ones in Vienna, and the rapid population growth in Vienna in the nineteenth century was not matched by a simultaneous growth in the total number of theatre seats, let alone those in the Burgtheater, which stayed more or less stable.[4] The story of theatre in nineteenth-century Vienna is not one in which the stage grew to greater and greater importance. But it is a story about how the artistic and institutional achievements of the late eighteenth century were retained and varied with unparalleled tenacity through several consecutive generations of playwrights, theatre practitioners, and spectators.

Moving beyond the mere assertion of the significant presence of theatre in the nineteenth century, this chapter analyses contemporary playwrights' and theatre practitioners' assumptions about theatre (that is, about both drama and performance) that supported the importance of the stage. Moreover, I ask to what extent we, today, in assessing nineteenth-century theatre's importance can rely on the explicit statements by writers and thinkers from that period. For as it turns out, the nineteenth century remained to a surprising degree unable to theorize the importance of its own theatrical practice, which it held so dearly.

By and large, writers thought about theatre with respect to the impact of individual plays on the audience, and they failed to consider the ways in which the newly established permanent theatres with their very large repertoires – in the case of the Burgtheater, there were close to 150 plays in any given year[5] – provided a space for a remarkably heterogenous debate. What made the theatres socially and politically relevant was, arguably, not the individual plays, but the diversity of views assembled across the various plays in the repertoire.

With this emphasis on the diversity in the repertoire, I develop an alternative not only to nineteenth-century theory of theatre, but also to more recent scholarship, which typically measures the political relevance of theatre by its relative transgressiveness. What matters is not only – and not primarily – the extent to which an individual dramatic work (or theatre production) departs from the cultural consensus, but the extent to which the diversity of positions across different plays undermines the very notion of such a consensus and shows the possibility for debate.

The Importance of Theatre through the Eyes of Nineteenth-Century Critics

The question of how contemporaries explained the importance of theatre is surprisingly, given the strong social presence of theatre in the mid–nineteenth century, not easy to answer. The function of theatre was not a topic of extensive explicit discussion in the middle decades of the nineteenth century. This is noteworthy also because the eighteenth century had produced several texts on that subject that remain canonical to this day: Gotthold Ephraim Lessing's *Hamburgische Dramaturgie* (*Hamburg Dramaturgy*, 1767–9); J.M.R. Lenz's *Anmerkungen übers Theater* (*Remarks on the Theatre*, 1774); and Friedrich Schiller's "Was kann eine gute stehende Schaubühne eigentlich wirken" ("What a Good Permanent Theatre Can Really Achieve," 1784) are famous examples.

In the mid–nineteenth century, there is very little to match these works by Lessing, Lenz, and Schiller. Writers, theatre practitioners, and scholars wrote in this century long histories of the genre of drama and of the institution of theatre, as well as of its most famous stages.[6] There was also some theory of drama (and especially of tragedy).[7] But there was relatively little discussion of the impact of theatre as an institution in which drama was performed.

To the extent that extensive critical or theoretical reflections on the practice and institution of theatre were produced, they tended to focus on the impact of individual dramatic performances. Because of this focus, these discussions missed what constituted theatre as an institution in which diverse groups of the population gathered again and again to watch a series of diverse dramatic productions. Nineteenth-century theatre was, to a degree unmatched by any other institution in society, a place for the unfolding of a rich and diverse discourse. While many people of the nineteenth century engaged in this practice as spectators or practitioners, they did not theorize theatre in this way. The nineteenth century was, at least when it came to the performing arts, apparently unable to grasp the heterogeneity and diversity on which it thrived. If we hope to understand what theatre meant for the nineteenth century, nineteenth-century writings on the theatre are of surprisingly little help. A brief review of two crucial mid-nineteenth-century texts about theatrical practice – Gustav Freytag's 1863 treatise *Die Technik des Dramas* (*The Technique of Drama*) and Richard Wagner's early essay *Die Kunst und die Revolution* (*Art and Revolution*, 1848) – can serve to illustrate how contemporary debate remained limited to the discussion of individual works.[8]

Although largely forgotten today, Gustav Freytag was perhaps the most widely read German-language writer of the nineteenth century and certainly the most important representative of the middlebrow national-liberal literature that featured prominently in the repertoire of the Burgtheater. Freytag was very successful as a novelist: his novel *Soll und Haben* (*Debit and Credit*, 1855) is generally considered the century's most widely distributed work of German-language fiction. But he also worked as a popular historian (notably with his voluminous collection *Bilder aus der deutschen Vergangenheit* (*Images from the German Past*, 1859–67), and as a playwright: Freytag's comedy *Die Journalisten* saw, in the Burgtheater alone, 165 performances between 1853 and 1912 (Rub 81), a number unmatched by any other contemporary playwright.[9] Given Freytag's astonishing and wide-ranging productivity, it is not surprising that his practically minded treatise *Die Technik* was also very widely known – as a matter of fact, among all of Freytag's works it arguably enjoyed the longest legacy.

Theatrical performance is central to Freytag's concept of drama. Breaking with a long tradition from Aristotle to Lessing that had considered reading an appropriate mode of reception, Freytag is deeply committed to drama as a genre meant for performance (*Die Technik* 288). Drama, Freytag urges, is intended to create an impact both on the intellect and on affect, and it can achieve this through performance, by working on the eyes as well as the ears (17–18). Freytag speaks in more detail about the ways in which drama is tied to the specific conditions of the stage, musing, for instance, on the possible length of dramatic performances. He refers with awe to the Ancient Greek practice of having a series of dramatic performances that lasted an entire day; he notes with respect that Shakespeare's plays often still required four hours; he states with resignation that in his own time, three hours appear to be the maximum, and that playwrights have to limit their play to about two thousand verses if they do not want to jeopardize the impact of their drama.

Impact (*Wirkung*) is the central concern in Freytag's book, and not only with respect to the length of performance. But this same category is almost always thought of in relation to individual plays, not to the theatre as a whole or even just with an eye to the question of how the impact of any one play depends on its interaction with other plays in a theatre's repertoire. Only once, and that only in passing, Freytag acknowledges the fact that theatres are home to a multitude of different productions. But even here, the implication is that this variety is a problem because it makes it difficult for new playwrights to stand out among the hodgepodge of traditions and ideologies:

> On the stage, there is a crowding of farce, opera, comedy; of form and ideology of multiple centuries. Everything aims to please; the newest and strangest, and whatever suits the great masses the best, pushes aside the rest.

> Auch auf der Scene drängen sich Posse, Oper, Komödie; Form, Weltanschauung verschiedener Jahrhunderte. Alles müht sich zu gefallen, das Neueste und Seltsamste, und wieder was dem großen Publikum am behaglichsten ist, stößt Anderes bei Seite. (Freytag, *Die Technik* 287)

Freytag was not alone in reducing the impact of drama to the impact of individual plays. In another well-known work of the period, Richard Wagner's early essay *Die Kunst und die Revolution* (1848), this same tendency is even more prominent. Essentially, Wagner deplores a decline of theatrical performance from its first great phase of blossoming in Ancient Greece. Wagner looks to Greece for a theatre of the people and for the people; for a theatre that presents its audience with a clear picture of itself, instead of providing thoughtless entertainment in the pursuit of profit; and for a theatre that combines the arts into a *Gesamtkunstwerk*, instead of partitioning drama and music into entirely separate genres. When the "entire population" ("ganze Volk"; Wagner, *Die Kunst* 30) came together in the Ancient Greek theatre, Wagner claims, that public was provided a chance to grasp its own being:

> The people [*Volk*] were coming to gather in front of the most powerful artwork, to know themselves, to grasp their own actions, to melt into one with their essence, their community, their God.
>
> [D]ieses Volk strömte [...] zusammen [...], um sich vor dem gewaltigsten Kunstwerke zu sammeln, sich selbst zu erfassen, seine eigene Thätigkeit zu begreifen, mit seinem Wesen, seiner Genossenschaft, seinem Gotte sich [...] zu verschmelzen. (8–9)

Theatre in Greece, or so Wagner claims, provides art for all instead of just for an affluent minority: "In the copious spaces of the Greek amphitheatre, the entire population attended the performances; in our exclusive theatres, only the wealthy part of the people loafs around" ("In den weiten Räumen des griechischen Amphitheathers wohnte das ganze Volk den Vorstellungen bei, in unsern vornehmen Theaters faulenzt nur der vermögende Theil desselben"; 30). To make theatre more widely available, Wagner demands that admission to theatre should be free of charge (58).[10]

However, even though Wagner's thought is clearly shaped by some democratic ideals in that he advocates universal access to a theatre of and for the people, he fails to appreciate the democratic practice that emerges from diversity on the stage.[11] And with that he also ignores the diversity that was already a reality in contemporary theatres. Wagner continues to think of the actions on the stage of a theatre in terms of a single work. The fact that the people uniting in front of the stage could experience, across the multiple productions, diverse perspectives and positions is never discussed. Wagner's ideal theatre would allow the *Volk* to know and celebrate itself in its own being.[12] But this being is very much thought of as a homogenous essence. The *Volk* would experience no discord between its own values and those on stage, or between the various values presented across different theatre productions.

The Politics of Transgression

More recent critics have, in a sense, taken the opposite approach to that of Wagner. Rather than seeing the political significance of drama and theatre in its potential to allow the audience to understand and embrace its own being, they found a theatre whose relevance lies in disrupting the audience's assumptions and reigning normative frameworks. However, even though their emphasis on disruption and transgression would have been alien to Wagner, they share with their nineteenth-century predecessor the fact that they too usually think of drama and theatre in terms of individual works and productions. There is relatively little appreciation of the historical fact that permanent European theatres of the nineteenth century (and beyond) were venues for a large and wide-ranging repertoire.

Since the second half of the twentieth century, the politics of theatre (as well as of other media) have often been measured by the extent to which a performance challenges prevailing structures and normative frameworks. Theatre as an institution to present society with a confirmation of their views and values, by contrast, is critically viewed as an aspect of conservative mass media, against which more ambitious art stands out. Through this lens, J.S.R. Goodlad, for instance, analysed in his much-cited 1971 study *A Sociology of Popular Drama* a "drama of reassurance."[13] Goodlad highlights the extent to which British audiences of popular plays and television dramas from the 1950s and 1960s found their norms confirmed in the fiction, while also noting, at least in passing, that the same could not be said of more ambitious art, which transgresses these norms.[14]

In the decades since Goodlad's study, some scholars have developed alternatives to the project of assessing the political significance of a work of literature on the basis of its relative conformity with the reigning normative framework. Yet in one way or another, these various alternative approaches remain bound to the categories of affirmation or transgression. Most prominent among these theories is the work of Jacques Rancière. Instead of looking at the normative content explicitly found in works of art (Rancière is not concerned with drama in particular), Rancière urges readers to appreciate how literature (as a form of art) participates in the project of a "Distribution of the Sensible" (7–45): below the level of the explicit negotiation of norms, literature significantly contributes to decisions over what can become perceptible.

Rancière is committed to a study of aesthetics as a study of "what presents itself to sense experience" (13) at various moments in history:

> [Aesthetics] is a delimitation of spaces and times, of the visible and the invisible, of speech and noise, that simultaneously determines the places and the stakes of politics as a form of experience. Politics revolves around what is seen and what can be said about it, around who has the ability to see and the talent to speak, around the properties of spaces and the possibilities of time. (13)

Rancière's emphasis on the political bases of various systems for making people or things visible or invisible, audible or inaudible, importantly expands our understanding not only of what constitutes politics, but also of why art, as a crucial site of aesthetic practice, fulfils an important political role. Building on Rancière, one could easily develop a system that interrogates why theatre – in addressing the various senses of sight, hearing, and potentially even smell, taste, or touch – has a particular significance for the theory and practice of the "distribution of the sensible." But in Rancière's framework, the relevance of artistic practice, including drama, is still understood by the ways in which individual works disrupt – or perpetuate – the established system of sense perception.

Another approach to the politics of art – more specific to theatre – has been developed by Chantal Mouffe. Like Rancière, Mouffe operates with a broad notion of the political. In contrast to Rancière, however, she is not primarily interested in the decisions over what is given access to our senses. Building on the work of the Italian Marxist philosopher Antonio Gramsci, Mouffe argues that in the notion of what a given society advances as their "common sense," there is a distinctly political project. Artistic practices, for Mouffe, carry with them the potential to undermine common sense. The arts can contribute to Mouffe's project of a "construction of multiple spaces of what I [Mouffe] call 'agonistic' spaces, where the dominant consensus is subverted and where new modes of identification are made available" (193).

The theories by Goodlad, Rancière, and Mouffe present three fundamentally different options for how to assess the politics of theatre. Depending on the framework we choose, we can look either at the governing norms (Goodlad), at what is allowed access to the senses (Rancière), or at the implicit understanding of what constitutes "common sense" (Mouffe). All these are highly meaningful questions for the study of art. Yet what is overlooked in all three approaches is that artistic works (here, dramatic plays) do not exist only in their relationship to the established moral framework of the audience that perceives them, but also in relation to other artworks perceived by that audience. This fact has special importance for (traditional, permanent) theatre, in which the plays are performed as part of a wider repertoire. The theatre is not only a place of collective reception, but it is also a place where frequently returning spectators are confronted with a plurality of experiences that remain interconnected through various means.

The Politics of Polyphony

The fact that contemporary as well as eighteenth and nineteenth century theories of the theatre are largely limited to the exploration of the effect of individual performances is remarkable. After all, theatres offer many performances – almost daily ones, in the case of the Burgtheater.[15] Especially in nineteenth-century court theatres, a significant part of the audience consisted of regulars. Whatever a theatre did or did not achieve thus must have to do not only with individual performances, but also with the cumulative effect of the multitude of performances to which it exposed its audience.

The first study that provided an in-depth analysis of this aspect of theatre is Marvin Carlson's 2001 monograph *The Haunted Stage*. Carlson is interested in the multiple ways in which every new theatrical performance carries with it traces of previous performances so that new works are (partially) viewed through the lens of – or in comparison to – older works. To be sure, something like this might be argued for every artwork. No new work of art operates in an art-historical vacuum. Each song evokes previous songs, each painting previous paintings, and certainly each novel previous novels. But what might be considered a general feature of artistic production and reception has, as Carlson argues, a particularly pronounced role in the theatre. Carlson claims that historically speaking, the literary genre of drama is already more invested in the repetition of existing themes than other literary forms. There is a great tendency in drama to restage existing dramatic subjects. The stories of Medea, Oedipus, Mary Stuart, and Faust have been the subject of countless plays, and there is nothing quite like that in either the traditional epic or the modern novel (though the case for lyric poetry may be more complex). Admittedly, as Carlson concedes as well, with the onset of realism in drama in the nineteenth century, there was a greater emphasis on the exploration of new, contemporary subject matter: for instance, neither ancient myth nor the great historical events of the European or national past tended to figure very prominently in the Burgtheater's popular *Konversationsstücke* ("conversation pieces"), set in contemporary spa towns or urban centres. And yet, as we will see in detail in chapter 6, central events of the German national past did continue to make their mark on the repertoire of the mid-nineteenth-century Burgtheater as well.

The echoing of past works in theatre productions – Carlson calls it "ghosting" – extends far beyond the dramatic text. It works, notably, through the actors who appear again and again in different plays, and whose new performances carry, for the audience, reminders of their past roles. Especially for a theatre like the Burgtheater, in which the same regular spectators watched, over years and decades, the same actors with their lifetime appointments occupy ever new roles, this kind of "ghosting" was certainly very pronounced. But the effect of ghosting does not end with the actors. Theatres in the nineteenth century often reused costumes, props, and stage designs, and all these too carried with them traces of previous productions. Finally, the building of the theatre itself, to which the audience returns, retains, for the spectators, memories of past plays.

Carlson's *The Haunted Stage* powerfully displays the various ways in which theatre performances are characterized by reminders of previous performances. But the key term of "ghosting" in Carlson's study overemphasizes the subconscious or unconscious effect of the repetition. What Carlson appears to have in mind is that the past retains a spectral presence in new plays. But there can also be a much more sober, conscious, and explicit awareness of older plays. Every new play that revisits a topic covered in another play invites comparison to that work, and, in some way, the new work can be perceived as a response to the old work.

The sense that the various plays performed in the Burgtheater were perceived in relation to one another does not mean that there was a direct dialogue between the plays. Generally, there was no explicit critical engagement of one play with another in the way in which such engagement existed in other fora – say, in the newspapers, coffeehouses, clubs, or societies. With some exceptions, the implicit and explicit references to other plays are unidirectional, from the Burgtheater's popular mid-nineteenth-century writers to the idolized Weimar playwrights of the previous generation. Schiller and Goethe as well as, to a lesser extent, the popular playwright August von Kotzebue (1761–1819), are often evoked in plays by signatory Burgtheater writers such as Friedrich Halm (1806–71), Eduard von Bauernfeld (1802–90), Johann Ludwig Deinhardstein (1790–1859), or Charlotte Birch-Pfeiffer (1800–68).[16]

Not only do Goethe and Schiller, of course, not reference popular writers emerging after them, but intertextual references between the popular writers of the mid–nineteenth century also remain relatively rare. The plays by Halm and Bauernfeld are a case in point. The Viennese playwrights Halm and Bauernfeld, born within a few years of each other, represent the opposite ends of the political spectrum of the Burgtheater, Halm occupying the conservative and Bauernfeld the progressive end. During the 1830s, forties, and fifties, the plays of both writers figured very prominently in the Burgtheater's repertoire. They surely knew each other well because they frequented overlapping social circles and because they collaborated as advisers to the Burgtheater director Franz von Holbein. More importantly still, they wrote for an audience whom they also knew to be aware of each other's plays. And yet there are, to my knowledge, no direct references in Halm's plays to Bauernfeld's plays, or vice versa. To the extent that mid-nineteenth-century Burgtheater plays were referenced by other playwrights, this happened largely by means of parody in the suburban theatres. Notably, Johann Nestroy was notorious for his parodies of his contemporaries Friedrich Halm and Friedrich Hebbel (Yates, "Dialect Satire" 45).

While there was no explicit dialogue between the performed plays, there was an implicit dialogue that emerged for the audience as an effect of the Burgtheater's repertoire. There was a polyphony of positions, and the fact that these positions were all given voice on the same stage and by the same ensemble united them as related contributions. At least the Burgtheater's many regular spectators could not have helped seeing the plays in relation to one another. It is important to bear in mind also that the repeated attendance at the same plays, which is a rare occurrence today, was rather common, at least for those who had seats or entire boxes reserved for them throughout the entire year. For these regular attendees, something approaching a figurative back and forth between the plays did emerge.

The various plays that were produced in the mid-nineteenth-century Burgtheater by the same ensemble and that often returned to similar topics and questions existed, for the Burgtheater's regular audience, in relation to one another. One of the most immediate and important effects of the plays thus derived from the extent to which they echoed – or departed from – previously performed plays on that stage. Through the repertoire, the audience was confronted with discourses unfolding in varying degrees of homogeneity or heterogeneity.

The measure of heterogeneity is a very powerful criterion in thinking about the political importance of theatre as an institution – a criterion that allows us to go beyond the effect of individual productions. What we should assess is the extent to which a theatre, through the diversity of its repertoire, suggests the possibility that the topics it discusses allow for a variety of positions and perspectives. In other words, we should not concern ourselves only with the political ideas of individual plays, whether expressed through a text's subject matter, plot, dialogue, or form; we should not concern ourselves only with the question of whether any idea we encounter in a given text is in itself conformist or progressive, challenging the status quo or trying to retain it. What we should also look at is the inner differentiation of a larger corpus of texts consumed by a specific audience. What makes a body of literature politically or socially important is that there are appreciable differences between the positions implicitly or explicitly proposed by different works. Through these differences, alternatives become visible, and it becomes clear that there is room for debate – and potentially, as a consequence, change. More important than either the precise content of an individual idea in an individual work or even the polyphony of ideas and voices in an individual work, the inner differentiation of a larger corpus of texts – corpus polyphony or *repertoire polyphony*, we may call it – prepares a room for political debate.

To some extent, I arrive at my concept of repertoire polyphony by way of necessity. The mid-nineteenth-century Burgtheater was far from being a wellspring of political radicality, and if radicality is the measure, then the Burgtheater was almost as apolitical as conventional opinion has it. That being said, to the extent that one does consider the multiplicity of different plays as the irreducible content of a permanent theatre, then the sole focus on radicality seems unsatisfactory. Is acting as an echo chamber of radical ideas the only politically meaningful act of an institution? To put it more carefully, an institution can foster critical discourse and debate not only by producing ideas outside the accepted spectrum, but also by showing a variety of different standpoints.

To produce a meaningful assessment of repertoire polyphony, which is the goal of the following chapters, it is important also to acknowledge what remained beyond the represented positions on stage. Otherwise, the very emphasis on diversity in a repertoire might reinforce the sense that whatever is represented on stage is the complete spectrum of possible discourse. It is crucial to counteract this impression by drawing attention to the many voices and thoughts that remained excluded, regarding both the selection of topics to be discussed and the positions on these topics. Concretely, in the following chapters, I highlight the debates on individual freedom and obedience (ch. 4), women's role in society (ch. 5), and national identity (ch. 6) as central topics that received discussion in the mid-nineteenth-century Burgtheater. All three topics were politically and socially central for nineteenth-century Austria. What is more, these were by no means harmless topics for the regime. The House of Habsburg was generally wary of nationalistic rhetoric because it saw in nationalism a threat to its multiethnic empire. Likewise, the discussion of the role of women, beyond undermining the general patriarchy, could easily become an allegory for more general debates on justice and liberty. At the same time, the social and political relevance of these topics should not blind us to the fact that other crucial topics were, by and large, successfully suppressed (or not even pursued by anyone): most importantly, the role of the Church and the legitimacy of monarchy, but also the rights of peasants, the importance of a constitution, and the justification for censorship.[17] Even within the debates that did find representation in the Burgtheater, moreover, not all was being said, and this, too, requires attention.

With the term "repertoire polyphony" as a measure of the heterogenous discourse on the stage of the Burgtheater, I borrow the concept of polyphony that Mikhail Bakhtin introduced in his analysis of Dostoevsky's novels. Bakhtin, however, developed his concept with reference to individual works, not larger corpora. Polyphony, for Bakhtin, is defined by the presence of a range of different, independent, and equal voices and standpoints in one literary work that are not meant to serve the overarching ideological position of the author.[18]

Bakhtin also argued that the polyphony of the modern novel put it in a sharp contrast with drama, because drama, in Bakhtin's mind, remains, as a rule, focused on the expression of a single idea. In a discussion of Shakespeare, whom Bakhtin cautiously entertains as an exception to this limitation of drama, Bakhtin explains the general nature of drama in following terms:

> First, drama is by its very nature alien to genuine polyphony; drama may be multileveled, but it cannot contain *multiple worlds*; it permits only one, and not several systems of measurement.
>
> Secondly, if one can speak at all of a plurality of fully valid voices in Shakespeare, then it would only apply to the entire body of his work and not to individual plays. In essence, each play contains only one fully valid voice, the voice of the hero, while polyphony presumes a plurality of fully valid voices within the limits of a single work – for only then may polyphonic principles be applied to the construction of the whole. (Bakhtin 34)

Bakhtin's understanding of drama as "alien to genuine polyphony" is by no means intuitive. Drama, as distinct from epic and novel, is typically characterized by the absence of a narrator so that there is, in some sense, very little in drama beyond a multitude of voices. To be sure, in other ways, the form of drama has traditionally been used for a relatively focused expression of a single idea. One might even say that it is the very fact of drama's formal polyphony that encourages, as a counterweight, the clear focus on a single idea. Classic German comedy of the eighteenth century especially was meant to focus on the critical depiction of one single vice. Likewise, the German *Schauspiel* (serious drama with a positive ending), which enjoyed great popularity in the nineteenth century, often centred on a positive central character who embodied one specific virtue: the brave honesty of Goethe's Iphigenie; the sovereign obedience of the titular hero of Friedrich Halm's successful drama *Griseldis;* and the serious and honest devotion of Hans Sachs in Deinhardstein's much-performed eponymous play all prove this point.

In tragedy, the matter is a little more complex, at least if one accepts Hegel's definition of tragedy as focused on the conflict of equally justified principles – a definition that still has currency in the latest scholarship on tragedy, as in, for instance, Simon Critchley's 2020 book *Tragedy, the Greeks, and Us.*[19] There are a number of tragedies from the eighteenth and nineteenth centuries that particularly make use of the notion of tragedy as a battleground between equally justified ideas to confront the reader or spectator with the difficult question of which – if any – of the positions represented by individual characters should be espoused. One may think here of the antagonism of Mary Stuart and Queen Elizabeth in Friedrich Schiller's *Maria Stuart*[20] (which premiered in Weimar in 1800) or between Georges Danton and Maximilien Robespierre in Büchner's *Danton's Tod* (*Danton's Death,* written in 1835). More complicated still, there are plays in which we are presented not with a limited number of incompatible but equally justified positions, but with a wider range of positions that are all, to varying degrees, unjustified. In the eighteenth century, *Sturm und Drang* plays by J.M.R. Lenz – notably *Der Hofmeister* (*The Tutor*) and *Die Soldaten* (*The Soldiers*) – provide examples of this trend; in the late nineteenth century, the social dramas by Gerhart Hauptmann such as *Vor Sonnenaufgang* (*Before Sunrise,* 1889) can be read in this manner. However, at least as far as the Burgtheater of the mid-nineteenth century is concerned, we can largely discount this last group of plays: Hauptmann, of course, did not write in the mid-nineteenth century; Lenz's *Der Hofmeister* was first banned by the censors and then fell into obscurity. Moreover, tragedy more broadly (as a genre that is likely to focus on a conflict between multiple justified positions) was not the leading genre in the repertoire of the Burgtheater. Although there are some prominent examples of highly successful productions of tragedy – Shakespeare's *Hamlet* and Schiller's *Maria*

Stuart were more successful than any comedy – overall, comedy and Schauspiel dominated the Burgtheater stage. With some qualifications and a certain lingering scepticism then, we might, for the purposes of this book, grant Bakhtin's point that polyphony is alien to the concept of drama.

Of crucial importance, however, is another thought that Bakhtin expresses in the passage previously quoted, namely the idea of polyphony at the level of the "the entire body of his [i.e., Shakespeare's] work." The curious idea of polyphony at the level of the oeuvre is not developed any further by Bakhtin, but it appears to rely on a few conditions that are worth spelling out. To the extent that one wants to regard such polyphony as a potential that is actually realized in reception, it requires, first, readers or spectators who are exposed to multiple works by Shakespeare without lengthy intervals so that they retain a good memory of the various plays and can indeed compare them. Second, readers or spectators would have to understand the identity of the author as a unifying principle of the plays so that they are motivated to compare the plays to one another. Third, one would have to establish that the same set of problems are addressed in various plays. Finally, and most crucially, these same problems would have to be discussed in a sufficiently heterogenous manner across the different plays so that one can speak of polyphony.

This is not the place to discuss the extent to which all four conditions are met in Shakespeare – or, more precisely, in the reception of Shakespeare at various points in history. By contrast, as the following chapters of this book demonstrate, all four criteria are meaningfully fulfilled at the level of the repertoire in the mid-nineteenth-century Burgtheater. Here we have a theatre filled with spectators who go to the theatre several times per week and potentially see performances multiple times so that they have many different plays simultaneously present to them; we have plays performed by the same set of actors on the same stage so that a comparison becomes almost unavoidable; we have similar topics discussed with considerable frequency; most importantly, we have a considerable range of positions concerning these recurring topics.

2 Making the Burgtheater Repertoire

The Burgtheater's repertoire presented remarkably diverse answers to some of the most pressing social and political questions of the mid-nineteenth century. Before exploring the debates over these questions, a few remarks about the repertoire in general are in order. These remarks can usefully be structured by two guiding questions: first, who determined the repertoire? And second, what characterized the repertoire in terms of the writers, genres, and traditions involved? In this chapter, I discuss the making of the repertoire, and I reserve the following chapter for an overview of the content of the repertoire.

Surprisingly, given that this appears to be a rather basic question of theatre history, relatively little research has been devoted to the making of repertoire.[1] And yet the process by which different plays make their way into the repertoire reveals much about the complex power dynamics in which a theatre operates. An analysis of repertoire-making in the Burgtheater shows that there was no single agent – either inside or outside the theatre – who could unilaterally control the repertoire as a whole. On the one hand, the Burgtheater was a lot less under the sway of court and censorship than is often claimed. On the other hand, while the Burgtheater directors were, relatively speaking, most involved in the determination of which plays to produce, their ability to change the overall repertoire remained limited both by the very large size of the repertoire that they needed to manage and by the various financial, political, and artistic constraints under which they operated. To a significant degree, the diversity of the Burgtheater repertoire was the fortuitous and almost unintentional product of this complex and dynamic process in which the repertoire emerged and developed.

There were many distinct people and offices who had some influence over the decision of what plays should be introduced and maintained in the Burgtheater – from the theatre and stage directors to the actors and the audience, and from the court bureaucracy to the emperor himself. It is not easy to disentangle which of these various agents prevailed at any specific point over a fifty-year period. One might simply expect the repertoire to be the result of the respective theatre director's decisions. But that expectation is more reflective of the present reality than of the theatres of the mid–nineteenth century. In his recent study of the repertoire of today's German state-owned theatres, Thomas Schmidt highlights the rather extreme influence wielded by the theatre director (*Intendant*) on the repertoire. On average, upon a change in the position of the theatre director, fewer than one production continues to be performed (Schmidt 174). The change of director signals a change of identity for the entire institution, and the director is allowed to make their mark by completely reinventing a repertoire in their first year – consequently, the number of new productions usually drops after the first year. Of course, even contemporary theatre directors do not operate in a vacuum. The expectations of state funders and critics (and, to a lesser degree, also of the audience) influence repertoire decisions as well (8). Nevertheless, in comparison to the mid-nineteenth-century permanent theatres (and, notably, the Burgtheater), today's theatre directors exercise a much greater influence.

All this is not to say that nineteenth-century Burgtheater directors were powerless. We can consistently observe for that period an increase in the number of new productions in the first few years of a director's tenure. The average number of new annual productions between 1814 and 1867 (that is under the artistic leadership of Schreyvogel, Deinhardstein, Holbein, and Laube) is roughly 19.5. By contrast, in the first three years of Schreyvogel's tenure (1814–16), twenty-eight, thirty-one, and twenty-six new plays were introduced. A more modest but still recognizable increase can be noticed for Deinhardstein's first three years from 1832–4 (twenty-three, twenty-two, twenty-two). Holbein introduced twenty-six plays in his first full year (1842) only then to decrease that number to sixteen, thirteen, and thirteen in the following years. Finally, Laube's first full three years (1850–2) saw twenty-three, twenty-five, and twenty-six new plays. Importantly, however, we do not see the simultaneous near-complete discontinuation of established productions, which is characteristic of today's theatres. Such a radical break would have been almost impossible given the extremely high number of different plays performed in the Burgtheater in any given year. For instance, in 1842, the first full year of Franz von Holbein's tenure (Holbein became the Burgtheater's director on 3 April 1841), we see the unusually high number of twenty-six new plays. Yet these twenty-six new productions represent only a small fraction of the total of 148 different plays performed in the Burgtheater that year[2] – a staggeringly high number when compared with today's theatres, but representative of the Burgtheater throughout the mid–nineteenth century.[3]

The Burgtheater had to cater to its regular – in many cases, daily – visitors by providing a very large repertoire. Beyond the specific power structures present inside and outside the theatre, it was the necessity of staging well over one hundred plays per year that made it unmanageable for any new theatre director to change the repertoire overnight. At best, he could focus on a different part of the repertoire as he inherited it from his predecessors. Heinrich Laube, for example, did just that, by not only introducing new plays by Goethe, Schiller, and Grillparzer, but also by bringing back to life plays that had already been introduced in earlier years and that had since fallen into neglect. In 1851, his second full year as theatre director, Laube not only introduced twenty-five new plays, but he also revived thirty-eight neglected plays (Wlassack 244).

Aside from the structural limitation on the theatre directors that was imposed by the large number of plays in the repertoire, the theatre directors also had to contend with a significant number of other crucial players both within the theatre and beyond who sought to make their preferences felt. Within the theatre, the directors had to navigate the considerable power of the actors and the *Regisseure* ("stage directors").[4] Outside the theatre, they were faced with the expectations of the court and the censorship office, the predilections of the audience, and the judgment of the newspaper critics. While I try to rank the influence of these players at the end of this chapter, the most important insight to be gained is that the decision making happened in a process of constant negotiation between the many agents involved, with variously shifting alliances between them. The theatre directors certainly had a very important role to play in this process, but in contrast to the reigning practice today, the repertoire was not the direct and (more or less) sole expression of the artistic vision of the theatre director. Instead, the repertoire emerged from a dynamic and somewhat inconsistent process of debate, innovation, and reaction. While the severely censored imperial stage should not be romanticized as a bastion of pluralism, the one-sided stereotype of the Burgtheater as a theatre in chains, under the sway of the Habsburg court, is equally misleading.

The Theatre Directors

Despite all the limitations of their decision-making power, the Burgtheater's theatre directors were the personalities most closely associated with the repertoire. In the years from 1814 to 1867, the four consecutive artistic leaders of the Burgtheater were Joseph Schreyvogel (1814–32), Johann Ludwig Deinhardstein (1832–41), Franz Ignaz von Holbein (1841–9), and Heinrich Laube (1849–67).[5] For the sake of terminological simplicity, I use the term "theatre director" indiscriminately for these four leading artistic personalities in the Burgtheater between 1814 and 1867, even though not all of them enjoyed the title of director. Only Franz von Holbein and Heinrich Laube were called *Direktor*. The "directors" before Holbein and Laube – that is, Schreyvogel and Deinhardstein – had more modest titles. Schreyvogel was *Theatersecretär* ("theatre secretary") and *Dramaturg* ("dramaturge"); Deinhardstein was "Vice-Director." In both cases, it was thus emphasized that the ultimate direction of the Burgtheater lay elsewhere, in the hands of the Habsburg court. This fact, however, did not fundamentally change when Holbein and Laube were allowed to call themselves *Direktor*. In fact, despite the less prestigious title, Schreyvogel was given significant room to design the repertoire (Wlassack 172). Conversely, when Holbein was appointed *Direktor* and thus nominally holding a higher position, the director's powers were simultaneously curtailed.[6]

Different directors exercised their power to determine the repertoire to varying degrees. We know that both Joseph Schreyvogel and Heinrich Laube devoted themselves wholeheartedly to this task and sought to define the Burgtheater through a careful management of the repertoire. Schreyvogel, a Kant enthusiast and respected artistic and intellectual force in Vienna for generations to come, was instrumental in bringing, against the resistance of the court, as much as he possibly could of the German classics (Goethe, Schiller, Kleist) onto the stage while also recruiting new Austrian talent. It was under his tenure that plays by Franz Grillparzer and Eduard von Bauernfeld made their first appearance in the Burgtheater.

Decades later, Heinrich Laube, too, took great pride in his work on the repertoire – notably by championing Shakespeare's works and by reintroducing Grillparzer, whose plays had fallen into neglect under the previous two directors. When, in 1867, Friedrich Halm, in his function as newly appointed *Generalintendant* ("general manager") of the court opera and court theatre, wanted to take away part of Laube's control over the repertoire and the casting of actors, Laube resigned (Wlassack 276). Laube thus signalled that he understood the design of the repertoire as one of his crucial domains.

Schreyvogel and Laube are the Burgtheater's decisive directors in the nineteenth century, making their mark through their persistent work on the repertoire during their long terms – both kept their positions for an astonishing eighteen years. Both Schreyvogel and Laube also came to the theatre as well-known liberals. People spoke about Schreyvogel as an admirer of Napoleon, and in his youth, Schreyvogel even had to leave Vienna for several years to escape the rising indignation over his journalistic activities (Lasher-Schlitt 269). Heinrich Laube had been part of the liberal *Jungdeutschen* group, and his works were banned from performance in Vienna between 1845 and 1848. While both Schreyvogel and Laube eventually lost the support of the court and were let go against their will, the fact that they were hired in the first place and managed to stay in their positions for such a long time is revelatory of the possibilities that existed for liberals in Habsburg Austria, and, notably, in the Burgtheater.

The two directors between Schreyvogel and Laube – Johann Ludwig Deinhardstein and Franz von Holbein – have received significantly less praise for their work, even though they both arrived in their positions as highly qualified theatre practitioners. Deinhardstein had proven his knowledge of the theatre as the author of some very successful plays. But as a director, he was considered lazy and largely inept. Allegedly, he preferred spending his time bird-hunting instead of attending rehearsals (Wlassack 188). Leaving the selection of the repertoire in the hands of the lower-ranking *Regisseure* ("stage directors") and neglecting the theatre's finances, the Burgtheater survived his tenure largely on the work inherited from Schreyvogel. Even so, it was under Deinhardstein that the young Friedrich Halm, who advanced to become one of the Burgtheater's signature Viennese playwrights of the nineteenth century, had his first plays performed.

Deinhardstein's mismanagement was tolerated for a full nine years. His successor, the diligent Franz Ignaz von Holbein, has been described as the polar opposite of the lazy Deinhardstein, but he too proved incapable of bringing the Burgtheater back to the renown that it had enjoyed under Schreyvogel. This is perhaps surprising because Holbein came to the position not only as a successful playwright, but, more importantly, also with an impressive record of theatre management. Before joining the Burgtheater, the sixty-two-year-old Holbein had been the director of Vienna's Theater an der Wien and, later, the director of the theatre of Bamberg in Bavaria, where he collaborated with E.T.A. Hoffman, and of the court theatre in Hanover.

While Deinhardstein reigned through neglect, Holbein acted as an experienced technocrat, bringing the theatre's finances back in order. However, as Eduard von Bauernfeld later described it, Holbein simultaneously deprived the theatre of its intellectual and artistic ambitions (Bauernfeld, *Gesammelte Schriften* 12: 184). Faced with a backlog of manuscripts that he had inherited from his predecessor, Holbein dutifully worked his way through them, although he was glad to receive assistance from the established Burgtheater playwrights Bauernfeld and Halm. And yet this negative portrayal of Holbein requires qualification. Even if it was a matter of chance that Holbein happened to be the Burgtheater's director in the revolutionary year of 1848, it was under his leadership that the repertoire immediately reacted to the revolution and the brief pause of censorship. The second new play performed in the reopened Burgtheater after the March Revolution was *Die Karlsschüler* by Heinrich Laube – a playwright who had, as noted, previously been banned from having his plays performed.

More interestingly, two of the decisive trends of the year 1848 – a privileging of tragedy over comedy and of originally German-language plays over translated foreign-language plays – were already happening to a degree under Holbein's directorship in the years prior to the revolution. German-language plays especially had suffered under Deinhardstein's leadership. In 1839, the ratio between German-language plays and originally foreign-language plays reached an all-time low, when only seven of the nineteen new plays of the year had originally been written in German. During the years of revolutionary freedom and national awakening, this ratio was reversed: eighteen out of the twenty-one plays in 1848 had originally been written in German; seventeen of the twenty-two plays in 1849; and nineteen out of the twenty-three plays in 1850. However, already prior to the 1848 revolution, in 1846, Holbein oversaw a repertoire in which fifteen of the seventeen new plays were German.

A similar trend – albeit less pronounced – can be observed for the representation of tragedy in the repertoire under Holbein. It is one of the most striking aspects of the history of the Burgtheater repertoire that the 1848 revolution led to a marked increase in tragedies. Indeed, 1848 is the only year in which more tragedies than comedies were introduced: the four new comedies faced six new tragedies. In the over fifty years between 1814 and 1867, there was no other year with as many new tragedies or as few new comedies. In each of the following two years, another five new tragedies were added, significantly above the average of around two new tragedies per year in the period from 1814 to 1867. This high number of new tragedies in the repertoire was eventually also reflected in the representation of tragedies on the daily playbills: in 1850, the Burgtheater performed a tragedy on seventy-nine of the 316 days it was open. In the time frame here under investigation, this number was higher only once: in 1863, the Burgtheater performed tragedies on eighty evenings. Under Deinhardstein's leadership, by contrast, tragedy had suffered. Both in 1837 and in 1841 no new tragedy had been introduced. While Holbein's arrival did not bring an immediate and radical reversal, there were again new tragedies in every year of his tenure. In 1844, three new tragedies came to the repertoire, the highest number since 1827, when there had been five new tragedies, and in that same year, the Burgtheater performed tragedies on sixty-three days – more than it had done in over a decade (in 1832, there had been sixty-six performances of tragedy).

In sum, Holbein's directorship of the Burgtheater was surprisingly in tune with the revolutionary artistic trends of 1848. But, and this is just as decisive, it is not clear whether the selection of the repertoire in the Holbein years was the direct product of Holbein's leadership, or whether it just happened *during* Holbein's time in the theatre. The changes under Holbein's directorship were likely also facilitated by several other people and groups who influenced decisions over the repertoire – notably the playwrights Halm and Bauernfeld, who advised Holbein on the repertoire, and those actors who, in their function as *Regisseure* ("stage directors"), were also tasked with the review of manuscripts for production.

The Actors

In the eighteenth century, German theatre troupes were often led by actors. While that ceased to be the case with the foundation of a larger number of permanent theatres around the end of the century, actors retained a significant influence over a theatre's decisions well into the nineteenth century. In his influential guide *Die Technik des Dramas* (*The Technique of Drama*, 1863), Gustav Freytag still advises emerging playwrights who hope to see their works performed that they send their new plays directly to leading actors (305).

What was true for nineteenth-century theatre in general was especially pertinent for the Burgtheater, which had always been considered a *Schauspielertheater* ("an actor's theatre"). The connotations of this term are, at least in the context of the Burgtheater, not altogether positive, because the term could also be used to highlight certain perceived weaknesses in other areas: acting, critics would charge, mattered more than content on this stage (see, for instance, Klingenberg 19).

Still, if the Burgtheater enjoyed great renown in the nineteenth century, this was in large part due to its actors, who were widely celebrated for their skill, and who were adored by the Viennese public. Each generation had its own stars, both male and female, and because many of these actors stayed for a long time (longer, in many cases, than the Burgtheater directors), they were able to leave a mark on the institution and to help establish a theatrical tradition in the Burgtheater.

Perhaps the greatest influence was made early on by two actors who stayed only a relatively short time: Friedrich Ludwig Schröder, a member of the Burgtheater ensemble from 1781–5 (Rub 228); and August Wilhelm Iffland, who had a number of guest appearances in 1801 and 1808 (Rub 233, 235). Schröder and Iffland both came to Vienna from the north (from Hamburg and Berlin, respectively), and they both represented what was then considered a naturalistic acting style.[7] This style was avidly imitated by other actors in Vienna and became a hallmark of the Burgtheater until at least the move to the large new Burgtheater on the Ringstrasse in 1888, whose initially poor acoustics made this acting style impractical.[8]

Importantly, the naturalistic acting style has been understood to be especially conducive to a particular type of play – bourgeois conversational drama (*bürgerliche Konversationsstücke*): "a kind of comedy of manners," as Yates defines this genre, "in which special weight was placed on the art of social conversation" (*Theatre in Vienna* 20). The writer Eduard von Bauernfeld – who was hugely popular in Vienna – became a particular master of this genre.[9] It was this genre for which the Burgtheater was best known in the mid–nineteenth century.

Beyond the way in which the Burgtheater's acting style was conducive to specific types of plays, there were still other ways in which the actors influenced the repertoire. Notably, the relative skill and fit of the actors was, at least indirectly, instrumental in deciding which play would become popular (and thus had a much higher chance of being retained in the repertoire). A prominent example is Friedrich Halm's first play, *Griseldis*. *Griseldis* failed to convince the audience on its first night. But on its second night, when a new actor, Julie Rettich, took over the leading role, it became a great success. (Rettich and Halm subsequently became close friends, and Rettich continued to play all the heroines of Halm's plays in the Burgtheater.) Rettich's performance is, undoubtedly, not the only aspect that contributed to the success of *Griseldis*, which also fared very well on other stages, where Rettich was not present. But the example of *Griseldis* can nevertheless serve as a reminder that the retention of a play could, at least on occasion, be promoted by a fortuitous casting choice.[10] There are other prominent examples from the period that further support this claim. It has been said, for instance, that Grillparzer's *Medea* (premiered 1821) retained its place in the repertoire due to the performance of the celebrated actress Sophie Schröder in the title role (who in the early 1820s was the highest earning of all actors, male or female; Wlassack 160).

The influence of the actors was potentially even more concrete. When Joseph II founded the Burgtheater in 1776, the actors had been given significant privileges. In the Burgtheater's early years, there was a council of older actors that chose which play would be produced in the Burgtheater. This system of leadership was strikingly democratic – but also somewhat cumbersome. Each week, a different secretary from among the ensemble would be appointed to communicate council decisions to court and public. No single actor was thus able to develop significantly greater power than the others. The system of the so-called *Wöchner* (literally, "weekler," from *Woche*, "week") was too impractical to last long.[11] Still, under Joseph II's reign, the council of actors with the *Wöchner* in charge was replaced by a smaller committee, consisting of five actors who were appointed for one year. The committee members were initially called *Inspizienten* ("inspectors"; Lothar 30) and later *Regisseure* ("stage directors").

Under Joseph II, this committee enjoyed great authority over all artistic matters. That power was much reduced when, beginning with Joseph Schreyvogel, artistic directors were hired in the Burgtheater. And yet the committee of the *Regisseure* continued to remain in place throughout the entire period here under investigation, and every new play that was being considered also went through this committee. It was not until the twentieth century that, during the directorship of Hugo Thimig, a "pure" stage director was hired – that is, a stage director who was not simultaneously also an actor (Klingenberg 81). Until that point, the arrangement of a play for performance fell into the hands of the actor-directors, the *Regisseure*. All that being said, the extent to which the committee of the *Regisseure* actively steered the repertoire in specific directions in the mid–nineteenth century varied and was, as far as I can see, probably quite limited. While, as mentioned earlier, Deinhardstein is said to have relied significantly on the help of the *Regisseure* to identify new plays for the repertoire, the same does not appear to be the case for Schreyvogel, Holbein, or Laube.

Last but not least, the influence of the actors was felt by the fact that they themselves regularly turned playwrights. Both Iffland and Schröder, who influenced the Burgtheater's acting style, also contributed many plays. Iffland contributed thirty-nine plays, which were performed a total of 1,329 times between 1784 and 1898, and was among the Burgtheater's most popular playwrights (Rub 272). Schröder was even more successful. His record shows fifty-four plays and 1,412 performances between 1778 and 1901 (280). The most prominent case of a Burgtheater actor-playwright for the period under investigation, however, is Johanna Franul von Weißenthurn, who was a member of the Burgtheater ensemble for astonishing fifty-three years, from 1789 to 1842 (in her time, she was the longest-serving actor of the Burgtheater).

Between 1800 and 1853, forty-eight of her plays saw a total of 912 performances (282).

The Playwrights

When considering who had the power to determine the repertoire, it is easy to forget that this determination did not happen in an artistic or literary-historical vacuum. Especially when it came to domestic productions, the selection of plays depended heavily on the supply by contemporary writers. Whoever had the power to choose new plays could only choose from what had (recently) been written. Despite the considerable number of dramas submitted to the Burgtheater (amounting to perhaps four times the number of new plays performed), there was a clear sense that the supply of quality plays was rather limited.[12] In the draft of a decree from 6 May 1817, Schreyvogel urged the stage directors to quickly seize whatever good play one could lay one's hands on: "Given the obvious scarcity of good plays, the very least that needs to be done, is to bring the good ones as quickly as possible to the stage" ("Bey dem offenbaren Mangel an guten Stücken ist das Wenige, was vorhanden ist, zum mindesten immer so schnell als möglich zur Aufführung zu bringen"; qtd. in Hadamowsky 326).

Much more so than today, many theatres depended on a large and frequently changing repertoire. Not before the second half of the nineteenth century had European cities grown to such an extent that a theatre could thrive on a very limited repertoire, filling the seats night after night with a new group of people enjoying the same few productions (Booth 331). The Burgtheater's audience in the mid–nineteenth century was constituted – not exclusively, but to an important degree – by regulars who wanted frequent updates to the programming. As noted before, in the average year between 1814 and 1867, the Burgtheater introduced about twenty new plays. And while that number fluctuated widely – between twelve and thirty-one – it is significantly higher than that of most theatres today. For instance, for the 2020/1 season, the main stage of the Burgtheater had planned only eight new plays.[13] More important still, in contrast to the nineteenth-century Burgtheater, where contemporary German-language drama was the main fare, today's Burgtheater is much more historically minded. Of the eight plays that were scheduled to have their premiere in the 2020/1 season, only one play was a (relatively) new drama originally written in German: Peter Handke's *Zdenec Adamec* (2020).[14] The remaining seven plays were made up of three older classics (Euripides's *Women of Troy*, Shakespeare's *Richard II*, and Calderón's *Life Is a Dream*); one newer classic (George Tabori's 1987 farce, *Mein Kampf*); two contemporary adaptations of classics (Mozart's *Zauberflöte* [*Magic Flute*] and Maxim Gorki's *Children of the Sun*); and one new German translation of a contemporary British play (Lucy Kirkwood's *The Welkin*).[15]

To provide the large number of new German-language plays it needed, the mid-nineteenth-century Burgtheater was dependent on prolific playwrights. Of course, some works also came from older European playwrights – notably from Shakespeare, Molière, Calderón, Lessing, Goethe, Schiller, and Kleist. In the nineteenth-century Burgtheater, plays by Shakespeare were performed more often than those of any German playwright, except for Kotzebue.[16] Additionally, some plays could be taken from contemporary writers abroad. These contemporary foreign playwrights came mostly from France. Close to one hundred different French playwrights were produced in the Burgtheater between 1814 and 1867 – many of them had only a single play performed on Vienna's main stage, and that only a handful of times.[17]

By far the most widely successful contemporary French playwright was Eugène Scribe (1791–1861). While Scribe is, at least in German-speaking Europe, largely forgotten today, he has been described as "the most popular European playwright of the nineteenth century" (Booth 327). Between 1821 and 1910, twenty-three plays written solely by him saw a total of 609 performances in the Burgtheater. At 151 performances, the suspenseful and tightly organized comedy *Das Glas Wasser, oder: Ursachen und Wirkungen* (*The Glass of Water, or: Effects and Causes*; in the French original, *Le verre d'eau ou Les effets et les causes*), which is set at the court of Queen Anne of England (r. 1702–14), was by far the greatest success among Scribe's plays. Scribe's *Le verre d'eau* premiered in Paris in 1840, and already in the following year, it was introduced in the Burgtheater as well as in other German-language theatres.[18]

In addition to these single-authored plays, Scribe also collaborated on many plays with other writers: between 1821 and 1898, forty-seven such co-productions saw a total of 1,081 performances (Rub 296). In the nineteenth century, performances of plays by Scribe (as well as by Scribe and collaborators) thus far outnumbered the combined Burgtheater performances of all major French playwrights still widely known today: Corneille, Molière, Voltaire, and Racine. The works of Voltaire (1694–1778), the most popular among these, came to twelve plays and 201 performances between 1776 and 1836 (Rub 297).

The significance of contemporary French playwrights as well as of European classics notwithstanding, under pressure to introduce about one new play every two weeks (remembering that the theatre was usually closed in July and August and during the Christmas holidays), the Burgtheater relied on its known and established German-language playwrights.[19] As a consequence, authors whose plays had a proven track record of success with the audience enjoyed considerable liberties. For established Austrian Burgtheater playwrights of the mid-nineteenth century – notably, Johanna Franul von Weißenthurn, Friedrich Halm, and Eduard von Bauernfeld – virtually every new play was performed in the Burgtheater. There was, in their cases, no real decision involved on the side of either the theatre directors or anyone else with a voice in the selection process. Even the otherwise ardent limits set by the censorship system seem to have been somewhat flexible in the case of these playwrights.

Eduard von Bauernfeld, one of the most popular Burgtheater playwrights – the Burgtheater showcased forty-eight of his plays in a total of 1,126 performances – serves as a good example. In his 1846 comedy *Großjährig* (*Age of Majority*), he managed to introduce in one of the main characters what was widely understood to be a caricature of the very embodiment of censorship, the state chancellor Klemens von Metternich. That such an affront was permitted by censors and the court is best explained by Bauernfeld's established position as a Burgtheater playwright. For the court was unquestionably aware of Bauernfeld's liberal politics and found little to applaud in them, either before or after 1848. When a search for a new dramaturge for the Burgtheater was started in 1849, Bauernfeld was ruled out on account of his suspect liberal politics (Wlassack 234). But while Bauernfeld was deemed unsuitable for further promotion, he was given considerable leeway as a playwright.

To be clear, not everything that Bauernfeld wrote was produced in the Burgtheater. On occasion, even Bauernfeld overextended his liberties and saw his plays banned from performance.[20] In other instances, Bauernfeld directly refrained from submitting his work to the Burgtheater. In 1862, for instance, Bauernfeld wrote a short dramatic satire that shows the Austrian Field Marshal Windischgrätz in heaven, arrogantly making his demands before God and teaming up with Don Quixote. But Bauernfeld wrote this satire only for his friends, and published it only much later, as part of his memoirs *Aus Alt- und Neu-Wien* (*From Old and New Vienna*) in 1873, when the censorship system had been abolished (Bauernfeld, *Gesammelte Schriften* 12: 307–14). Bauernfeld knew better than to submit a text like this to the Burgtheater – even though at least parts of the audience surely would have welcomed the piece.

In many cases, of course, the Burgtheater playwrights wrote their works in a manner to directly meet the expectations of the theatre leadership, the censors, and the audience. As their plays were, with the possible exception of those of Grillparzer, primarily meant for the

(Burgtheater) stage, it would have made little sense for them to write a text that would not pass the censors or that they knew would be unpopular with the audience. With the introduction of the royalties system in the Burgtheater in 1844, the popularity of a play also had direct financial benefits to its author. Rather than being paid a flat sum for their play, as was previously the case, the playwrights now received, depending on the length of their play, between 3 and 10 per cent of the gross income of the evening: 10 per cent for plays that filled the entire evening; 6 per cent for plays that were accompanied by another play; and 3 per cent for a play that needed to be accompanied by a play of two or more acts (Wlassack 209).[21]

The Court Bureaucracy, the Censors, and the Emperor

Austria's system of censorship was infamous in Europe. In the nineteenth century, Austria was called the "China of Europe": the system of censorship was seen as constituting a wall around the country that was reminiscent of the Great Wall of China. Things really changed only in 1867, when Austria introduced a constitution that included the monarchy's first comprehensive catalogue of human rights and, along with that, also freedom of the press. Theatre censorship, however, continued long after that, until 1926 – although it appears to have been practiced much less strictly after 1867 (Yates, *Theatre in Vienna* 42–8).

The Austrian system of theatre censorship went back to the mid-eighteenth century. In 1751, Empress Maria Theresia introduced a censorship requirement for all manuscripts meant for print as well as for all printed works imported from abroad. Initially, plays that were seen fit for publication in print could also appear on stage. By 1770, an additional censorship review specifically for performance was introduced (Bachleitner, "Die Dialektik von Gehorsam"). From that time on, the censors' approval was necessary both for the printed publication of a play and for the performance of plays, and it was noticeably stricter for performance than for print.

The only exception to this practice in the mid-nineteenth century was in the immediate aftermath of the 1848 revolution. Freedom of the press had been one of the foremost concerns of Viennese liberals in the years leading up to 1848, and, right at the beginning of the revolution, in March 1848, Emperor Ferdinand gave in to the demand to abolish censorship, including theatre censorship. But this freedom was short-lived. Almost immediately after the defeat of the revolution in November 1848, some censorship measures were reimposed. Two years later, in November 1850, under Ferdinand's conservative successor, Franz

Joseph, theatre censorship received new official codification through the *Theaterordnung* ("Theatre Order") (Yates, *Theatre in Vienna* 42).

In his influential memorandum from 1795, the Austrian censor Franz Karl Hägelin determined two reasons why a "much stricter" ("viel strenger"; qtd. in Yates *Theatre in Vienna*, 246) treatment of the stage was warranted. First, performance, Hägelin argued, had a stronger impact than reading because performance also affected the ears and eyes, and "even aims to enter the spectator's will to bring about the intended emotions, which a mere reading does not achieve" ("und sogar in den Willen des Zuschauers treten soll, um die beabsichtigten Gemütsbewegungen hervorzubringen, welches die bloße *Lektüre* nicht leistet"; qtd in Yates 246). Second, Hägelin claims, censors were able to restrict access to books to only certain types of readers, "whereas the theatre was open to the whole public, to people of all professions, of all classes, and of all ages" ("da hingegen das Schauspielhaus dem ganzen Publikum offen steht, das aus Menschen von jeder Klasse, von jedem Stande und von jedem Alter bestehet"; qtd. in Yates 246–7).

There is some room to question the factual basis of at least Hägelin's second argument for the stricter treatment of performance than of print. For while there was a system in place to distinguish between books that were categorically banned (these books were labelled *damnatur*) and those banned only for the largest part of the population (*erga schedam*), Hägelin's optimism that the access to books was easy to control seems surprising. Conversely, it is also not clear that theatre really was, as Hägelin suggests, open to all. Not everyone had the financial means and leisure to access the theatre. By that logic, one would have to make some allowances for such seemingly exclusive institutions as the Burgtheater. While the Burgtheater's audience was much more diverse than is conventionally claimed, it was not equally attended by people of *all* walks of life.

But perhaps it is more productive to read Hägelin's statements not so much as reflections of the reality of media consumption or the possibilities of control, but as value statements about literature and theatre. As the leading scholar of Austria's censorship system, Norbert Bachleitner, argues, censorship is expressive of a very high estimation of the power of literature (Bachleitner, "Die Dialektik von Gehorsam"). And if the theatre received especially close scrutiny by the Austrian censors, this can be read as a sign of the especially high status that theatre enjoyed. Theatre, in Hägelin's censorship memorandum no less than in Friedrich Schiller's famous and enthusiastic essay of the previous decade – "Was kann eine gute stehende Schaubühne eigentlich wirken" ("What a Good Permanent Theatre Can Really Achieve," 1784) – was seen to have a real impact on the moral fabric of society. To prevent theatre from exercising the influence that the censors believed it to have – or, rather, to ensure that this influence was used to steer society in the right direction – the plays not only had to pass a process of approval before performance, but there were also censors present during the performances to confirm that the text was not changed at the last minute and to guarantee that actors did not improvise.

While the underlying beliefs of the censors are open to doubt, the power of the censors was real, and their influence on the repertoire was felt. Many of the *Sturm und Drang* dramas of the 1770s – now classics of German literature, regularly read in school and performed on stage – were prohibited by the Austrian censors. The prohibition happened either immediately upon publication as, for instance, in the case of J.M.R. Lenz's comedy *Der Hofmeister* (*The Tutor*, 1774), or with some delay, as Schiller's drama *Die Räuber* (*The Robbers*, 1784) was banned in 1804, twenty years after it was written (Bachleitner, "Die Dialektik von Gehorsam" 288).[22] For the period between 1814 and 1867, there are also a few prominent examples of new plays that did not pass the Austrian censors. As already noted, Heinrich Laube's plays were banned from performance between 1845 and 1847. Meanwhile, his printed works appeared with a range of restrictions. His comedy *Gottsched und Gellert* (first performed in Dresden in 1845 and first published in Leipzig in 1847), for instance, received the verdict *erga schedam*, thus allowing its distribution only to "especially reliable" ("besonders verlässlichen") citizens.[23]

Franz Grillparzer also faced considerable headwind from the censors. His best-known play today, the tragedy *König Ottokars Glück und Ende* (*King Ottokar's Rise and Fall*; written in 1823), was initially turned down by the censors as a manuscript for the stage (although it could be published in print). Only after a more favourable assessment by Emperor Franz's private physician, Friedrich Freiherr von Stifft, as well as an intervention by the emperor's wife, Caroline Augusta, did Grillparzer's play receive the permission to be performed (Bachleitner, *Die literarische Zensur* 252–3). It saw its premiere in the Burgtheater in February 1825.

Prominent as these examples are, most contemporary texts did pass the censors,[24] so that censorship did not completely change the literary landscape – or at least not in the form of direct prohibition.[25] Moreover, for more extreme examples of the censors' powers, one has to look beyond the Burgtheater to Vienna's suburban theatres. Famously, Johann Nestroy, the star playwright and comic actor at the Theater an der Wien, was imprisoned for his behaviour on stage, albeit only for a few days.

When we think today of state influence on theatre in nineteenth-century Austria, the censors, as part of the *Polizeihofstelle*, the court police office which assumed responsibility over theatre censorship in 1803, first come to mind (Bachleitner, *Die literarische Zensur* 242). However, technically the most immediate influence came from elsewhere. As discussed earlier, the title of director did not officially apply to all of those four leading artistic personalities working in the Burgtheater between 1814 and 1867: only Holbein and Laube carried the title *Direktor*; before them, Schreyvogel and Deinhardstein were merely *Theatersecretär* and *Dramaturg*. In this period, the Burgtheater was under the direct supervision of the so-called *Oberstkämmerer* ("grand chamberlain"), the second-highest position at the court, which had significant responsibility over the emperor's treasury.[26] The *Oberstkämmerer* was at the same time appointed *Oberster Hoftheaterdirektor* ("highest court theatre director"). Additionally, before Holbein was appointed director in 1841, there was another authority between the *Oberstkämmerer* and the theatre secretary: to make matters even more perplexing, this intermediary position was for some years filled by the *Oberstkämmerer* himself.[27] Finally, there was also a position of vice-director, which, at the emperor's directive and in an effort to save money, was eventually cut in 1829 (Hadamowsky 337–8).

Officially, censorship for the Burgtheater was the domain of the *Oberstkämmerer*, although in practice it was generally handled by the *Polizeihofstelle*, which was responsible for censorship in Vienna's other theatres (Bachleitner, *Die literarische Zensur* 242). Beyond censorship questions, the precise division of labour and of decision-making power between the various offices overseeing the Burgtheater repertoire depended on changing policies over the years as well as on the preferences of individual members of the leadership. For example, the long-serving *Oberstkämmerer* Johann Rudolf Czernin (in office, 1823–45), took for many years a great interest in the repertoire. But in 1834, at the age of almost seventy-six, he cited poor eyesight to justify that he was no longer able "to occupy myself with reading so many insignificant and often unsuitable plays" ("mich fernerhin [...] mit der Durchsicht so vieler und häufig nicht geeigneter Theaterstücke zu befassen"; qtd. in Hadamowsky 340). He thus tasked the theatre secretary, Deinhardstein, with deciding over the entire repertoire, directing him only to be guided by the following principles: honour of the Burgtheater, financial advantage, and strict objectivity (Hadamowsky 340). Before Czernin's withdrawal, the theatre secretary's role had already consisted in the review of – albeit not the final decision over – newly submitted manuscripts as well as older plays that were potentially suited for performance (Hadamowsky 338–9). In most cases, the theatre secretary's recommendations were likely accepted. Czernin's successor in the office of *Oberstkämmerer*, Count Moritz Dietrichstein (in office, 1845–8), again initially took a greater interest in the artistic matters of the Burgtheater, before leaving these tasks in the hands of the director (then, Holbein) and the *Regisseure* ("stage directors") (Wlassack 217).

Beyond these various court offices, the emperor himself also had a direct influence on the repertoire. This was particularly pronounced under Joseph II, the founder of the Burgtheater. Not only did the plan for all new plays go to Joseph for approval, but in 1782, he also wrote a memorandum that stipulated rather precise rules for the Burgtheater's repertoire. Among the rules set out in the memorandum were, for instance, the determination that Wednesday be reserved for tragedy, and that premieres of a play were to take place on a Monday (Link 485–6).

In the middle decades of the nineteenth century, the emperor played a less direct role in the programming decisions of the repertoire, and Joseph's rules, too, had long been forgotten. Franz Joseph (r. 1848–1916) especially did not greatly concern himself with the arts (Klingenberg 55). The case for Franz I (r. 1792–1835) is more subtle. While he was not as invested in the theatre as Joseph II had been, he did worry about its costs and was simultaneously eager to see the Burgtheater satisfy the highest artistic expectations. When, in 1827, a significant renovation and expansion of the Burgtheater was contemplated that would have seen the court theatre and court opera combined into one building, Franz personally weighed in and asked for direct access from his imperial apartment in the *Hofburg* to his box in the Burgtheater. Eventually, the entire renovation plan was abandoned (Hadamowsky 337). More negatively, Franz's influence was felt in connection with Grillparzer's *Ein treuer Diener seines Herrn* (*A Loyal Servant of His Master*, premiered 1828). Although this play passed the censors' review and was produced in the Burgtheater, it there met with the displeasure of Emperor Franz, so that it disappeared from the repertoire for some years after its initial performances.[28] Less radically, the emperors could also effect changes in the wording of individual plays. For instance, when attending Friedrich Halm's *Griseldis* (premiered 1835), Emperor Ferdinand I (1835–48) was offended by the fact that King Arthur's wife knelt before Griseldis, the daughter of a charcoal burner. In subsequent performances, the queen was seen bowing instead of kneeling (Wagner, "Navigating and Owning Obedience" 248).

The Audience

In the mid–nineteenth century, the decision over what was introduced to the Burgtheater and, even more so, over what remained in the Burgtheater, depended to a large extent on the audience.[29] While a certain number of seats and boxes had to be reserved – free of charge – for the court, most attendees had to pay an entrance fee, either through subscriptions for theatre boxes or individual seats or – and what in terms of revenue was significantly more important – through individual ticket sales. In 1851, for instance, subscriptions created a revenue of 74,000 guldens while the daily ticket sales grossed 125,000 guldens (Wlassack 245). Interestingly, the seats that were sold on a daily basis through the box office were largely the cheaper seats in the back rows of the parterre and high up in the galleries, populated by the least wealthy members of the audience. In economic terms, in other words, the least affluent spectators were most important to the financial viability of the Burgtheater, and these spectators certainly made their influence felt – against the preferences of the generally much more powerful occupants of the prestigious boxes. If contemporary testimony is to be trusted, it is thanks to the preferences of the more liberal and more education-minded visitors in the cheap seats that both the genre of tragedy and the literature of Shakespeare and of the German classics (Lessing, Goethe, Schiller, Kleist) retained a still relatively strong foothold in the theatre. It was on nights on which the classics and their contemporary heirs – Franz Grillparzer and Friedrich Halm – were played that the box office saw its greatest returns (Yates, *Theatre in Vienna* 64).

The theatre relied heavily on ticket sales for its operations, and the court kept a watchful eye on the ebbs and flows of the theatre's revenue. While it is common to distinguish during this period between Vienna's court theatres – that is the Burgtheater and the Kärntnertortheater (which served as the opera house) – and Vienna's commercial theatres, the court theatres also had to operate under significant economic pressures. At least for the Viennese context, it is not possible to say definitively that while commercial theatres designed their repertoire to please their audience, the court theatre chose their plays so that they would please their court donors.[30]

In the mid–nineteenth century, roughly 50 per cent of the theatre's income was coming in through ticket sales and subscriptions while the remaining 50 per cent was being supplied from the emperor's treasury.[31] Only during the commercially exceptionally successful years of Laube's directorship did about two thirds of revenue come from ticket sales and subscriptions (Wlassack 245). The (in most years) even share between subsidies and ticket sales in the Burgtheater was typical for German-language court theatres of the period (Kord, *Ein Blick* 22).

To appreciate the significant degree to which the mid-nineteenth-century Burgtheater relied on its own revenue, it is also instructive to recall that in the early twenty-first century, the Burgtheater received about eight times more money through state aid than through ticket sales.[32] The reliance on subsidies in today's Burgtheater is particularly high, even among public theatres, but it is not a complete outlier. One would look in vain for a state-owned theatre in German-speaking Europe today that produces half of its income from ticket sales.[33]

Mediated through the relatively high reliance on the box office, the public's aesthetic preferences had a considerable influence on programming decisions in the nineteenth century. Intriguingly, the Burgtheater attracted a relatively diverse audience, and the different parts of the audience had their own artistic preferences and political leanings, and they each made these different sentiments heard. Contrary to common perception, the Burgtheater neither served merely as a private club for the aristocracy, nor did it manage to produce a feeling of "classlessness" in the audience.[34]

The Burgtheater's audience has been the subject of some considerable popular and scholarly interest. Perhaps the most concise introduction to the diverse character of the audience can be found in two anonymous articles dating from 17 and 24 March 1861, and published in the Viennese journal *Recensionen und Mittheilungen über Theater und Musik*.[35] These articles provide us with an overview not only of the different parts of the Burgtheater audience, but also of the very diverse ways in which these different parts of the audience reacted to what they experienced on stage. The two articles are a rich resource, even if their satirical tone and their hyperbolic generalizations clearly signal that their claims should be taken with a grain of salt.

The articles begin with an account of *Das Logenpublikum*, the select group of spectators inhabiting the boxes, which consisted of the aristocracy and "haute finance" ("Das Burgtheaterpublikum" 161). There were a total of seventy-five boxes across four ranks (from the ground level parterre up to the third gallery), in addition to two larger royal and imperial boxes, placed prominently directly opposite the stage on the second gallery and directly next to the stage on the first gallery (see fig. 2.1). In 1851, the Burgtheater advertised the boxes on the lower three ranks for an annual fee of one thousand guldens, to be paid in two instalments. The boxes on the third gallery, which were furthest removed from the stage, cost eight hundred guldens (also payable in two instalments).[36] This was an exorbitant price for most people in Vienna, even if one acknowledges that the fee was not raised over the decades: almost forty years earlier, in 1812, boxes had been rented out for one thousand guldens per year (Wlassack 115). By way of comparison, Franz Grillparzer's gross annual salary as a civil servant in the Habsburg bureaucracy (including all supplemental payments) grew over the course of his forty-year career from four hundred guldens in 1815 to 2,400 guldens in 1856 (Heindl 187). Even the high-ranking *Hofräte* ("court councillors") earned in the 1840s "only" about five thousand guldens per year (183) – still surely not enough to spend one thousand guldens on the luxury of a box in the Burgtheater.

This inordinate annual fee for the boxes stands at a great distance from the modest price to be paid for a single performance in the cheapest seats, high up in the galleries. In 1822, tickets for these seats were sold for twenty kreuzers (Wlassack 158; one gulden equalled, in Austria, sixty kreuzers), which would have been affordable for wide swaths of the Viennese population. There is evidence of simple journeymen from the suburbs visiting the Burgtheater at least occasionally (Stauss 16).[37] The lowest entrance fees were reserved for members of the military, who enjoyed a reduced rate since 1815. For soldiers below the rank of *Hauptmann* ("captain"), a ticket could be acquired for as little as ten kreuzers (Wlassack 115). The military was also to be observed on the stage itself. Until 1851, soldiers were allowed to raise their income by working as supernumeraries – a service for which they received seven kreuzers per performance (Wlassack 159).

Some seats that were sold on a daily basis were again relatively expensive. To spend an evening in the front rows of the parterre, one had to pay one gulden. For five guldens, that is fifteen times the price of the cheapest seat, one could reserve a theatre box for one night (the fact that a box was thus paid off only after two hundred evenings is, incidentally, indicative of the very regular attendance expected of its subscribers).

The anonymous author of the articles in *Recensionen und Mittheilungen*, who was writing for a middle-class readership with intellectual aspirations, speaks disdainfully of the very wealthy part of the audience in the boxes and its alleged lack of all appreciation for serious theatre. The "modern barbarian" ("moderne Barbar"; "Das Burgtheaterpublikum" 162), the author writes, "rejected with indignation" ("mit Entrüstung zurückgewiesen"; 162) the idea of sincere thoughts of a sincere poet. Neither Shakespeare, Goethe, Schiller, nor Lessing found applause in the boxes. The preferred fare was contemporary comedy.[38] When a classic play ("ein klassisches Stück"; 162) was performed, by contrast, the boxes often remained empty – or, if they were occupied, the distinguished men and women in them disturbed the rest of the audience by talking, moving around, and by "rattling their ice cream spoons" ("Klirren mit dem Eislöffel"; 162).

Paradoxically, it was these most exclusive seats in the Burgtheater that were simultaneously also most likely to be filled by some of the lowest-ranking members of the audience. For in the absence of the aristocrats and wealthy bankers, the boxes were regularly occupied by those employed by the elite box-holders: secretaries, tutors, governesses, and maids ("Sekretären, Hofmeistern, Gouvernanten und Kammerfrauen"; "Das Burgtheaterpublikum" 162). It is important to recall here that, in contrast to the reigning practice today, subscribers had permanent access to their seats. For as long as their subscriptions lasted, the boxes remained exclusively theirs, and even a significant number of seats in the parterre were locked to ensure the exclusive rights of those who had secured them for the year (these were the so-called *Sperrsitze*, literally "locked seats").

The writer of the article speaks disdainfully of the secondary audience members, who occupied the boxes in the absence of their employers, apparently seeing in their presence just more evidence for the ignorance of the elite owners of the subscriptions. However, the practice of passing on tickets to relatively low-ranking employees, which is frequently described in contemporary accounts, crucially diversified the Burgtheater audience and is enough to cast some doubt on the reigning stereotype of the Burgtheater as the exclusive place of the wealthy and powerful. There were many more who were entertained, enraged, or bored by the Burgtheater than those for whom it was primarily built. The secondary occupants of the boxes are probably the most prominent group to be named, but one may also think of those attending performances to serve the audience. Famously, one of the best-known comic playwrights of the Austrian nineteenth century, Ferdinand Raimund, became acquainted with the theatre by selling pastries to the Burgtheater's audience in the first years of the nineteenth century.

To be clear, neither modest salespeople amid the audience nor the secondary occupants of the boxes had much impact on the decisions concerning the repertoire. In contrast to the eighteenth-century British novels that discovered in female servants a significant new readership and that paid tribute to this readership in the stories told (Samuel Richardson's *Pamela* is the most famous example; Watt 47), little such influence can be claimed for the repertoire of the Burgtheater. Nor are we permitted to draw on these relatively few men and women to say that the Burgtheater was generally open to all classes. The presence of some pastry sellers and tutors does not compensate for the absence of farm and factory workers for whom the theatre was beyond reach – both physically and financially. And yet, in the period, these unintended spectators still contributed to the diversity of the Burgtheater's audience.

Even if, as we saw, subscribers of the boxes did not attend the Burgtheater every single day, the practice of reserving certain seats and boxes for the exclusive use of the subscribers was reflective of the reality that (a select class of) people went to the theatre much more frequently than is common today, when a subscription typically buys access only to a handful of performances per season. And even though the subscriptions were a less lucrative source of revenue than daily ticket sales, these frequent visitors had a decisive influence on the repertoire insofar as it was for their sake that the theatre had to present, for weeks on end, a different play each night. Moreover, the necessity for such a great variety limited the time available to prepare for a play, and this, in turn, also limited the kinds of plays that could be produced. Performing demanding plays by Schiller or Kleist, which feature long and complex dialogue, on a daily basis would have overtaxed not only the audience but also the memory of the actors.

One large step below the boxes in prestige and price was the so-called "erstes Parterre" ("first parterre"). It consisted of a total of 167 locked seats (*Sperrsitze*) divided across twelve rows (see fig. 2.1). These seats were occupied by men from various positions in the military and civil service, as well as by members of the lower aristocracy. To my knowledge, women did not commonly enjoy the privilege of locked seats in the mid–nineteenth century. They were to be seen either in the boxes or in the open seats in the back rows of the parterre.

In comparison to the audience in the boxes, the men in the locked seats are described as more attentive to the actions on stage, albeit still lacking any actual refinement. According to the anonymous author of the articles for *Recensionen und Mittheilungen*, the two most prominent groups in the "erstes Parterre" were *bonvivants* and retired court councillors ("Lebemenschen und alte Hofräthe"; "Das Burgtheaterpublikum" 177). The former are depicted as frivolous spectators, interested largely in the actresses. The old councillors, by contrast, were "true, old friends of the theatre" ("der echte alte Theaterfreund"; 177), who nostalgically thought of the good old days of the Burgtheater in prior decades. But the "erstes Parterre" also included a range of other men: "higher ranking civil servants still in office, some of the more intelligent military officers, members of the lower nobility, important merchants, wealthy citizens" ("active höhere Beamte, intelligentere Militärs, kleiner Adel, große Kaufleute, reiche Bürger"; 177). Finally, the "erstes Parterre" also accommodated the professional critics, who receive, in these articles, the most damning portrait as an envious group of failed playwrights.

Finally, after the discussion of the boxes and the "erstes Parterre," the anonymous author turns to the back rows of the parterre, the so-called "zweites Parterre" ("second parterre").[39] This part of the audience receives enthusiastic – albeit somewhat patronizing – praise as naive and good ("unbefangen und gut"; "Das Burgtheaterpublikum II" 178). In the men and women of the "zweites Parterre," the author discovers an echo of Shakespeare's original audience that, the author tells us, only needed a sign with a name on it to believe itself in the location of the play on stage. What is more, this part of the audience is claimed to find great pleasure even in tragedy.[40] We are not told anything specific about the social background of the audience, but the image evoked here is that of an uneducated audience of modest social standing, which the author feels comfortable to address with informal pronouns.

In their review of the Burgtheater audience, the anonymous author reconstructs almost the entire social spectrum of Viennese society, from the very modest to the highest elite, and they claim an inverse correlation between social standing and literary taste. This claim is in keeping with other accounts of the period. When, in 1834, members of the high nobility took offence at the short comedy *Damen unter sich* (*Women Among Themselves*) by the French playwright Emmanuel Dupaty (1775–1851), then-director Deinhardstein allegedly told them that the "true rabble was sitting in the boxes from the first rank up and ended in the gallery" ("dass der eigentliche Pöbel in den Logen des ersten Ranges beginne und auf der Gallerie aufhöre"; Costenoble 195).

The image of the Burgtheater as a vessel for all walks of life, which the anonymous author conveys, is exaggerated. Already the fact that the author fails to specify any of the professions of those sitting in "zweites Parterre" should cause suspicion. If the author had given any such information, as they do for the other parts of the audience, they probably would have had to concede that most of the men and women sitting there were still of a middle-class background (as noted earlier, attendance on the part of the working class is proven, but it likely remained the exception; Stauss 16).

Even with this important qualification in mind, the articles from the *Recensionen und Mittheilungen* do make clear that the audience of the Burgtheater was rather heterogenous and certainly not a monolithic assembly of the rich and powerful. It was much more than merely "an institution for the private entertainment of the well-fed aristocracy" ("Privatunterhaltungsanstalt einer satten Aristokratie"; Engländer 195), as some evil tongues would have it. Even if the image of the Burgtheater as an equivalent to the (nearly) all-inclusive Globe Theatre of Shakespeare's London is an exaggeration, the fact that such an exaggeration could be printed in a Viennese newspaper suggests that it was not too far from the truth for at least parts of the readership to accept it.

We possess another clear proof of the audience's diversity from two decades earlier, in the account of a prominent foreign visitor to the Burgtheater in 1845. The traveller in question is Karl Gutzkow, a member of the group of liberal *Jungdeutschen*, who also had several of his plays performed in the Burgtheater. By far the most successful of these plays was the tragedy *Uriel Acosta* (1846, premiered in the Burgtheater in 1849). *Uriel Acosta* focuses on the (Jewish) mentor of Spinoza, Uriel Acosta, and makes a plea for religious freedom (albeit at the cost of a prejudiced depiction of the larger Jewish community as dogmatic and money-driven).[41] On his visit to Vienna in 1845, Gutzkow saw in the Burgtheater Eduard von Bauernfeld's drama *Ein deutscher Krieger* (*A German Warrior*), which had premiered in the Burgtheater the previous year, and which reached fifty performances over the following twenty-one years.[42] As Gutzkow describes it in his travelogue, Bauernfeld's play, which centres on an episode of insubordination of a patriotic officer in the Thirty Years' War, polarized its audience. Members of the aristocracy, seated in their boxes, were outraged by the applause that the play received further below, slammed their doors, and cried out: "It's getting worse and worse!" ("Es wird immer ärger!"; Gutzkow 186). Gutzkow cites the aristocracy's indignation largely as evidence of their reactionary character. More interesting than that indignation, however, is the fact that this indignation stood in sharp contrast to the reaction in other parts of the audience. There was, as Gutzkow's account makes clear, a marked internal differentiation of the Burgtheater audience.

As Gutzkow's description suggests, the interior hierarchy of the audience space, with its division between the boxes and the two levels of the parterre, reproduced some of the interior frictions within Viennese society more broadly, even if the lower and lower middle classes remained still largely excluded from the Burgtheater. The plays performed on stage functioned – intentionally or not – as a catalyst to make the conflicts between the different groups of society visible in the different reactions from different parts of the audience.

The heterogeneity of the Burgtheater's audience importantly shaped that theatre's repertoire. Because the audience did not speak with one voice, it was virtually impossible for the Burgtheater to cater to the entire audience's tastes in a straightforward way. More precisely, almost the only way in which the Burgtheater could cater to its audience's tastes was by offering a diverse repertoire – understanding that some parts of the audience would always remain unsatisfied.

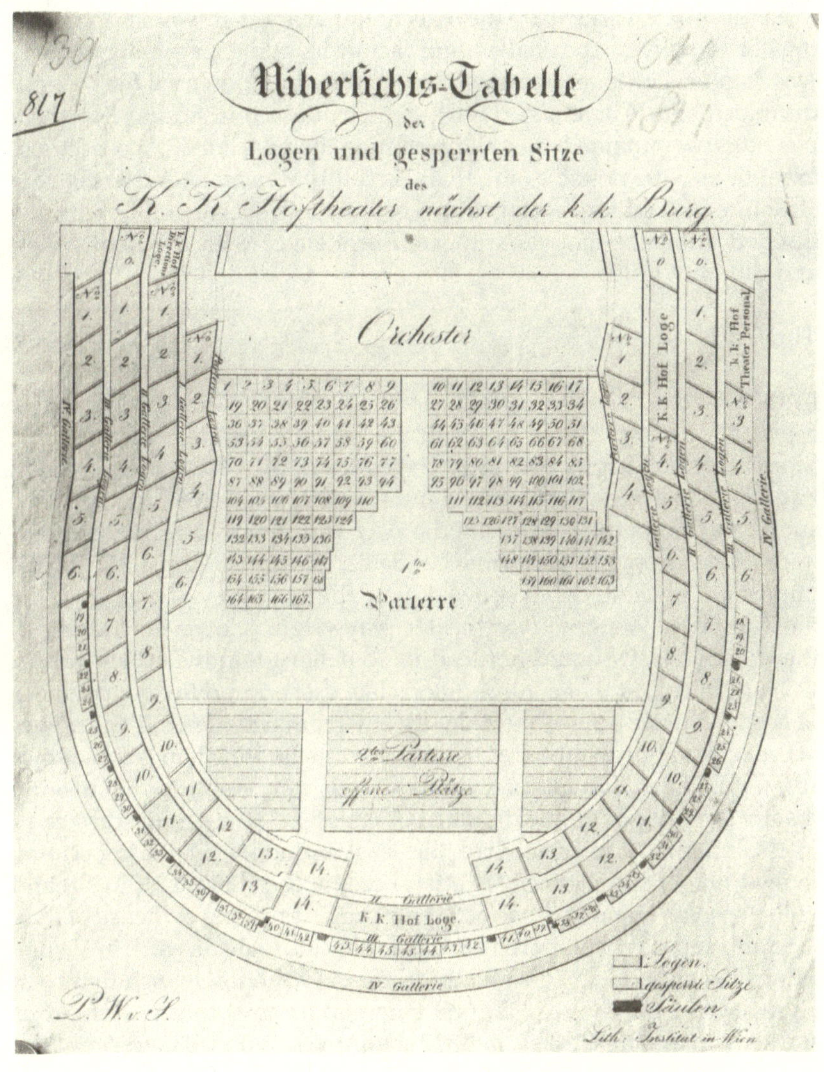

Fig. 2.1. Seating plan of the Burgtheater after the renovations of 1794. Note on this undated image: "Übersichtstabelle der Logen und gesperrten Sitze" ("Overview of the boxes and locked seats"; see Link 452). Austrian National Library/Vienna Picture Archive 129.051-B.

At this point, I anticipate the objection that another way for the Burgtheater to address the challenging fact of its audience's heterogeneity was to offer light entertainment that avoided all potential for political disagreements. There is certainly some truth to this. Scenes like those by Gutzkow remained more the exception than the norm. And yet those exceptions were possible, and this possibility was grounded in the very structure of the Burgtheater, which catered to a socially and politically divided audience that came to the Burgtheater with different beliefs and different tastes.

The Critics

In 1836, Eduard von Bauernfeld used his dramatic satire *Der literarische Salon* (*The Literary Salon*) to mock the leading Viennese theatre critic Moritz Gottlieb Saphir alongside the editor of the *Theaterzeitung*, Adolf Bäuerle. The two newspapermen immediately protested, and, with the support of Emperor Ferdinand, the play was removed from the repertoire after one single performance (Yates, *Theatre in Vienna* 64). In this important incident, critics showed their ability to prevail over even the most popular Viennese Burgtheater playwright. However, striking as this episode is, it should not lead us to believe that the critics' power was unlimited, or that confrontations like that around the performance of *Der literarische Salon* occurred with any regularity. Overall, the power of the critics appears to have been much more limited than is sometimes suggested, even though they were certainly very important in making theatre a matter of public discourse.[43] Among all the groups discussed in this chapter, the critics had the least influence on the repertoire. Indeed, the critics themselves often became the subjects of harsh and violent censure, and the case of Saphir provides ample evidence of that.

Saphir repeatedly suffered attacks for his journalistic work in Vienna as well as elsewhere.[44] Originally from an Orthodox Jewish family in Hungary, Saphir (1795–1858) first emerged as an author of humorous stories written in Yiddish. In 1822, he moved, upon Bäuerle's invitation, to Vienna and began writing for the latter's *Theaterzeitung*. In 1825, Saphir was already forced to leave the city, with, as Lothar Kahn writes in one of the very few scholarly articles devoted to this fascinating figure, "the curses of the theatrical world upon his head" (Kahn 251). According to an unconfirmed account, Saphir's departure was "accompanied by secret nocturnal beatings" (251). For the next several years, Saphir worked as a theatre critic in Berlin, first gaining the favour of the Prussian king Frederick William III and then losing it again, eventually being expelled from the Prussian capital in 1829. Saphir next moved to

Munich, where he met a similar fate, drawing upon himself the rage of his one-time benefactor, King Louis I, who, it is claimed, even imprisoned him for some time. In 1834, Saphir returned to Vienna. If he now managed to stay in that city for longer and retain the favour of those in power, it was by professing his support for the politics of the conservative state chancellor Metternich, while continuing to anger many playwrights.

The position of the critic, as Saphir's extreme example shows, was not easy. Saphir won his popularity with the readers through his harsh attacks, but these same attacks also made him vulnerable. It has been critically pointed out that Saphir was a writer without clear and firm convictions (he is even rumoured to have accepted payment in return for good reviews; Kahn 247). However, this apparent lack of a political or aesthetic backbone was also the result of the uncertain status of the mid-nineteenth-century critic, who, while often a bane of the theatre practitioners, was under immense pressure from various sides. Lacking the reliable salaries and pensions that those employed by the Burgtheater enjoyed, the critic had to produce a large amount of exciting prose, while also bearing in mind the repercussions from the playwrights, actors, directors, and, potentially, those in power (between 1828 and 1843, six of Saphir's printed works did not pass the Austrian censors).[45] Finally – and this is especially important to appreciate the very limited sway critics held over the repertoire in Vienna – the censors did not allow any critique of the Burgtheater director in the press (Klingenberg 45). Any principled attack on the repertoire as a whole was thus made impossible, insofar as this repertoire was, at least officially, associated with the director. All the critics could do was to speak out against individual plays and productions.

As noted at the outset of this chapter, it is not easy to assess the relative power of the various agents over the Burgtheater repertoire in the years from 1814 to 1867. What is most certain and most decisive is that there was no single force that could swiftly and unilaterally shape the repertoire as a whole. Nonetheless, a few important nuances can be observed. The artistic leaders of the Burgtheater (Schreyvogel, Deinhardstein, Holbein, and Laube) were most directly involved in decisions over the repertoire, and they were, contrary to what has been claimed, no mere puppets who implemented decisions of the court. Still, their powers were, especially when compared to today's theatre directors, limited by a range of different groups and agents. If one wanted to rank these various influences on the Burgtheater directors (accepting the uncertainty in this endeavour), it appears that the most decisive impact came from the audience and the playwrights: these two groups were crucial in deciding the Burgtheater's cycles of supply and demand. It is especially important in this context to emphasize the writers, whom one might be tempted to overlook or take for granted in analysing a theatre's management of its repertoire. A theatre with as large a repertoire as the Burgtheater's functioned, to some extent, simply as a forum for the literary production of the period and was thus heavily dependent on what was being written. The most important point to note about the audience, on which the Burgtheater relied financially for about half of its revenue, is that the audience was itself divided both in terms of rank and of taste, with the result that there was a demand both for the politically conservative and for the progressive, for contemporary entertainment as well as for classical drama.

All other groups were less decisive. The actors, while instrumental in making individual plays fail or succeed and in establishing a characteristic mode of presentation throughout all plays, had, by the mid-nineteenth century, only occasionally a more direct influence on decision making.[46] Court and censorship, for their part, undoubtedly forced the exclusion of some plays and topics: had it not been for the censors' stricture, we would have seen earlier a critical discussion of the Catholic Church especially.[47] Yet by and large, there is little to suggest that the repertoire would have looked radically different in the absence of these controlling forces. An even lesser role in repertoire making was played by the critics. While they were crucial in bringing the public's attention to theatre productions (in ways that were not always to the liking of those working in the theatre), there is scant evidence that they directly shaped the repertoire on a regular basis.

3 The Scope of the Burgtheater Repertoire

Difficult as the question of who determined the repertoire in the mid-nineteenth-century Burgtheater is, already the few points that we can state with relative certainty have a direct bearing on what the repertoire looked like and how it was perceived. The theatre directors were the most important people among those concerned with the inclusion of new plays and the retention of old plays. But they lacked the means to single-handedly shape the repertoire. They were faced with numerous other agents, who again were sometimes divided among themselves (which is especially true for the Burgtheater's diverse audience). As a result of this complex structure, the Burgtheater's repertoire existed, to some degree, as an unwieldy and heterogeneous corpus that resisted any attempt at swift unilateral action. To put it more positively, the Burgtheater successfully navigated numerous competing expectations – expectations for internationalism as well as for of nationalism, for entertainment as well as for education and the cultivation of the classics, for comedy as well as for tragedy. If the Burgtheater did manage to respond to all these diverse demands it was not least because of the remarkable size of its repertoire. In this chapter, I outline the diversity of the Burgtheater repertoire in general terms, before devoting the rest of this book to a more focused analysis of the ways in which the Burgtheater treated specific topics of contemporary social and political concern.

The limited power of the theatre directors provides one of the keys to understanding the Burgtheater's repertoire. It was largely as a result of the directors' narrow possibilities that the repertoire was not perceived as emerging from the creative and conceptual work of one single agent. Although many of the Burgtheater directors were themselves playwrights, there is relatively little indication that they saw their directorship as a direct artistic outlet. We know that at least Heinrich Laube's successor, the highly successful Burgtheater dramatist Friedrich Halm (in office, 1867–8), detested his position because he saw in it a fundamental obstacle to his work as an artist; he much preferred his previous position as head of the court library, which, in his mind, was also more conducive to his writing.[1]

Just as today's idea of the theatre director as the supreme artist of the institution remains relatively alien to the mid-nineteenth-century Burgtheater, so today's idea that we can put a label on the repertoire is not yet applicable to that earlier period. In the past few years, such labels have become very common in German-speaking Europe. According to one survey, 70 per cent of German state theatres use labels as a convenient tool at the intersection of conceptual artistic work and marketing practice (though the Burgtheater has resisted this trend so far). The Schauspiel Leipzig, for instance, used the slogan "Fear or Love" ("Angst oder Liebe") in the 2017/18 season. In 2018/19 season, that theatre adopted "I I I I" ("ICH ICH ICH ICH"). The label for the 2019/20 season was "Together/Ensemble" ("Miteinander/Ensemble"). However general these labels may be, they determine some form of emphasis, and they encourage the reception of all plays from the specific perspective of the chosen umbrella term, on which the theatre can then elaborate in publications and events throughout the year.

Such a practice would have been inconceivable for the mid-nineteenth-century Burgtheater, which managed a large, diverse, and slowly mutating repertoire and in which theatre directors often decided ad hoc about the submissions they received. This does not mean that plays necessarily entered the repertoire overnight or that there was no thought about the repertoire as a whole, but concrete decisions often happened on an individual basis (play by play), and, at least after the foundational years under Joseph II, there was never again a consistent and fully implemented redesign of the entire repertoire.

The Burgtheater's European Repertoire

While decisions over new plays were often made ad hoc, there were still moments in the mid–nineteenth century at which some more general reflections and even decisions over the repertoire were being ventured. Most prominently among those times are the early years of Heinrich Laube's directorship – even though Laube's conceptions were not as innovative or radical as he himself made them out to be. Laube envisioned a repertoire that would stand out for its wide international range – and eventually he believed to have attained this goal. Indeed, Laube insisted that the comprehensiveness of the Burgtheater repertoire was unmatched anywhere in Europe. In his 1868 book on the Burgtheater's history, he writes:

> For some years, the Burgtheater has been offering the most comprehensive repertoire not only in Germany, but in Europe. The Théâtre-Français, our great competitor, cannot, on account of its strictly Romance character, move beyond Romance limits; it cannot appropriate anything foreign in the way we can. And there is no other competitor. The German theatres have all fallen back in that respect; the English stage is in ruins; and the Spanish and Italian stages are under the sway of the French.

> Das Burgtheater hat seit einer Reihe von Jahren das umfassendste Repertoire gebothen, nicht nur in Deutschland, sondern in Europa. Das Theatre français, unser großer Rival, kommt wegen seines formell abgeschlossenen romanischen Wesens nirgends über romanische Grenzen hinaus und kann sich Nichts aus der Fremde aneignen, wie wir es vermögen. Und ein anderer Rival ist nicht vorhanden. Die deutschen Theater sind darin sämmtlich zurückgeblieben, die englische Bühne ist verfallen und die spanische wie die italienische sind französirt. (Laube, *Das Burgtheater* 159–60)

In emphasizing the Burgtheater's broad international repertoire, Heinrich Laube points to one of the key features of that institution. And yet his comments require at least some further specifications: not to show them as unfounded, but to clarify where the limits of the Burgtheater's internationalism were, and to avoid a misleading image of radical exceptionalism. When Laube, for instance, claims that the other German-language stages did not keep up with the Burgtheater's broadening of the repertoire, it has to be acknowledged that, in general terms, an international character was typical of other leading German stages in the mid–nineteenth century as well. Both Shakespeare and the contemporary French conversation plays in the manner of Scribe were widely popular in German theatres of the period. Moreover, Laube's map of Europe remains rather narrow. He does not include any Central and Eastern European countries and territories – even though there, too, he would have been able to observe a more international repertoire.

Even with these qualifications in mind (and I will add a few additional ones in just a moment), Laube's proud claim about the breadth of the Burgtheater repertoire is indicative not only of his ideals, but also of the general direction that the repertoire actually took. What this breadth meant more precisely becomes clearer in Laube's oft-cited declaration about his goals when he took over the theatre in 1849:

> My ideal was to be able say, after a few years, to every guest from abroad: Stay for one year in Vienna; you will see all plays of a classical or at least lively [*lebensvoll*] nature that German literature has produced in the past one hundred years; you will see what Shakespeare has bequeathed to us Germans; you will see everything from the Romance people that can be assimilated to our way of thinking.
>
> Mein Ideal war, nach wenigen Jahren jedem Gast aus der Fremde sagen zu können: Bleibe ein Jahr in Wien und du wirst im Burgtheater Alles sehen, was die deutsche Literatur seit seinem Jahrhunderte Classisches oder doch Lebensvolles für die Bühne geschaffen; du wirst sehen, was Shakespeare uns Deutschen hinterlassen, wirst sehen, was von den romanischen Völkern unserer Denkweise angeeignet werden kann. (Laube, *Das Burgtheater* 159)

Laube's commitment to a European repertoire has justly received much praise, even from such a staunch critic as Gerhard Klingenberg, who otherwise describes the Burgtheater as a helplessly narrow-minded and reactionary institution (56–7).

But, again, it should also be acknowledged where the limitations of Laube's internationalism are. Just as Laube failed to consider the internationality of Eastern and Central European theatres when praising the unmatched scope of the Burgtheater repertoire, he also disregarded the works of Hungarian and Slavic playwrights. No originally Russian play was performed in the Burgtheater until 1884, when Gogol's *The Inspector* was performed. The first originally Polish play arrived in 1878 (Alexander Fredro's comedy *Mädchenschwüre* [*Girls' Oaths*]). During Laube's eighteen years in office, there was also no play originally written in Czech or Hungarian (though under Schreyvogel in the 1820s, one originally Czech play had been introduced, without much success).[2]

The failure to better include Central and Eastern European playwrights is one of the great missed opportunities for the prestigious institution in the heart of the multiethnic Habsburg Empire. It is also striking that as much as the Habsburg court is said to have been wary of nationalist tendencies, as far as I have seen, it never used its influence on the Burgtheater to include a greater number of playwrights from its various territories. While the Burgtheater's neglect of the drama from its Eastern neighbours was in line with other German-language stages of the period, Laube's claim to internationalism was still conceived within a typical, but nonetheless problematically narrow, understanding of European literature.

More surprising perhaps than the neglect of Eastern European literature is, at least from today's perspective, the fact that Laube (quite like his predecessors) also turned a blind eye to the plays of Greek and Roman antiquity. Plays from ancient times arrived in the Burgtheater late in the nineteenth century, and, even then, they were not crowned with much success. Between 1814 and 1867, the only production of a play from antiquity was of Terence's comedy *Die Brüder* (*The Brothers*; orig. *Adelphoe*) in 1841, and it vanished after only four performances.[3] Sophocles and Euripides did not make an appearance until the 1880s. Aeschylus had to wait until 1900 (Rub 305). This neglect of the Ancients is surprising insofar as, by the mid-nineteenth century, their exemplary status had long been established. The idea that the Greeks should serve as a model for drama had not only been important for Goethe and Schiller around 1800 (as well as for Enlightenment thinkers across several generations before them), but it was also fully established as a fact in the writings of the great theatre practitioners of the mid-nineteenth century. In his 1849 essay *Die Kunst und die Revolution*, Richard Wagner described Greek tragedy as the unmatched pinnacle of dramatic art. And Gustav Freytag based his 1863 primer *Die Technik des Dramas* on the plays of Sophocles alongside those only of Shakespeare, Lessing, Goethe, and Schiller. Remarkably, Freytag notes in the introduction to his book that he wanted his examples to come from "universally known" ("allbekannte"; *Die Technik des Dramas* 6) works, and he apparently included Sophocles's plays under this rubric. All that being said, the neglect of classical antiquity in the Burgtheater was in line with the practice of other leading contemporary theatres. Even in Weimar, the epicentre of classicism, performances of the Greeks and Romans remained the great exception before the last third of the nineteenth century.

A closer look at Laube's programmatic claim also makes clear that he conceived of the variety of the Burgtheater's repertoire very clearly through the lens of a German national identity. As he states, plays especially in the Romance languages should be accepted only to the extent that they could be aligned with a presumed (albeit in no way defined) essence of the German spirit. The breadth that Laube aimed for thus cannot be understood as guided by a desire for true cultural diversity. Instead, his goal remained largely to explore resonances between a rather narrow corpus of other European literatures and German national culture.

Finally, despite Laube's prominent claims about his ambitious goals for the repertoire of the Burgtheater, what he professed was largely in line with the repertoire that he inherited from his predecessors. A closer analysis of the Laube years shows that there is no significant international expansion of the repertoire. The Burgtheater repertoire was international before Laube, and it stayed international under Laube. While he continued with some successful English, Spanish, and Italian playwrights introduced before him (Shakespeare, Calderón, Goldoni), the eighteen Laube years brought no new Italian or English playwright and only two new Spanish playwrights to the Burgtheater.[4] The only literary tradition for which Laube significantly and disproportionally increased the number of playwrights is the French – the very tradition that was, apart from originally German-language drama, already best established. In the eighteen years under Laube, thirty-nine new French playwrights were introduced. That is about twice as many as Schreyvogel introduced in the same amount of time, as well as about twice as many as Deinhardstein and about four times as many as Holbein had introduced, adjusted for the years they were in office.[5] In general, the share of plays originally written in a language other than German remained in the Laube era more or less in line with that of previous decades. While in the three directorships before Laube, international plays accounted for about 38 per cent of all newly introduced plays, in the years under Laube, international plays represented roughly 36 per cent of new plays.[6]

Because of all the above, it is prudent to approach Laube's statement about the Burgtheater's internationalism under his reign with some scepticism. Yet to avoid a misunderstanding, the Burgtheater certainly *was* remarkable for its inclusion of playwrights from different countries. Thanks to the significant size of its repertoire, it was able to perform, in addition to a long list of German plays, many recognized classics from England, Italy, Spain, and France, as well as a notable selection of contemporary French entertainment. But it bears emphasis that this feature long predated Laube's tenure, and that this internationalism operated within the confines of a clear hierarchy in which many Central and Eastern European literatures remained excluded.

Entertainment and Classical Education in the Burgtheater

As we saw, Laube's treatment of drama translated from other languages was largely similar to that of his predecessors. What did constitute a slightly more noticeable shift was the renewed emphasis on the German classics under his direction. For already in his first full year in office (that is, 1850), Laube added three major German classics to the repertoire: Goethe's *Faust, Part One*; Schiller's *Die Räuber* (*The Robbers*); and Kleist's *Der zerbrochene Krug* (*The Broken Jug*) (Rub 79). But here again, it is worth noting that not only had all these playwrights been prominently featured before, but also that Laube's innovation only continued an increased emphasis on German classics that had been ushered in by the new nationalist sentiment and simultaneous temporary abolishment of censorship in the aftermath of the 1848 revolution. Still, in 1848, immediately after the March Revolution, the Burgtheater had first performed a play about Schiller (*Die Karlsschüler* by Heinrich Laube) and then all three parts of Schiller's *Wallenstein* (Rub 75–6).[7]

Conversely, Laube also did not abandon the Burgtheater's longstanding devotion to lighter entertainment. One of the hallmarks of the Burgtheater throughout the mid–nineteenth century was that it managed to maintain a large repertoire that covered both lighter entertainment and aesthetically and intellectually more ambitious drama. Theatre in the nineteenth century in general, we should recall, functioned as entertainment in ways in which this is no longer the case for major state-sponsored German-language theatres today. The repertoires of the period were filled with many plays whose purpose was to amuse rather than to advance education, philosophical reflection, or political agitation – although the ambition to work towards these latter goals was also well established and addressed in a smaller number of plays. Scholars of nineteenth-century German-language literature, notably Susanne Kord, have emphasized the hierarchy that existed between these two forms of plays: plays of entertainment meant for stage performance on the one hand; and more serious plays that invited reading as another appropriate mode of reception on the other hand. Kord distinguishes, in German, between *Theater* (understood as ephemeral entertainment meant primarily for performance) and *Drama* (understood as longer-lasting and more demanding literature meant primarily for reading and worthy of theoretical reflection) (*Sich einen Namen machen* 69–70).

Essentially all nineteenth-century writers of *Theater*, men as well as women, are forgotten today: certainly in terms of theatre productions and the reading practice of the general public, but largely also as objects of scholarly discussion. Among the only exceptions to this are three popular actor-playwrights of Goethe's generation: August von Kotzebue (1761–1819; represented in the Burgtheater with 114 plays), the most successful of all writers of *Theater* of his age, and, in 1797–8 also the Burgtheater's *Theatersecretär* ("dramaturge"); August Wilhem Iffland (1759–1814; represented in the Burgtheater with thirty-nine plays); and Friedrich Ludwig Schröder (1744–1816; represented in the Burgtheater with fifty-four plays).[8] But there were many writers of *Theater* besides and after Kotzebue, Iffland, and Schröder who figured prominently in German-language theatres of the mid–nineteenth century, including the Burgtheater, and often with a staggering number of plays. If we focus only on those German-language playwrights who had twenty or more plays performed in the Burgtheater in that period, we arrive at the following list: Eduard von Bauernfeld (1802–90; forty-eight plays); Roderich Benedix (1811–73; thirty-four plays); Charlotte Birch-Pfeiffer (1800–68; twenty-five plays); Johann Ludwig Deinhardstein (1794–1854; twenty-seven plays); Ernst Raupach (1784–1825; twenty-eight plays); Carl Töpfer (1792–1855; twenty-three plays); Johanna Franul von Weißenthurn (1772–1847; forty-eight plays); Friedrich Wilhelm Ziegler (1759–1827; thirty plays).[9] This list includes not a single author of what Susanne Kord would likely classify as *Drama*. The large number of an author's plays in the repertoire is perhaps the easiest indicator for their identification as writers of *Theater*.

The lines between *Drama* and *Theater*, however, are not always clear. Nor is it in all cases evident that *Theater* had a lesser status than *Drama*. We find writers of *Theater* who took great pride in their work as a form of art meant for performance. Deinhardstein, for instance, defended aspects of his successful play *Hans Sachs* by referring to the requirements of the stage (x–xii). Importantly, his reference to stage practice does not come in the tone of an apology, but rather in the tone of an instruction, reminding critics of the principles of his art. Incidentally, Deinhardstein devoted one of his plays entirely to the topic of theatrical performance, and this play became his most popular piece in the Burgtheater. This is the comedy *Garrick in Bristol*, which focuses on a fictional episode in the life of the famous eighteenth-century actor David Garrick (1717–79). During his lifetime, Garrick was instrumental in improving the social standing and artistic recognition of actors, and in his play, Deinhardstein makes the question of the social prestige and artistic relevance of acting a major concern. Deinhardstein's work, in other words, was very proudly *Theater*.

Just how blurry the distinction between *Drama* and *Theater* is also becomes clear when we turn to the playwright Friedrich Halm. Halm belongs among the small group of nineteenth-century Austrian playwrights who largely abstained from writing comedy (the preferred genre of *Theater*) and at least during his lifetime as well as shortly afterwards, Halm was considered a serious and significant writer of *Drama*. His early play *Griseldis* became classroom reading in nineteenth-century England, and when, in 1888, the new Burgtheater opened on the Ringstrasse, he was deemed worthy of being represented in one of only nine busts of the greatest playwrights of all times – an honour that none of the evident writers of *Theater* received. There is thus good reason to see in Halm an author of *Drama* – and yet that might be the wrong category. After all, Halm was forgotten relatively quickly after his death in 1871: around 1900 he was already considered outdated, and his plays had vanished from the stage (see Wagner, "Zur Gehorsamskritik"). There also never emerged any Halm philology that is worth that name, and Halm's brief inclusion in British university curricula notwithstanding, there is little to suggest that Halm's printed plays found a wide readership, even in his own time. In retrospect, Halm remained, by and large, a phenomenon of the nineteenth-century stage, even if his contemporaries who attended his plays would have likely judged otherwise, putting him, instead, more in line with authors such as Friedrich Hebbel or Franz Grillparzer, whose literary status as writers of serious and lasting drama only grew after their death.

A final point to consider in the dichotomy between *Drama* and *Theater* is that it was not uncommon for popular Burgtheater playwrights to produce two versions of their play, one for the stage and one for reading. In some printed plays, playwrights signalled passages or scenes that could or should be cut during performance, be it because those passages were, dramatically speaking, less promising or because they could cause problems with the censors, who had stricter standards for performance than for print publication.[10] By signalling the passages to be cut, the playwrights made clear both that they were writing with the stage in mind *and* that they envisioned a life for their plays outside of performance, in the realm of *Drama*.

While many playwrights of *Theater*, who are forgotten today, featured prominently on nineteenth-century stages (including the Burgtheater), authors we now tend to regard as classics were marginalized in many theatres of the period. In Zurich's main theatre of the mid–nineteenth century, the Aktien-Theater, for instance, Goethe, Schiller, Shakespeare, and Lessing were hardly performed at all.[11] Even though parts of the educated middle class increasingly sought out the theatre to encounter classic playwrights, whom it predominantly knew through reading, nineteenth-century theatres still largely sought to satisfy a demand for entertainment. As noted earlier, this had as much to do with the audience's tastes as with the practical limitations of the theatres. Performances of the classics with their often rather lengthy dialogue were too taxing for an ensemble that had to move quickly from one play to the next. As we have seen, the mid-nineteenth-century Burgtheater with its well over one hundred different plays in any given year had a much larger repertoire than any theatre today. This, alongside the fact that there were significantly fewer rehearsals than is common today (rarely more than a handful), made it very difficult to stage plays that required memorizing long stretches of text (Kord, *Ein Blick* 23). Instead, theatres preferred lighter plays, which were typically shorter and which distributed the dialogue among more characters.

The Burgtheater, however, was different from Zurich's Aktien-Theater and many other commercial theatres in that demanding plays by the classics did have a significant presence. As in some other court theatres, plays largely meant for entertainment succeeded in the Burgtheater alongside the formally and intellectually more demanding classics. As a matter of fact, hardly any playwright was more successful in the Burgtheater in the long nineteenth century than Schiller, who saw 1,911 performances across nineteen different works between 1787 and 1912 (Rub 279). Moreover, what stands out in the case of Schiller – and, to a lesser extent, the same is true for the other classics as well – is that his plays were much more consistently successful than those of the popular playwrights. Kotzebue, for instance, by far the most popular playwright of the period, reached 3,872 performances, but he needed 114 plays to get there (Rub 274). In other words, his plays averaged about thirty-four performances, whereas Schiller's plays saw on average 101 performances. If we exclude Schiller's translations as well as his fragment *Demetrius* and the performance of his poem *Die Glocke* (*The Bell*) from our calculation, Schiller's average increases to about 143 performances.

For other popular playwrights of *Theater*, the average number of performances per play was even lower than Kotzebue's. Bauernfeld's plays saw, on average, twenty-four performances; Charlotte Birch-Pfeiffer's, twenty-three; and Roderich Benedix's, nineteen (Rub 266). And while Schiller's success rate was uniquely high, other recognized playwrights of *Drama* still fared significantly better than even the most successful writers of entertainment. Shakespeare's twenty-seven plays averaged about eighty-one performances and Grillparzer's fifteen plays reached about sixty-six performances each (Rub 270). Goethe's fifteen plays in the Burgtheater saw, on average, fifty-nine performances.

The classics, in sum, had a very solid standing in the Burgtheater. And that is noticeably true also for those classic plays that could have easily been regarded as politically problematic by the Habsburg court and its censorship office. Of all of Schiller's plays, his most successful was *Maria Stuart*: a tragedy about the execution of a deposed queen at the hands of an unscrupulous Elizabeth I of England. It is hard to imagine subject matter that would have been more offensive to a court that was highly suspicious of any references to royalty on stage. And yet it was this play that saw 235 performances in the nineteenth-century Burgtheater.

The censors were certainly aware of the challenges in Schiller's plays, and they did not simply choose to ignore these challenges because of Schiller's singular standing as the embodiment of the greatness of German literature. As a matter of fact, because the censors were watching with an especially strict eye over the Burgtheater (as well as the court opera house), some of Schiller's plays (*Die Räuber*, *Wilhelm Tell*) were first performed elsewhere, in the Theater an der Wien (Wlassack 133). But the artistic leaders of the Burgtheater persisted and eventually did manage to produce these plays on Vienna's main stage. In 1810, for instance, the censorship office rejected Ferdinand Pálffy's request to stage *Maria Stuart* in the Burgtheater, a rejection confirmed by the emperor when it was appealed (Yates, *Theatre in Vienna* 32). In 1814, Pálffy tried again, and succeeded. While the censorship office was able to cut or alter some passages, the impact of these interventions was limited in the case of a play that much of the audience knew through reading. All too easily, the audience could fill in what the censors sought to extinguish. Additionally, there is anecdotal evidence to suggest that, at least in some cases, the actors in the Burgtheater may have managed to bring across the original content even where this had been altered by the censors.[12]

There is a similar story to be told about Goethe as about Schiller. Goethe's early *Sturm und Drang* play about a rebellious knight, *Götz von Berlichingen*, was, at 128 performances, his third-most successful piece in the Burgtheater, with *Faust, Part One* and *Egmont* having been shown more often (Rub 270). Admittedly, *Götz* premiered only in 1830, over half a century after Goethe had written that drama in 1773, and even then, some changes had to be made to the manuscript.[13] Notably, one of the play's villains, the Bishop of Bamberg, lost his clerical position in the Burgtheater production, where he was turned into a landgrave (Yates, *Theatre in Vienna* 34). But again, this change was likely obvious to many in the Burgtheater audience because the print version appears to have circulated freely in Austria at the time.[14]

In short, while obstacles for productions of the classics were significant and the alterations made to the plays noteworthy, it is an exaggeration to claim, as W.E. Yates does in his seminal study of Viennese theatre, that "the treatment of the German classics made nonsense of the original intention that the Burgtheater should function as a national theatre" (*Theatre in Vienna* 34). With significant delay and through much compromise, the Burgtheater did become in the mid–nineteenth century one of the major stages for the performance of the classics. Indeed, during Heinrich Laube's directorship, the Burgtheater became, as even Gerhard Klingenberg concedes, the uncontested leader in the production of German classical drama: "Since Laube, the Burgtheater is *the* German-language stage for the classics" ("Seit Laube ist das Burgtheater *das* Klassiker-Theater deutscher Sprache"; 57).

The Genres of the Burgtheater

The Burgtheater managed not only to accommodate a demand for lighter entertainment alongside a commitment to the German classics, but it also showcased a robust coverage across the dominant genres of the period: comedy, drama (*Schauspiel*), and tragedy. This is important to emphasize because it goes against the common (negative) stereotype of the Burgtheater as a platform for comedy (see, for instance, Hellbach 21). Those in the nineteenth century who wanted to denigrate either Austrian theatre in general or the Burgtheater in particular reduced it to a stage for comedy – comedy here being understood as a deeply apolitical genre, offering entertainment without raising any serious concerns. In a regime that was suspicious of any political subject matter, all that could be performed, it was claimed, was allegedly unpolitical contemporary Austrian comedy.

Karl Gutzkow's report of his journey to Vienna in 1845 is a case in point. The initially pleasant scene at the Austrian border on the way to Vienna, Gutzkow writes, threatened to become sombre when he declared having books with him, for "this giant state with its colossal Hungarian grenadiers is scared of books as if they were ghosts" ("Vor Büchern hat dieser Riesenstaat mit seinen kolossalen ungrischen Grenadieren eine wahre Gespensterfurcht"; 152). But when Gutzkow said that his books were comedies, the officer lightened up. In clear defiance of the historical record, Gutzkow claims:

> They are not afraid of plays for the theatre there. Of course, Metternich and Sedlnitzky [Count Sedlnitzky, who from 1817 to 1848 was head of the court police office, which oversaw censorship] do not allow the performance of a single Shakespeare piece in which an ambiguous [*zweideutiger*] king or evil minister appears. But what one commonly calls "comedy" in Austria – a bit of Bauernfeld, some Grillparzer, a little Raimund, and a lot of Nestroy – that is permitted, and the suitcase passed a barrier of twenty customs officers.

> Vor Theaterstücken haben sie dort keine Furcht. Metternich und Sedlnitzky lassen zwar kein einziges Shakespeare'sches Stück aufführen, in welchem ein zweideutiger König oder schlechter Minister vorkommt,

> aber was man gewöhnlich in Oesterreich Komödien nennt, ein bisschen Bauernfeld, etwas Grillparzer, ein wenig Raimund und viel Nestroy, das läßt man zu und der Koffer wanderte durch eine Barriere von zwanzig Mauthsoldaten. (152–3)

Contrary to what Gutzkow claims, Shakespeare's tragedies with morally ambiguous kings were among the most popular plays on that stage. Notably the production of Shakespeare's *King Lear* with Heinrich Anschütz in the role of the old king (introduced in 1822) became one of the most written-about productions not only in the Burgtheater, but in all of German theatre in the nineteenth century. Likewise, Gutzkow's insinuation that Nestroy or Bauernfeld were harmlessly apolitical reveals a very limited understanding of these dramatists (that said, Nestroy's plays were not produced in the Burgtheater until 1901; Rub 277).

And yet it is true that comedy featured very prominently in the Burgtheater repertoire. Between 1814 and 1867, the share of comedies among the plays introduced into the repertoire averaged around 55 per cent. Drama (*Schauspiel*) represented about 26 per cent, and tragedy about 11 per cent of new plays (see fig. 3.1).[15] However, the share of comedies is somewhat inflated because comedies could either be filling an entire evening or be performed as part of an evening's programming. While it was not uncommon to see two or even three shorter comedies performed on a single night, there was never more than one tragedy on display – simply because there were no one- or two-act tragedies. Moreover, the most successful plays of the period were tragedies, not comedies. There was no comedy that matched the success of Shakespeare's *Hamlet*, Schiller's *Maria Stuart*, or Goethe's *Faust*.

While there was some fluctuation, the share of comedy, tragedy and *Schauspiel* remained, overall, fairly stable over the decades. The only tentative trend to be noticed is that the years under Deinhardstein (1832–41) saw a dearth in the introduction of new tragedies. But even this apparent outlier turns out to be less stark if we consider not only the number of new plays across different genres, but also the daily playbills (remembering that the repertoire always included a very large number of previously introduced plays). While on average, tragedy was on stage on about fifty-four evenings each year between 1814 and 1867, in the Deinhardstein years, this average was lowered to about forty-seven evenings – a difference that, possibly, was not very noticeable for the average member of the audience.[16] The assertion, made some decades later in 1876, that under Deinhardstein comedy "reigned with almost unchecked power" ("das Lustspiel herrschte mit fast unumschränkter Macht"; Wlassack 189) is an exaggeration.

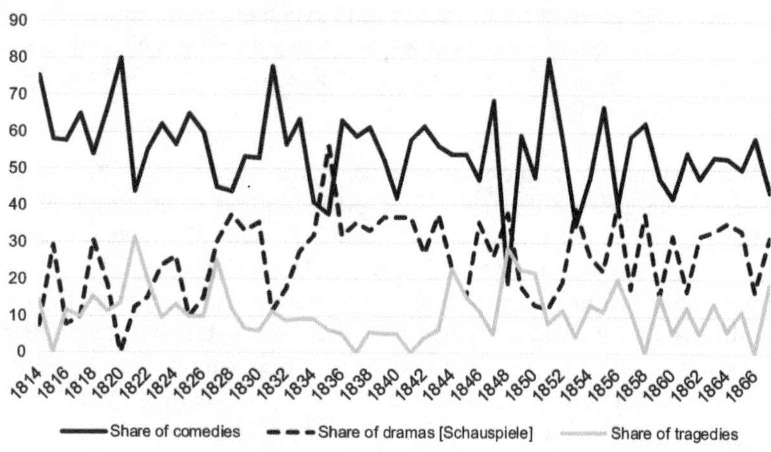

Fig. 3.1. Share of comedy, drama, and tragedy among the newly introduced plays in the Burgtheater, 1814–67. Data based on the information in Rub.

Crucially, the Burgtheater's relative preference for comedy was typical of the period's theatres – even of the more prestigious court theatres. A comparative glance at Weimar's court theatre in the years of Goethe's directorship (1791–1817) shows a nearly identical distribution of genres. During Goethe's tenure, 393 plays were introduced. Of these, 224 (or 57 per cent) were comedies and farces; 104 (26.5 per cent) were dramas (*Schauspiele*); and 60 (15.3 per cent) were tragedies (Kindermann, "Notwendigkeit und Aufgaben" 165). At the Hoftheater Karlsruhe, tragedy was probably even more sidelined than at the Burgtheater. In 1830, among 123 evenings on which the Hoftheater Karlsruhe opened its doors to the public, only nine evenings presented a tragedy – entire months passed without the performance of a tragedy. And even if this number may be untypically low for the Hoftheater Karlsruhe,[17] there is no indication that tragedy ever became more prominent than the competing dramatic genres or that it was more prominent than in the Burgtheater.

If anything is notable in the comparison between Vienna's Burgtheater and that of the court theatre in Karlsruhe, it is the difference in absolute numbers. Because of the Burgtheater's large repertoire, and because the Burgtheater performed almost daily, it was able to show tragedy more frequently and in a greater variety. In the year 1847, for instance, in which tragedies were performed on only thirty-nine evenings (thus below the Burgtheater average), there were still fourteen distinct tragedies on the playbills. The Burgtheater thus remained an important stage for tragedy. Tragedy was performed about once a week, and at least the regular visitors could count on seeing roughly a dozen different tragedies each year. Comedies, of course, were performed much more frequently and in much greater variety. But that was the norm for the period in general, and, given the different patterns of theatre attendance from the period, this is also rather understandable. It seems hard to imagine an audience that attends the theatre day after day and still prefers tragedy as its main fare.

In later chapters, I will present further statistical work about the Burgtheater's repertoire, notably concerning the representation of female playwrights (ch. 5) and the representation of German-language drama (ch. 6). But the patterns that we will observe there largely match what we have found in this chapter, namely that the Burgtheater repertoire was sufficiently broad and sufficiently uncontrolled to accommodate a number of competing trends and directions. As we saw in this chapter, the Burgtheater could pride itself on its large international repertoire, and yet the majority of the repertoire generally remained German. Similarly, the Burgtheater served a demand for entertainment, and yet it became the leading stage for the classics, which it produced with great success. Finally, while the Burgtheater was generally a stage for comedy, tragedy still retained a strong presence.

4 Mourning and Reforming Obedience

Questions on the validity and justification of obedience to authority held centre stage in the repertoire of the mid-nineteenth-century Burgtheater, and the answers that these questions received differed appreciably. To be clear, the positions here explored were not radical, even by the standards of the time. What could be said in the Burgtheater was a far cry from the thoughts harboured in the contemporaneous radical student circles around, for instance, the Jena university teacher Karl Follen (1796–1840), who insisted on the absolute primacy of the conscience over any codified secular or divine law, and whose ideas also found some resonance in Vienna (Siemann 590). What was debated in the Burgtheater was also at a great remove from the ideas of avant-garde playwrights of the period – be it Georg Büchner or Christian Dietrich Grabbe (neither of whom was performed in the Burgtheater in the nineteenth century). And yet, the repertoire of the Burgtheater was not as conformist or uniformly conservative as one might imagine it to have been under the regime of censorship and political repression that had a long tradition in Austria and that saw a further intensification after the assassination of the playwright August von Kotzebue by the radical student Karl Ludwig Sand in 1819.[1] While striking an overall moderate tone, the Burgtheater neither evaded the question of submission to authority, nor did it unequivocally preach obedience. Appreciating the diversity of positions in the Burgtheater helps us recast the image that is commonly held both of this theatre and of the Restoration period more broadly. Analogous to Wolfram Siemann's recent reinterpretation of Chancellor Metternich as significantly less reactionary than is conventionally stated, we can see the Burgtheater as well as a decidedly more heterogenous and politically engaged institution than most studies to date have made it out to be.

This chapter lays out the principal positions that defined the debates on obedience in the Burgtheater of the mid–nineteenth century. Based on readings of four popular productions between 1822 and 1846 (of plays by William Shakespeare, Franz Grillparzer, Friedrich Halm, and Eduard von Bauernfeld), this chapter creates an abstract matrix in which the main lines of discussion about obedience become visible. While there are other plays from the repertoire that cover broadly similar trends and that might have served as examples, the selected plays represent the most iconic playwrights of the mid-nineteenth-century Burgtheater.[2] Shakespeare was, after Kotzebue, the most widely performed author in the nineteenth-century Burgtheater, and the production of his play *King Lear*, on which I focus in this chapter, rose to great fame in this period. Franz Grillparzer was the most significant serious Austrian playwright of the time, regarded both by himself and others as the legitimate heir of Goethe and Schiller in the mid–nineteenth century. Eduard von Bauernfeld and Friedrich Halm, finally, are the main Austrian playwrights of nineteenth-century liberal middlebrow dramatic literature, representing the progressive (Bauernfeld) and conservative (Halm) ends of the liberal spectrum.

What clearly emerges from the analysis in this chapter is not only that obedience was actively being debated on Vienna's main stage, but also that this debate was surprisingly complex and nuanced. What we witness is not a camp of staunch liberals striving to overcome all established systems of obedience, pitted against their blindly submissive conservative counterparts celebrating the rationality of the established system of governance. The question was not whether obedience, simply and generally, was a good or a bad thing. What the following interpretations highlight instead is that obedience was discussed both with a historically more complex and a theoretically more specific focus.

There were at least two categorically different – albeit interrelated – strands of discussion. The first of these strands historicizes obedience as a thing of the past, potentially lost to the present age, for better or worse. The second strand focuses on reform and asks in what form obedience would have to be restructured to become an acceptable liberal virtue for a post-Enlightenment society. Both of these strands or discourses – that of mourning obedience as a thing of the past, and that of reforming it – show strong signs of internal differentiation. There is a range of plays in which obedience is mourned as a virtue lost to older times, but this same mourning is tinged with varying degrees of ambivalence. And among those plays that introduce a reformed notion of obedience as compatible with liberal striving, this new-found synthesis is endorsed, again, to very different degrees. That is to say that not only did each individual play and production have some degree of ambiguity, but that there was also, and more importantly, a marked ambiguity or polyphony on the level of the repertoire. And it was arguably thanks to these different stances on clearly recurring questions in otherwise very different productions that the Burgtheater could incite and sustain a political debate whose complexity and nuance has often been lost in intellectual historians' focus on the more well-known sites of political debate, including coffeehouses, clubs, newspapers, and universities.

Mourning Obedience

There is a story to be told of the mid–nineteenth century (and especially of the Burgtheater of the period, as well shall see) that would focus on the mourning for obedience as a guiding principle of personal and social relations, as well as on fantasies to reinstitute this principle – even if only to resist it. In this narrative, the nineteenth century appears as the long hangover after the Enlightenment exultation of the previous century. A cursory glance at major German-language novels of the mid–nineteenth century does much to underscore this vision of the period. Gottfried Keller's seminal novel *Der grüne Heinrich* (*Green Henry*, 1854–5; rev. 1879–80) tells the story of Heinrich Lee, who grows up without father and without direction and who pines for the "sweet feeling of obedience and lust for freedom" ("süßen Gefühle des Gehorsams und trotziger Freiheitslust"; Keller 643). Gustav Freytag's bestselling novel *Soll und Haben* (*Debit and Credit*, 1855) envisions a state in which such obedience is actually still possible. Freytag tells the story of Anton Wohlfahrt, the son of a dutiful civil servant who matures as the equally dutiful clerk of a well-established merchant. With more nuance than in Freytag, we find this idyll of obedience also in Adalbert Stifter's quintessential Austrian novel *Der Nachsommer* (*The Indian Summer*, published two years after Keller's and Freytag's novels, in 1857), which tells the story of Heinrich Drendorf, whose educational journey is successfully prepared by his regimented upbringing in the household of his merchant father.

Interestingly, Stifter's novel captures this image of the nineteenth century as one characterized by the mourning for authority and obedience in an episode about one of the most remarkable productions in the Burgtheater of the nineteenth century, Joseph Schreyvogel's 1822 staging of Shakespeare's *King Lear* (Stifter, *Der Nachsommer* 187–95).[3] The much-cited *Lear* episode in Stifter's novel conveys a vivid impression not only of the discourse on authority and obedience, but also of the social world of the Burgtheater in which this discourse found its stage. For Heinrich introduces his account of the production of *Lear* with a broader survey of his experience with theatre. Growing up, we are told, Heinrich's merchant father did not expose him much to the theatre. Never did the father take Heinrich to the suburban theatres, whose reputation and moral worth was, presumably, far too uncertain; and not once did the boy see the (more expensive) opera or ballet, which, we are meant to understand, remained more firmly in the hand of the aristocracy. If his father took him to the theatre, it was to the court theatre (that is, the Burgtheater), the meeting place of the educated, the noble, and the wealthy. This court theatre, Heinrich states, was the model institution for all of Germany. As a young adult, Heinrich retains the habit instilled by his father: if he goes to the theatre, he goes to the Burgtheater. And in a way that can be deemed typical of the educated middle classes, for whom, in contrast to the aristocracy, the Burgtheater did not normally form part of their daily routine, Heinrich prefers plays of clear educational or moral value (i.e., not the contemporary French and Austrian comedies) – the same plays to which his father had already taken him.

Shakespeare's *Lear* was, of course, one of these plays that, because of its status as a classic, had the potential to draw an audience beyond the aristocratic Burgtheater regulars. But it is, more importantly in our context, also a quintessential play about the decline of obedience as a defining virtue in human relationships, in the family as well as in politics. Recall here the famous opening of the play, in which the old King Lear summons his three daughters – Gonoril, Regan, and Cordelia – to divide his kingdom among them. We witness in this scene Lear's tragic failure to define his relationship to his daughters in terms of obedience. Pondering over how to divide his realm, he asks his daughters to express their affection for him:

> LEAR. Tell me, my daughters,
> Which of you shall we say doth love us most,
> That we our largest bounty may extend
> Where merit doth most challenge it. (*Lr.*, 1.44–7)[4]

The keyword in Lear's demand is "love," and it is in terms of love that his older two daughters, Gonoril and Regan, answer him. They each invoke a love for their father and king that is so immeasurably great that it defies expression. With that, they satisfy the father's expectations, and each receives a part of his kingdom. Only the youngest daughter, Cordelia, answers Lear's question not in a vocabulary of affection, but of strictly measured obedience.[5] More precisely, she grounds her love in an underlying system of duty: "I love your majesty/According to my bond, nor more nor less" (1.83–4). Famously, Lear finds Cordelia's response unsatisfactory, and, in anger, he divides her part of the realm among the other two daughters.

Much ink has been spilled in attempts to answer the question of why Lear behaves the way he does at the outset of Shakespeare's tragedy. In Stanley Cavell's seminal essay on *Lear*, "The Avoidance of Love" from his 1969 book *Must We Mean What We Say?*, Cavell lists the three most common responses to this question in the following terms: "Lear is senile; Lear is puerile; Lear is not to be understood in natural terms for the whole scene has a fairy tale or ritualistic character which simply must be accepted as the premise from which the tragedy is derived" (286). Cavell is not satisfied with any of these approaches. To counter them, he presents a sophisticated analysis in which Lear's odd behaviour becomes legible as a function of shame, or, as the title of Cavell's essay puts it, as an avoidance of love. Lear, Cavell thinks, knowingly accepts the insincere expressions of love from Regan and Gonoril because he cannot bear the exposure of the self that comes with true love.

Cavell's analysis is as beautiful as it is intriguing. But it pays surprisingly little attention to the fact that the alternative laid out at the outset of the play, is, at least on the surface, not primarily between sincere and insincere love, but between (personal) love and (generalized) duty as the foundations of human relationships. It is love – be it sincere or not – that Lear fatefully chooses, and with that, Lear becomes, arguably, an emblem of the modern self. Lear's behaviour, in other words, is neither puerile, nor senile; nor is it a product of shame or a meaningless premise for the plot: his behaviour, instead, is *modern*. The opening of Shakespeare's plays stages one of the fundamental distinctions of Christian Europe – between the old bond of law, duty, and obedience, and the new bond of love – and it highlights the pitfalls in rejecting duty and obedience (or in failing to discover the true love that consists in and through these values).

Lear's inability to see the value of a traditional language of obedience over a modern discourse of love is his *hamartia*, his tragic guilt that implicates him in his own demise. For a little later, he is horridly abused by Regan and Gonoril. Upon receiving their inheritance, they refuse to host him and his retinue of knights according to his standing, and eventually they abandon him in inclement weather outside. Only too late, when Cordelia has already left for France, and when Regan and Gonoril, whose hyperbolic language of affection has proven hollow, resist their father's pleas, does Lear invoke obedience to parental authority as a category. Demanding divine intervention in his altercations with his daughters, Lear exclaims:

LEAR. O heavens,
If you do love old men, if your sweet sway
Allow obedience, if yourselves are old,
Make it your cause! Send down and take my part. (*Lr.*, 7.346–9)

Lear's cry for obedience comes too late. His daughters cannot be reined in anymore, and indeed, they themselves soon prove incapable of controlling their lands. Fooled by their greed as well as by their jealous (and extramarital) love for the "bastard" Edmund, they drown their kingdom in violence and chaos, eventually dying through murder (Regan) and suicide (Gonoril). *Lear,* to sum up this brief interpretation, is at its core a tragedy about the danger of defining relationships in terms of love instead of in terms of obedience. This makes *Lear* one of the great conservative myths, criticizing the modern age's preference for love over obedience.

This tragedy about the demise of obedience became one of the defining productions of the Burgtheater of the nineteenth century. The play figures as perhaps the greatest achievement in Schreyvogel's 1814 to 1832 tenure at the Burgtheater (Williams, *Shakespeare on the German Stage* 115), and Heinrich Anschütz's performance of the title role over almost forty years (until 1860; Großegger 234) was, in the nineteenth century, one of the most written-about in German theatre (Williams, *Shakespeare on the German Stage* 118). It turned out also to be one of the defining roles for Anschütz himself, who had joined the Burgtheater only in 1821, one year prior to the premiere of *Lear,* and who had originally been hired to fill the role of the young hero (in the period, actors were usually employed to fill a specific type). It was Schreyvogel's idea to move the only thirty-six-year-old actor already into the role of the heroic father ("Heldenvater"; Wlassack 153) and Lear was his first attempt at this type (152–3).

With 130 performances between 1822 and 1909, *Lear* was one of the most-performed Shakespeare plays in the Burgtheater. In the entire decade of the 1820s, there were only three plays that would eventually see more performances: aside from the 1828 *Hamlet* (which had 190 performances), these were the 1827 *Wilhelm Tell* by Friedrich Schiller (139 performances) and the 1821 *Käthchen von Heilbronn* by Heinrich von Kleist (150 performances). The other 182 new productions in the ten years from 1820 to 1829 were performed less often.

What then explains this great resonance of *Lear* in Vienna? Simon Williams, in his study *Shakespeare on the German Stage* (1990), argues that the success of *Lear* was "due mainly [...] to the poetic world of decline so attractively conjured up by [the main actor] Anschütz" (119). But perhaps it is possible to point to something slightly more specific than a general feeling of Habsburg decline, which, in any case, is much more typical of the later nineteenth and early twentieth centuries. In 1822, the decline of the Habsburg Empire was still in the very distant future. In these years, Austria was, under the guidance of Metternich, a powerful political player, and it dominated decision making in the German confederation.

Alternatively, *Lear*'s success may have been due less to a general feeling of decline and more to a specific sense of loss of authority and obedience as guiding principles in personal and social relations. As the novels by Keller, Freytag, and Stifter suggest, the mid–nineteenth century was preoccupied with sentiments of such a loss, and Shakespeare's play clearly speaks to these feelings. There are no direct reception documents – no newspaper reviews or statements from later memoirs – that directly support this explanation of *Lear*'s popularity. However, it proves instructive, both to confirm our explanation of the popularity of the *Lear* production with the Viennese audience and to refine it, to go back to Stifter's novel, where our discussion of *Lear* started. One peculiarity about Stifter's fictional account of the *Lear* production is the great extent to which the descriptions of the actions on stage are embedded in a narrative of paternal guidance. For not only is the very act of theatregoing introduced as an effect of the education that Heinrich received from his father, but also the specific visit to the performance of *Lear* is associated with the father. Heinrich hears of the performance only through an announcement in his father's morning papers, and, upon returning home late from the performance, Heinrich turns down the supper that his mother had kept for him, to instead ask his father for an edition of Shakespeare's works in the original English (the father grants the request, and Heinrich takes out the books from his father's library).

What stands out about this framing of the *Lear* episode in Stifter's novel is that King Lear himself is, for lack of a better word, a rather terrible father and king – not only unjust, but also incapable. Shakespeare's play has, on the surface, nothing much flattering to say about either Lear's paternal or his monarchical authority. The play consists, as I suggested earlier, in the critique of a paternal figure who fails to give obedience precedence over affection. What then does it mean that this play is framed in a narrative of successful and unquestioned fatherly guidance?

The point for Stifter is not to create a stark contrast between a good and a bad father: there is nothing in the narrator's comments that would support this claim. Lear is, in the words of Stifter's narrator Heinrich, rash and imprudent, to be sure, but still worthy of love ("hefti[g] leichtsinni[g] und doch liebenswürdi[g]"; Stifter, *Der Nachsommer* 190). Heinrich's positive relationship to his father appears to be mirrored in his affection for Shakespeare's hero, not contrasted with it.

Confronting this curiously warm paternal framing of a play that is ostensibly centred on a failing monarchal father and on a demonstration of the primacy of obedience, we are forced to refine our analysis of Shakespeare's play. It proves useful to that end to engage in a simple hypothetical exercise: what would have occurred if Lear had valued Cordelia's well-measured assertion of duty over Gonoril's and Regan's hyperbolic expressions of love? In some sense, of course, this would have been the better thing for Lear to do. But we would then have no real plot to speak of, or at least no tragic plot in a technical sense: even if Gonoril and Regan had, in that scenario, rebelled against their stern father, Lear himself would not have borne any direct responsibility. More importantly, the king, while being blameless, would also have appeared much less likeable in this scenario. It is his tragic failure to understand the primacy of obedience that makes him a likeable character to a modern audience. That is the central – and, indeed, tragic – paradox of this play: Lear's greatest strength and weakness are united in his inability to sustain obedience as the highest value.

Shakespeare's play achieves the paradoxical result of asserting a conservative appreciation of obedience to paternal and royal authority while at the same speaking to a modern predilection for love over obedience. Obedience is mourned as a lost virtue in *Lear*, but it is mourned, surprisingly, while at the same time celebrating modern affection, high as the price may be. King Lear is loving to death (or, as in the case of the Burgtheater production with its more conciliatory ending, *almost* to death, for Schreyvogel knew well that he could not let the monarch die in the emperor's theatre without causing affront).[6]

Given this paradoxical tendency of Shakespeare's tragedy both to hold obedience to paternal and monarchic authority in great esteem *and* to paint a positive picture of the monarch who fails to appreciate the value of obedience, it should not surprise us that Austria's emperor and the Viennese censors were perfectly satisfied with this play. In Shakespeare's *Lear*, kings really cannot go wrong. As sensitive to any potential questioning of historic or contemporary monarchs, domestic or foreign, as Austria's censors normally were, in this case they saw no reason to intervene. Instead, Schreyvogel was expressly lauded by his aristocratic superiors and given a cash bonus of six hundred guldens for his work on the Shakespeare play (Schreyvogel 377).

The theme of mourning obedience, which defines, in all its ambiguity, Shakespeare's Early Modern tragedy, was also present in productions of contemporary plays in the Burgtheater. The most important instance of this is a tragedy by the principal Austrian playwright of the period, Franz Grillparzer (1791–1872). In Grillparzer's *Ein treuer Diener seines Herrn* (*A Loyal Servant of His Master*), which premiered in the Burgtheater six years after *Lear* in 1828 (that is, still under Schreyvogel's leadership), we see in even more pronounced fashion that obedience is nostalgically marked as a virtue of older times. Obedience here is embodied in the tragedy's main character, Count Bancbanus, played by Heinrich Anschütz – the very actor who had also performed in the role of King Lear. Bancbanus, the king's most loyal servant, is an elderly man, critical of the newspeak of his time, and physically infirm (even though he is, incidentally, only approaching sixty years of age). "I am an enemy of innovation" ("Ich bin ein Feind von Neuerungen"; Grillparzer, *Diener* 8), he declares already in the play's opening act. But while his unfailing obedience to his king is, on some level, lauded as a virtue, unmatched in the younger generation, it is also clear that it is Bancbanus's obedience that causes his – and not only his – suffering. The death of both his wife and of the queen over the course of the play can, as we shall see, be linked to his unrelenting adherence to the king's commands and rules. Although the theme of *Diener* – the relative virtue of obedience – is thus closely related to that of *Lear*, Grillparzer's tragedy presents us with the inverse evaluation of obedience from the one we saw in Shakespeare. Whereas Lear's tragic guilt is to value love over duty, Bancbanus errs in the opposite manner: his unfailing service to his master and his disregard for the demands of love constitute his tragic guilt. The fact that these two plays were performed side by side, and under the auspices of the emperor, on the stage of the Burgtheater is testimony to the fact that this institution fostered a surprisingly lively debate on the appropriate stance to authority. The two productions with the same main actor had the potential to mutually enforce the importance of their main concern (that is, how to evaluate obedience) while at the same time confronting the audience with markedly different perspectives on this question. They encouraged debate on the relative virtue of obedience, and in a sense, they themselves already performed such a debate.

In the play, Bancbanus's dutiful service to his master, the medieval Hungarian King Andreas, is put to a severe test. As King Andreas leaves Hungary with his army to restore order in rebellious Galicia, Bancbanus is tasked to aid the queen in keeping peace in the king's homeland. Bancbanus is wholly devoted to the task, and as an orderly bureaucrat, he follows due procedure, including all necessary paperwork, in dealing with the many supplicants who approach him. While the rest of the court begins to run wild as soon as the monarch has left, Bancbanus deals with each supplicant according to the rules and expectations set out by the king. At the same time, however, Bancbanus neglects his wife, Erny, who becomes, quite against her will, drawn into the court's merrymaking.

Bancbanus's single-minded devotion to the duties of his office comes at a cost. Not only is he derided by the younger members at court, but, more importantly, he also fails to protect his wife from abuse. As Erny escapes from the court's celebrations, very agitated and with several suitors still following her, Bancbanus remains cold. Erny pleads to be allowed to stay with her husband. But he reminds her of his duties (as well as hers) and sends her away. He shows great indignation over Erny's failure to appreciate both his dutiful service and that service's ultimate goal: to keep the promise to retain peace in the king's land during the monarch's absence:

I promised it,
I swore to the king upon his departure
That I would maintain peace in his land,
And I will keep that promise, happen what will.
I will pursue my duties; you, go, and pursue the celebrations.

Ich hab's versprochen
Dem König angelobt bei seinem Scheiden
Den Frieden zu bewahren hier, die Ruh,
Und werd' es halten, trifft was immer zu.
Dem Dienste folg' ich; folg' dem Feste du!

(Grillparzer, *Diener* 48)

In these lines from the second act, Bancbanus's tragic guilt – as well as the tragic irony of obedience in the play – is prepared. By sending his wife back to the feast, Bancbanus not only abandons her, which leads her, a little later, to commit suicide to escape rape and abduction from the queen's unruly brother, Otto, but Bancbanus also jeopardizes the peace that he vowed to maintain in the king's realm. For as the news spread of Erny's untimely death, Bancbanus's brother and brother-in-law seek revenge on the king's family. It is, ironically and tragically, Bancbanus's extreme commitment to maintain order and peace (and the resulting neglect of his wife), that undermines this peace.

Bancbanus remains a faithful servant of his master and seeks to prevent this revenge, but infirm as the old man is, he fails: he faints when his brother and brother-in-law and their men begin to attack the castle. In the ensuing conflict, Bancbanus sides with the king's family, trying to protect the queen as well as her son, Bela, and even her brother Otto, who directly contributed to the death of Bancbanus's wife. But Bancbanus's efforts are met with only mixed success. While Otto and Bela survive, the queen is killed.

The queen's death is significant in this context, even though it happens, as far as the immediate action is concerned, accidentally (the brothers aim for Otto, but, inadvertently, they kill the queen). It reinforces the tragic core of this play, for in the brief opening scenes in which we encounter the king before he leaves for Galicia, he shows himself to be guilty of the same error as Bancbanus: a disregard of affectionate bonds in favour of relationships defined by duty. In his very first words on stage, the king rejects his wife's wish to stay any longer with her, invoking the call of duty: "Beloved wife! You know that my duties are pressing" ("Geliebtes Weib! Du weißt es drängt die Pflicht"; Grillparzer, *Diener* 18). And in the ensuing dispute between king and queen, he denies her wish for him to choose her favoured brother Otto, instead of Bancbanus, as his representative during his absence. The king is thus portrayed to have a similarly single-minded devotion to his duties as Bancbanus, and, like Bancbanus, he must pay for this devotion with the death of his wife.

It is tempting to interpret Bancbanus's and the king's suffering not in terms of a classic tragedy, but in terms of a Christian martyr play, and the consequences of this interpretation are far-reaching. Whereas a classic tragedy implies some limited guilt of the tragic hero (the hero's *hamartia*, in Aristotle's words), a martyr play does not. The martyr dies holding on to the one and only true faith. Read as a martyr play, Grillparzer's loyal servant is blameless: he simply has to suffer for remaining a faithful servant of his lord. His obedience is not tinged by guilt.

At least one aspect of *Diener* invites such a reading as a martyr play. Bancbanus's revenging brother and brother-in-law are called Simon and Peter, evoking the biblical Simon Peter, the disciple who – very much against Jesus's will – violently attacks the Roman guards when they come to arrest Jesus. If one follows this line of reasoning, Bancbanus appears as the suffering Christ. And, indeed, Bancbanus, like Jesus, does implore his allies to abstain from all violence against his enemies.

However, there is good reason to be suspicious of a reading of Grillparzer's tragedy as a martyr play. Not least of all, Bancbanus does not primarily suffer himself (in the way a martyr does) but has others suffer in his stead. He fails, at least for a significant period of time, in his task of peacekeeping, and both his wife and the king's wife die in the process. Moreover, despite Bancbanus's seeming abstention from all direct violence, his preference for relationships defined by duty over those defined by affection is itself marked as a violent usurpation of his wife's agency. Not only does he neglect his wife in their marriage, but the marriage itself is revealed as a problematic bond of duty, not affection. As we are told by Bancbanus himself, their marriage was demanded by

Erny's father, an old friend of Bancbanus's, on his deathbed. Bancbanus was, he claims, reluctant to go through with it given the significant difference in age, but go through with it he did. And while Erny, at the time and according to Bancbanus's narrative, had asked Bancbanus to fulfil her father's demand, it is stated in none too subtle terms that her desire was directed at the queen's brother – her later aggressor, Otto. For as we learn elsewhere from Otto, Erny had, before her marriage, stolen some of Otto's hair, which he had sent as a gift to his sister. Even later, when already married, Erny returns, significantly enough, Otto's pressing of her hand during a dance. It is important to stress that these signs of affection are cited by Otto himself in justification of his harassment. To take this evidence at face value means to become complicit in Otto's abusive stratagems.[7] But Erny does not directly deny Otto's claims about her past behaviour, and the effect in the play is clearly to cast doubt on the legitimacy of her relationship to the much older Bancbanus. Erny's relationship with Bancbanus is built on her obedience to her father, and obedience thus overreached itself once again.

Critical as the play is of obedience, this critique is never clearly foregrounded; it certainly never becomes an outright "message." As surprising as this might appear considering the previous remarks, the play has largely been understood as a nostalgic celebration of loyalty to monarchy. At the time of its first appearance, the censorship office let it pass without any concerns, and Emperor Franz I applauded it, at least at first (Prutti 390). Contemporary liberals criticized the play for its alleged celebration of submissiveness (Reichert 70). And even in 1937, the Germanist Richard Alewyn still called Grillparzer's tragedy the most pro-monarchical play written since the French Revolution (Alewyn 282; qtd. in Prutti 371). It took critics until the final decades of the twentieth century to highlight elements in the play that undermine this affirmative reading of Bancbanus's obedience.[8]

Grillparzer expressed himself with fine nuance about the question of how to evaluate Bancbanus. In his autobiography, he recalls that the play was accused of "servile submissiveness" ("knechtische Unterwürfigkeit"; Grillparzer, *Selbstbiographie* 182), to which he responds – only partially refuting the charge – that he himself was thinking rather of "the heroism of duty" ("Heroismus der Pflichttreue"; 182). Yet to avoid an all too clear endorsement of Bancbanus, Grillparzer adds that the sentiments of the play's main character should not be confused with that of the play's author, "for despite all his good character traits, he [Bancbanus] is described as a rather narrow-minded old man" ("da er bei all seinen Charaktervorzügen zugleich als ein ziemlich bornierter Mann geschildert ist"; 182).

Grillparzer's curious comments aside, the fact that the play was initially mainly received as an uncritical celebration of obedience does not have to surprise us. Notably the ending of the play does much to conceal the subversive potential inherent in this tragedy of obedience. As the king returns, the raging conflict with the rebels is brought to a halt and Bancbanus is praised for his actions. The king even wants to reward Bancbanus by making him the second-highest-ranking man in the realm. And while Bancbanus declines this advancement (citing his infirmity as a reason), he, too, upholds in the tragedy's final words the role he has held throughout, as "Ein treuer Diener seines Herrn" (Grillparzer, *Diener* 147). Focusing on these final moments alone, one might well think that the old virtue of obedience, though severely tested, reigns supreme in this play.

But, again, doubts must remain. The conciliatory ending cannot fully blind us to the fact that Bancbanus's implication in the death of his wife – tragic (and thus limited) as this implication may be – is associated with his single-minded devotion to the very virtue of obedience that the play ostensibly holds up in such great esteem. And, as discussed, we can identify this same tragic guilt also in the figure of the king.

Obedience, in other words, remains far from unquestioned, and at least some of Grillparzer's contemporaries appear to have been aware of this. At least Emperor Franz I, as Grillparzer tells us in his autobiography, quickly revoked his initial praise of the play and tried to stop its circulation (*Selbstbiographie* 180–2). In this, however, he devised the most benign form of censorship, offering to purchase Grillparzer's original manuscript of *Diener* along with all of the copied manuscripts in the possession of the Burgtheater – allegedly to place them in the emperor's private library.[9] When this plan was brought to Grillparzer, the playwright was dismayed by the idea of being paid to bury his work, and he explained that he was no longer in full control of this text. Even if he submitted his manuscript to the court, Grillparzer pleaded, this would not prevent further circulation. The emperor's plan was not pursued much further, and the matter was set aside. In 1830, two years after the first performance, a printed edition appeared without, as Grillparzer states, any intervention by the censors (182). Yet in the Burgtheater the play disappeared after fourteen performances, about a year after its opening night (it was then taken up again, under Heinrich Laube's directorship, in 1851 and eventually reached forty-seven performances before 1903).

What makes the story about the emperor's wavering endorsement of *Diener* so important is that it reveals the inconsistencies and uncertainty of the powers governing over the Burgtheater. While, generally speaking, all subversive productions were banned or heavily censored, there was considerable room to sustain on stage a lively and controversial debate on one of the topics that the authoritarian Metternich system should have been most loath to tolerate, namely the question of the relative advantages of obedience to authority. Even plays that had, as in the case of Grillparzer's tragedy, actually displeased the emperor, were, at least occasionally, tolerated.[10]

One can give the central events in Grillparzer's tragedy almost any spin one wishes. The fact that obedience makes Bancbanus guilty does not necessarily imply a critique of obedience – no more, at least, than Lear's tragic preference for love over duty inevitably shows love in a critical light; as discussed earlier, Lear's mistaken predilection for love is precisely what draws us to him. It is part of the irony of tragedy, which Peter Szondi highlights with such great eloquence in his seminal work *Versuch über das Tragische* (*Essay on the Tragic*, 1961), that the behaviour undertaken for the best reasons can turn out to trigger the tragic demise. It would thus be misleading to read Grillparzer's play one-sidedly as a secretly subversive script that, in the guise of a conservative praise of duty, advances a radical critique of obedience. But in its productive ambiguities, the play does put obedience up for debate, and it is itself recognizable as part of a debate in the Burgtheater to which *Lear* belongs as well. It is part of this debate both because it mirrors concerns over obedience as a virtue of the past and over the hierarchy of duty and love as guiding values that also shape Shakespeare's tragedy, and because it shows these topics in a way that is very different from – indeed, as I suggest, the very inverse of – *Lear*.

Reforming Obedience[11]

Shakespeare's *Lear* and Grillparzer's *Diener* give us a sense of how the Burgtheater of the 1820s provided a stage, for many decades to come, for the mourning of obedience as a lost virtue of older times: a form of mourning, however, that is full of ambivalence and that accommodates a range of critical undertones in its very praise of obedience. But the melancholic discourse of a decline of obedience – no matter how ambivalent this melancholy may be in individual plays – was not the only, and, arguably, not the most prominent way in which authority and obedience were being discussed in the Burgtheater. Instead, what appears to have been the centre of discussion was an attempt to rethink the meaning or functioning of obedience so that obedience could be aligned with a post-Enlightenment sense of individual agency. For mid–nineteenth century Austrians, the point was not so much simply to stress the freedoms afforded by obedience. That was, at that time, arguably already an outdated idea, more typical of the previous century. Kant's classic essay "Was ist Aufklärung" ("What Is Enlightenment," 1784), for instance, comes to mind here, in which the acceptance of a system of obedience in the realms of military, bureaucratic, and church practice was to guarantee a free exchange of ideas among scholars. With variations, similar thought also ran through the Austrian Enlightenment philosophy of Joseph von Sonnenfels.[12]

There is no doubt that this general idea of securing certain freedoms by giving up others did not suddenly die out at the turn to the nineteenth century. It is still present, for instance, in Hegel's justification of obedience to state laws in his *Grundlinien der Philosophie des Rechts* (*Elements of the Philosophy of Right*, 1820). Obeying the state's laws is, according to Hegel, what secures us the protection to exercise a free life as citizens.[13] But even in Hegel – in his *Grundlinien* as well as in his *Vorlesungen über die Philosophie der Geschichte* (*Lectures on the Philosophy of World History*) – we are pointed in a different direction. Obedience to state laws and institutions does not merely make room for freedom; it itself *is* freedom. In his *Vorlesungen*, Hegel states: "Freedom is nothing more than a knowledge and affirmation of such universal and substantial objects as law and justice, and the production of a reality which corresponds to them – i.e., the state" (Hegel 134). This idea of a complete synthesis of obedience and freedom is also what already characterizes Friedrich Schiller's aesthetic and political deliberations in *Über die ästhetische Erziehung des Menschen* (*On the Aesthetic Education of Man*, 1794; see, most recently, Robanus): in Schiller's ideal state, people will choose of their own volition what they are bound to do.

It was this idea of a possible synthesis of freedom and obedience that became popularized by nineteenth-century poets, novelists, and playwrights – also, and especially, in the Burgtheater. Thus Friedrich Halm notes in his poem "Wollen und Sollen" ("Will and Duty") that all human happiness consists of wanting to do what one has to do ("Es gibt kein Glück auf Erden/Als wollen, was man soll!"; Halm, *Werke* 7: 16). What Schiller had phrased as a political utopia is here rephrased as simple advice for the good life in the present Habsburg state. There is in Halm, who made a stellar career as a civil servant in the Habsburg bureaucracy (becoming the long-standing director of the court library, and, for a short while, from 1867 to 1868, also the director of Burgtheater and court opera), an unmistakable comfort with the powers in place. A similar sentiment is also expressed in Halm's poem "Prometheus," a rewriting of Goethe's rebellious *Sturm und Drang* poem of the same title. Where Goethe stresses a longing for autonomy, Halm emphasizes the acceptance of authority. As a matter of fact, Halm describes the severe suffering that Prometheus must endure for having stolen fire from the Gods as an essentially apt punishment (Halm, *Werke* 7: 23–5). But the acceptance of authority that we encounter in Halm's writings does not imply that Halm renounces freedom as an important value. What he seeks to establish is the possibility of realizing one's freedom in the very submission to someone else's authority.[14]

At first sight, it may not be evident why this discussion of obedience should have been central to discussions among Viennese liberals. If anything, we might associate such reflections more with Prussian or Protestant philosophy in the line from Kant to Schiller and Hegel. What Viennese liberals gathering in coffeehouses and reading clubs had on their minds in the years leading up to the 1848 revolution, was, for the most part, much more concrete: they talked about the freedom of the press and the implementation of a binding constitution. Elsewhere in Habsburgs lands, the system of feudal bonds was under scrutiny, as was the question of the role that each of the eleven nations in the empire should be allowed to play (Judson, *Habsburg Empire* 155–6; Kann 300). The much more abstract debate over the meaning of obedience, by contrast, seems to be rather far removed from all these pressing practical concerns. And yet the problem of obedience was one of the fundamental underlying topics of Austrian liberalism.

In Vienna, as elsewhere, liberals remained, by and large, loyal to monarch and monarchy (one important exception to that is, of course, Hungary, where the striving for freedom was essentially a striving for independence). Liberty, went the prevailing idea, should be maintained through a constitutionally stabilized Habsburg monarchy. When the news first spread of the 1848 revolution and its initial success (freedom of the press was granted; a constitution was promised; and Prince Metternich, architect of the restoration, had to resign as chancellor after twenty-seven years in office), they were met in many places in Austria with hymns praising Emperor Ferdinand (Judson, *Habsburg Empire* 169–70). Even in the first wave of revolutionary excitement, the victory of liberalism was not understood to undermine the established authorities, but to reaffirm their legitimacy.

This liberal monarchical sentiment, however, did not prevail in all places and at all times. Instead, there was appreciable disagreement within the liberal camp. This diversity of opinion is well illustrated by successful plays by two of the period's most popular Viennese playwrights, the drama *Griseldis* (1835) by Friedrich Halm and the comedy *Großjährig* (*Age of Majority*, 1846) by Eduard von Bauernfeld. Both of these plays, which were produced under Schreyvogel's successors,

Johann Ludwig Deinhardstein (1832–41) and Franz Ignaz von Holbein (1841–9), respectively, concentrate on the question of whether the obedience demanded of the main characters can, at the same time, be thought of as a product of their free will. But whereas Halm's drama answers this question largely in the affirmative, Bauernfeld's comedy shows this synthesis in a much more critical light.

The drama *Griseldis*, written in classical blank verse, was Friedrich Halm's highly successful first play. It premiered in the Burgtheater in December 1835 and saw ninety-one performances before it was removed from the repertoire in 1882 (Rub 65). It is based on one of the quintessential European myths of obedience, the story of the young wife Griseldis whose submissiveness is tested in a series of cruel trials by her husband. This narrative entered literary history in the fourteenth century as the last of the one hundred tales in Boccaccio's *Decameron*. It found wider dissemination through its Latin adaptation as an independent story by Petrarch ("A Fable of Wifely Obedience and Devotion," written 1373, first printed 1470), which in turn inspired numerous works throughout the Middle Ages and Early Modern period. Understandably, this story did not receive much attention in the century of the Enlightenment, which could not find much of value in this tale of obedience. It was only in the first decades of the nineteenth century that the story of Griseldis made its comeback into European cultural history. And, while there were some nineteenth-century precursors (for instance, Otto Heinrich von Loeben's 1819 narrative *Markgraf Walther und Griseldis*), one can attribute this comeback in large part to Friedrich Halm. Halm's *Griseldis*, though mostly forgotten today, was at the time a phenomenal commercial success in the Burgtheater,[15] and it was widely translated, read, and performed across Europe (Wagner, "Navigating and Owning Obedience"). In the early twentieth century, Halm's reintroduction of the Griseldis story found a late echo in Gerhart Hauptmann's comedy *Griselda* (1909) and Hedwig Courths-Mahler's popular novel *Griseldis* (1917).

What Halm achieved in his play, and what arguably explains part of its success, was to reframe Griseldis's obedience in a way that allowed contemporaries to see in it an acceptable form of modern agency. In 1846, Saint-René Taillandier, a leading French observer of the Viennese stage, enthusiastically praised Halm for attenuating Griseldis's submissiveness:

> One must thank Mr. Halm for the noble thought that he has so ably brought to the stage. The Griseldis character is now complete; resignation is no longer degrading itself to complete surrender of right and will. The Middle

> Ages could not demand more of Griseldis. Today her humility appears – thank God – much more sublime, blended with such pure dignity.

> Il faut remercier M. Halm de la noble pensée qu'il a si bien portée sur la scène. Maintenant la figure de Griseldis est complète; la résignation ne s'abaisse plus jusqu'à l'abandon absolu du droit et de la volonté. Le moyen-âge pouvait bien ne pas demander davantage à Griseldis; aujourd'hui, grace à Dieu, son humilité paraît plus sublime unie à une dignité si pure. (Taillandier 179)

While Petrarch's Griseldis (and it is on Petrarch's version that I rely for contrast) was not quite as passively submissive as Taillandier makes her out to be, it is true that obedience is conceived of rather differently in Halm's play. Petrarch and Halm differ in where they accord room for freedom in Griseldis's behaviour. Whereas Petrarch shows Griseldis's freedom aside from her obedience, for Halm, Griseldis's very obedience becomes an expression of her agency. She reveals her freedom in the act of obedience, instead of in the aspects not bound by obedience.

This difference between Petrarch and Halm is illuminating because it allows us to see what was specifically new in the nineteenth-century way of conceptualizing obedience. It is thus worth looking at Petrarch in some more detail, even if it appears to lead us astray from our main focus on the Burgtheater. Petrarch opens his story with a scene of obedience that contains, in a nutshell, the structure that the story repeats many times over. The marquis Walter, we are told, is pressured by his subjects to marry. What they ask of him is that he "should take thought of marriage and bow [his] neck, free and imperious though it be, to the lawful yoke" (Petrarch 292). Walter's response to his subjects' demand to "bow his neck to the lawful yoke" is characteristic of what obedience means throughout this story. At the same time that he readily "bows" to their demand, he gains the concession that the choice of his partner will be up to him. Obedience, in Petrarch's story, always comes in tandem with the plea for a concession, thus marking a space for freedom in addition to obedient behaviour.

The marquis Walter uses the concession that he has obtained in a striking way, marrying the daughter of the poorest man within his domains. What draws Walter to this woman, Griseldis, is that she embodies obedience to the utmost. Still, for reasons that are not revealed, after the wedding Walter tests just how obedient his wife really is. In these ordeals, Griseldis proves her obedience at the same time that she demands a small concession (just as Walter had done at the outset).

In the first test, Walter sends one of his servants to Griseldis to demand that she surrender to him her firstborn daughter, apparently to give her up forever. Griseldis readily accepts the order, but she manages to arrive at one small accommodation. She tells the servant: "Go, and whatever our lord hath laid upon you, see that you perform it. One thing I beg of you: take care lest beasts or birds tear her [the daughter's] little body, and this, only if no contrary orders have been laid upon you" (Petrarch 300). Griseldis is not insubordinate, but she navigates a room for agency within the confines of obedience. There are, for Griseldis, always possibilities to act and realize her will, however minimally, while obeying.

A little later, Griseldis is subjected to another test. This time, her husband sends her away from his palace, claiming that he wants to remarry. Griseldis has to leave, and she must return everything that Walter has ever given her. Because Griseldis entered into the marriage dressed in clothes that she had received from her future husband, this would leave her with nothing. Once more, Griseldis obeys, but not without uttering a small demand:

> "Wherefore, if it please you – but not otherwise – I pray and beseech you, as the price of the maidenhood which I brought hither and do not take hence, bid me keep one shift, out of those I have been wont to wear, that I may cover therewith the belly of her who was once your wife." (Petrarch 306)

Griseldis's demand for just one piece of clothing is, of course, so modest that it seems to serve almost to underscore her obedience more than to qualify it. But perhaps this is the point. Petrarch explores the ways in which agency and obedience become *almost* indistinguishable. The complete union of obedience and agency, however, remains the peculiar trait of Halm's *Griseldis*. For Petrarch, there is always still a small formal difference between the acquiescence to a demand and the performance of freedom through the counter-demand for some concession.

The fact that Griseldis's agency and obedience are closely tied to each other (without becoming identical) is made even clearer in the final test to which Griseldis is subjected. At Walter's new, staged wedding, he not only demands of Griseldis to be a servant, but he also asks her if she approves of his new wife. Griseldis's response is a masterpiece of ingenuity:

> "Surely," said she, "no prettier or worthier could be found. Either with her or with no one, can you lead a life of tranquility and happiness; and that you may find happiness is my desire and my hope. One thing, in all good

> faith, I beg of you, one warning I give you: not to drive her with the goads with which you have driven another woman. For since she is younger and more delicately nurtured, I predict she would not be strong enough to bear so much." (Petrarch 309)

This final test is not one of obedience in quite the same way as in the previous instances. There is no direct command that Griseldis is asked to obey. Still, in Walter's question, there is an implicit command for Griseldis to suppress her own feelings for the sake of her former husband: she has to approve of a new marriage that is meant to be painful to her. In Griseldis's response, we see, once more, the characteristic combination of obedience with the demand for a concession. She approves of the new wife (and thus obeys the implicit command), and she asks for a concession: not to test the new wife as severely as she has been tested.

On the surface, one might read Griseldis's demand as a sign of the utmost readiness to submit herself entirely to the wellbeing of others. But there is more to say about this. It is important not only that Petrarch once more includes some request, thus stressing the connection between Griseldis's obedience and her agency (represented in her ability to ask for and obtain concessions) – but read closely, there is also something surprisingly subversive in Griseldis's humble request to spare the new wife. By asking that the new wife not be submitted to the same ordeals, Griseldis, in a way, makes it impossible for Walter to remarry. For how could he then be sure that his new wife is as obedient as Griseldis? There is thus also something joyfully ambiguous to Walter's reaction to Griseldis's response. Immediately after hearing Griseldis's words, he ends her trial, exclaiming: "It is enough, my Griseldis! Your fidelity to me is made known and proved" (Petrarch 309). At the risk of subverting the intended meaning of this scene, one can say that Griseldis, while appearing obedient, has made clear to Walter that he has little other choice than to take her back as his wife – provided that he wants the most obedient wife. Through the humble plea for milder treatment of the new wife, Griseldis thus demonstrates her efficient agency, regaining her husband. The essential point in all of this is not only that Petrarch's story insists on freedom as a necessary ingredient of obedience, but also that this freedom is realized *aside* from obedience, in the concessions that accompany all instances of obedience. This changes fundamentally in Halm's version, in which Griseldis's freedom is represented as being realized in her obedience, not aside from it.

When Halm approached the Griseldis tale in the 1830s, he made at least three important changes to the plot that all serve to locate Griseldis's agency more firmly within her obedience. The first of these changes consists of a multiplication of legitimate authorities. Whereas Petrarch limits himself to the portrayal of Griseldis's obedience to her husband, Halm emphasizes the conflict between different sources of authority that all – justifiably, in some limited sense – demand obedience of Griseldis. Specifically, Griseldis finds herself torn between the demands of her husband and those of her father. Halm devotes the long first scene of the second act to this conflict, the very first scene in which Griseldis appears on stage. As we learn in this scene, Griseldis's father scorns his daughter for putting her husband over her parents. This introduction of a conflict between paternal and spousal authority arguably serves to imbue obedience itself with agency. By showing Griseldis's obedience to her wifely duties as the result of a necessary decision between husband and parents, Griseldis's obedient behaviour becomes interpretable as a free act. This is entirely different from Petrarch's story, in which Griseldis's agency consists not in her obedient behaviour, but in the concessions that she secures while being obedient.

It is therefore only fitting that these concessions, which are of great importance to Petrarch's text, are consistently omitted in Halm's play; this forms the second innovation in the Austrian play. This is already true for the initial exchange between Griseldis's future husband and his subjects. In Halm's play, the husband never explicitly acquiesces to his subjects' demand and thus does not have to ask for a concession. More significantly, Halm cuts the plea for a concession from the scene in which Griseldis is asked to abandon her child. Unlike Petrarch's Griseldis, Halm's does not ask to have the child protected from wild animals. Halm makes up for this omission by adding a prolonged scene in which Griseldis protests the demand to give up her child. From expressing disbelief to contemplating resistance, Griseldis explores different avenues that would allow her to keep her child. Only when she is falsely made to believe that keeping her child would put her husband at risk does she surrender her.

It would be wrong to attribute Halm's handling of this scene only to his underlying concept of obedience. Likely, Halm found it psychologically improbable, morally problematic, and dramatically unsatisfactory that a mother surrenders her child as willingly as Petrarch's Griseldis does. In staging Griseldis's conflict, Halm can show a psychologically more realistic portrait at the same time that he gains a dramatic exchange for this potentially undramatic subject matter. But another important implication of Halm's change is that, once more, Griseldis's obedience becomes readable as an *act* – resulting from deliberation and contrasted with alternative forms of behaviour. Her agency lies not in asking for concessions that she is afforded due to her obedience, but in the obedient behaviour itself.

With much consistency, Halm also removes the concession in the scene in which Griseldis is sent away by her husband with nothing other than what she had brought into the marriage.[16] In Petrarch's story, let us recall, Griseldis is outfitted by her husband before entering his home, thus bringing absolutely nothing herself into the marriage – a fact that in some way necessitates Griseldis's request to keep one piece of clothing when she is sent away. Halm, by contrast, makes sure to change the plot so that this demand is no longer called for. In his version, Griseldis enters the marriage with a humble wool dress and an apron of her own, and she can thus simply accept the dismissal and leave in her old clothes.

The most significant way in which Halm recasts the meaning of obedience in his play consists of the different ending that he invents. Rather than returning to her husband, as Petrarch's Griseldis does, Halm's Griseldis leaves her husband when she finds out that her obedience was merely being tested in a frivolous wager (the wager itself being another invention of Halm's). The fact that Griseldis abandons her husband has routinely been read as a significant increase of Griseldis's agency, reflecting the burgeoning emancipation of women in the nineteenth century (see, for instance, Zanuchi 200, Skrine 145, and Reitani 227). However, Griseldis does not simply remove herself from the jurisdiction of conjugal authority. Quite to the contrary, Griseldis refuses to return to her husband because she wants to hold on to the "divine image" ("göttergleichem Bild"; Halm, *Werke* 2: 137) that she previously held of her husband:

> I could not wander hand in hand with thee,
> And feel that heart was coldly turned from heart.
> [...] – My self-respect –
> My life – its closing scenes – all, all must rest
> Upon the God-like image of my dreams –
> Rest on thy image; let me then preserve it,
> Sparkling and bright, as now it fills my soul.
> (Halm, *Griselda* 128)

> Ich kann nicht mit dir gehen, Hand in Hand,
> Wenn Herz vom Herzen nüchtern sich gewandt,
> [...] Es hängt mein Leben,
> Die Achtung meiner selbst, mein letztes Streben,
> An meiner Träume göttergleichem Bild,
> An deinem Bild! – O laß mich es bewahren,
> Wie's hell und funkelnd meine Seele füllt.
> (Halm, *Werke* 2: 137)

Griseldis's refusal to unite with her husband is done in the name of self-respect; but this self-respect is identified with her dependence on the divine image of her husband. Critics who wanted to see in Halm's play merely a moment of increasing individual freedom and of female emancipation have not paid sufficient attention to this enduring authority of the ideal husband. In a sense, Griseldis's refusal to be with her husband is the ultimate confirmation of his previous authority. Griseldis's agency does not consist, as for Petrarch, in the freedom to act also outside of authority; instead, up to the very end and including the refusal to be with her husband, Griseldis's actions are obedient acts. Griseldis's departure from her husband is in line with her previous obedience to her idealized husband, not a rupture with it.

Halm's successful first play is a prime example of what it could mean for nineteenth-century writers to reform obedience so as to reintroduce it as an otherwise lost virtue. Halm himself came back to this idea repeatedly, most explicitly in his 1848 comedy *Verbot und Befehl* (*Prohibition and Command*), a parody of the Austrian bureaucracy that reveals the inefficiencies of an authoritarian system that works against – rather than through – the will of its subjects and that culminates in a successful reform of the system of governance. As in *Griseldis*, Halm celebrates here the possibility of a synthesis of freedom and obedience.[17]

As the note by the French critic Taillandier quoted earlier suggests, contemporaries experienced this new synthesis of freedom and obedience as an attenuated form of obedience, more compatible with modern expectations of a sovereign subject. There is good reason to be sceptical of such an assessment. Petrarch's marking of wiggle room within obedience might point us to a realm of freedom that, while being modest, is at least more certain and perhaps more productive. Halm's modern synthesis of freedom and obedience, by contrast, remains possibly very little else than an internalization of an external system of command. Indeed, one of the great critical insights of scholars of the second half of the twentieth century is to have "debunked" the nineteenth-century discourse of subjectivity and autonomy as one of an internalization of authority. Michel Foucault thus analysed how nineteenth-century men and women became "the principle[s] of [their] own subjection" (Foucault 202–3). The most effective control, the nineteenth century learned, was indirect, relying on workers, prisoners, and citizens controlling themselves.

But already in the nineteenth century, and already in the Burgtheater repertoire, there was a critical awareness of the shortcomings of the new-found synthesis of freedom and obedience. Even Halm – one of the most popular Burgtheater playwrights – sometimes failed to find resonance with his modern recasting of obedience. This at least would explain why his comedy *Verbot* fell flat with the audience when it premiered on 29 March 1848, shortly after the onset of the 1848 revolution. After just four performances (hardly more than the three performances that almost all new productions were granted), the comedy was taken off the repertoire. At least at that point, the Viennese audience was looking for slightly more radical fare, which the relaxation of censorship in the immediate aftermath of the revolution also permitted: the first play to premiere after Halm's comedy was *Die Karlsschüler*, a play about the rebellious young Friedrich Schiller, written by the *Jungdeutschen* Heinrich Laube, whose plays had been banned from the Burgtheater since 1845.[18]

However, even some two years before the March Revolution, in 1846, when the censorship system was still firmly in place and the revolution seemed far off, the Burgtheater staged in Eduard von Bauernfeld's comedy *Großjährig* a play that was remarkably critical of Halm's easy synthesis of freedom and obedience. This play premiered in the Burgtheater on 16 November 1846; it saw thirty-five performances in under four years until it was taken off the repertoire in August 1850.

The plot of Bauernfeld's comedy follows a relatively simple dialectic structure. It is the story of a submissive young man who suddenly feels the urge to break free until he finally learns to see – and enact – a possible synthesis of freedom and obedience. The central character is the young baron and civil servant Hermann, who is still under the tutelage of a Herr Blase. Blase plans to declare Hermann of age (the Austrian term for this is "großjährig," hence the title of the play), but at the same time, he wants to retain his influence over Hermann and the latter's considerable estates. To that end, Blase aims to arrange a marriage between Hermann and his (that is, Blase's) niece Auguste, who is under his tutelage as well. Through family ties, Hermann would thus continue to be tied to Blase. The challenge for Blase, in whom Bauernfeld's contemporaries saw a rather thinly veiled caricature of the emperor's chancellor, Prince Metternich (Horner 114–15), is clear: how can one ensure that the bonds of obedience remain unbroken when citizens nominally become free.

While the obedient Hermann appears ready to comply with the marriage plans of his foster father, Auguste – a prototype of the confident young woman striving for independence, who appears in many plays of the period – is not interested in a marriage with the submissive civil servant. But when she confronts Hermann directly with the inferiority of his life as a bureaucrat, a taste for freedom begins to awaken in him, too. In a monologue near the end of the of the first of two acts, Hermann reflects: "But why am I a civil servant, after all? Why? To what end? It was the will of my father. Alas, it was his will that I should be without will! But I do will! I have the will to will!" ("Aber warum bin ich denn eigentlich ein Beamter? Warum? Wozu? – Es war der Wille meines Vaters. – Ach, es war sein Wille, daß ich keinen Willen haben soll! – Aller [sic] ich will! Ich will wollen!"; Bauernfeld, *Gesammelte Schriften* 5: 226). Soon, Hermann's "will to will" finds expression in radical protest. He abandons his job in the Habsburg bureaucracy, and he rebels against Blase by stating his intent to manage his estates himself and by revoking his interest in marrying Auguste. This outburst of independence proves too much not only for Blase, who fears for his influence over Hermann's wealth, but also for Auguste, who is now quite drawn to a man of such vocal independence. It has to be noted, however, that Auguste, a woman without her own financial means, faces the question of independence in different ways from Hermann, who is a man and rich enough not to need a salary or someone else's financial support. While Bauernfeld does not develop these economic differences in any detail, he at least hints at the fact that the debate about freedom and obedience is not fruitfully conducted in a social and cultural vacuum – a point to which we will have to return in much more detail in the following chapter.

After the sudden change in Hermann from passive submissiveness to a rebellious search for freedom – a change from thesis to antithesis, as it were – the play ends with the logical, though imperfect, synthesis: an (uneasy) union of freedom and obedience. How exactly we understand this synthesis determines the interpretation of the entire play. Afraid to lose Hermann completely, Auguste seeks help from Blase's assistant, Spitz (as the clever sidekick with a dog name, we might see a nod to Goethe's Mephisto here, who famously appears in the form of a poodle in *Faust*). And in a just a few short words, Spitz does succeed in bringing Hermann and Auguste to a mutual expression of their love for each other. Hermann's plans to break free are now reined in. He even appears to renounce his plans for a year-long journey for which Auguste had given him permission – he claims to have already become the "the new man" ("neu[e] Mensch"; Bauernfeld, *Gesammelte Schriften* 5: 263) he might have become through his travels. At the end of the play, Hermann and Auguste thus agree, of their own volition, to the very behaviour that the despotic Blase had tried to force on them at the outset. In the end, the obedient behaviour is implemented, but in a fashion wholly different from what Blase himself had planned – not as the result of a direct order, but as the result of the young couple's independent free will.

Blase, who cannot believe the lucky turn of events, asks his assistant Spitz for confirmation: "Herr Spitz! Is it really so? We are necessary again?" ("Herr Spitz! Ist's denn wirklich? Wir sind wieder notwendig?";

Bauernfeld, *Gesammelte Schriften* 5: 264). Spitz reassures Blase with a surprisingly ambiguous response: "The status quo is established" ("Der Status quo ist hergestellt"; 5: 264). Blase, perhaps not entirely satisfied with the ambiguity of this response (a status quo can normally only be retained, or established again – but not *established*), simplifies Spitz's statement: "Things remain as they were" ("Es bleibt beim Alten"; 5: 264). But this simplification triggers the protest of Blase's antagonist, the family friend and avowed liberal Schmerl, who counters Blase's interpretation by saying: "No, we are advancing! This is thanks to us – the what-is-it-called – the opposition!" ("Nein, es geht vorwärts! Das hat man uns zu danken – der Dings da – der Opposition!"; 5: 264). After these words, the curtain falls, and the two opposed interpretations of Spitz's assertion that the "status quo is established" – as either a return to the old or the onset of a new paradigm – remain unreconciled.

It is noteworthy also that Bauernfeld had originally contemplated Blase's final words ("Things remain as they were"/"Es bleibt beim Alten") as the title of his play – but then decided against it (Horner 115). Ostensibly, Bauernfeld was not satisfied with a too one-sided interpretation of the play's synthesis of freedom and obedience. By and large, this synthesis is the object of ridicule in *Großjährig* – but Bauernfeld apparently did not wish to go so far as to suggest that the new synthesis was identical to the old status. In comparison to Friedrich Halm, Bauernfeld invites a much more critical perspective on this synthesis, but even in this critical perspective, a door is left open for the viability of the new, "reformed" notion of obedience according to which freedom and obedience can successfully be reconciled.

In the readings of *Lear*, *Diener*, *Griseldis*, and *Großjährig* in this chapter, an abstract matrix emerged that allows us to see, in broad outlines, some of the dominant ways in which obedience was mourned and reformed in the repertoire of the Burgtheater (as well as important variations within these approaches). While this abstract matrix of mourning and reforming can provide useful guidance in further explorations of the repertoire, it is also clear that to nineteenth-century playwrights and their audiences, obedience was much more than merely an abstract problem. The question of how to think of obedience was at the heart of some of the most pressing cultural topics of the period, notably those concerning women's role in society and those concerning the meaning of individual agency within the ideological context of nation and empire. It is to these social and political topics that we now turn.

5 Performing the Women's Movement

In the middle decades of the nineteenth century, the question of how to navigate obedience overlapped in important ways with the debate over women's role in society. The women's movement was gaining momentum at this time, and women's demands to realize an active life outside the confines of the role of the obedient wife began to receive greater attention. The theatre, as one of the few public institutions in which men and women closely interacted and collaborated, was especially well attuned to these debates.

Plays on the Burgtheater stage of the period abound with critical as well as affirmative references to the contestation of gender norms. While these works generally end on a sceptical note concerning women's demands for independence and equality, they also seek to justify women's subordination as potentially compatible with a liberal framework. Women's submission to their fathers and husbands was, in other words, represented as something that could align with a certain understanding of individual liberty: women's acceptance of their roles as wives was envisioned as the product of free choice. Concretely, plays often started on the premise of a woman's refusal to marry, and they quite reliably ended with the respective woman's voluntary acceptance of a husband.[1] Concerning the precise path to marriage, however, there exist significant differences between the plays, and these differences have important implications for the broader understanding of women's agency.

To map out the Burgtheater's debate about women's role in society (that is, to identify what the contested points were and how far the positions differed from one another), this chapter reviews the most frequently performed plays of each of the three most successful female playwrights in the Burgtheater between 1814 and 1867: the comedy *Das letzte Mittel* (*The Last Resort*) by Johanna Franul von Weißenthurn (fifty-nine performances between 1820 and 1865; Rub 50);[2] the comedy *Der Majoratserbe* (*The Tenant in Tail*) by Amalie von Sachsen (twenty-seven performances between 1845 and 1877; 73); and the drama *Die Grille* (*The Cricket*)[3] by Charlotte Birch-Pfeiffer (123 performances between 1857 and 1902; 85). Yet the debate over women's role in society was not just a topic for female playwrights but also featured prominently in some of the most popular comedies by male playwrights. Here again we see a considerable range of approaches, neatly captured in the contrast between two extremely popular comedies of the period: Roderich Benedix's infamously conservative comedy *Doctor Wespe* (101 performances between 1843 and 1896; 72) and the much more conciliatory comedy *Bürgerlich und Romantisch* (*Bourgeois and Romantic*) by Eduard von Bauernfeld (156 performances between 1835 and 1912; 65).

Additionally, this chapter situates the debate on women's role in society on stage at the Burgtheater within the contemporary Austrian debates on women's rights off the stage. Moreover, it presents a survey of the representation of women in the Burgtheater. For the question of women's role in society was not merely the subject matter of the plays in the Burgtheater, but also concretely lived out in the degree to which women were allowed to participate in this institution.

Women in the Burgtheater

Depending on what aspect of the Burgtheater one considers, women were quite differently represented. On the one extreme is theatre leadership, which remained exclusively male. It took until 2014 for the first woman, Karin Bergmann, to become director of the Burgtheater. Female leadership in German-speaking theatres of the nineteenth century more generally was an exception, but it was not entirely unheard of, and it could look back on an even more robust tradition in the previous century. The most prominent case of a female director in the mid-nineteenth century is that of the very popular actress and playwright Charlotte Birch-Pfeiffer, who headed the Aktien-Theater in Zurich from 1837 to 1843.[4]

While women were generally excluded from the Burgtheater leadership, there was, among the ensemble, something approaching equal representation – albeit with significant fluctuations. In 1814, the Burgtheater employed twenty-four male actors and twenty-one female actors; in 1848, there were thirty-two men and seventeen women; in 1867, the Burgtheater had nineteen men and nineteen women permanently employed as actors.[5] And while male actors generally received higher salaries than female actors, at least in some years the best earning actors in the Burgtheater were women.[6] This numerical analysis of the ensemble does not convey a complete picture, and it does not allow us to conclude that women's status as actors was equal to that of men. For instance, female actors were, to my knowledge, not included into the circle of *Regisseure* ("stage directors"), which also had some say over the repertoire.[7] Still, it is hard to think of an industry in the nineteenth century that saw more equal representation or where women enjoyed an equal degree of agency as they did on stage, and there is little indication that the Burgtheater was an exception in this respect.[8]

Women, of course, were present not only on stage at the Burgtheater, but also in the audience, watching and discussing the performances. Unfortunately, there is no precise data concerning the representation of women among the spectators. But what information there is suggests that, while women may not have been in the majority, they were not a small minority either, and they appear to have exercised a significant influence.[9] In the mid–nineteenth century, women formed a very important part of literary readership (Stein 250), and they also made their presence felt in the theatre, including the Burgtheater. Heinrich Laube notes already for the 1820s, albeit critically and derisively, the crucial impact of the female audience on the fortunes of a play: "success with women makes for the broadest success" ("die Theatererfolge bei den Frauen sind die breitesten"; Laube, *Das Burgtheater* 109; see also Kord, "The Curtain Never Rises" 371). Incidentally, one of the few visual representations of the Burgtheater's auditorium – in an 1825 painting attributed to the Viennese artists Eduard Gurk and Joseph Gurk (fig. 5.1) – also gives us a good indication of the presence of women. In this painting, female spectators appear not only in the company of men, but also together with other women, and even by themselves.

The matter of women's representation in the Burgtheater is probably most complex when we look at the repertoire. On the one hand, drama was traditionally considered a male genre. In contrast to the novel, where women were more easily accepted as authors, the strict logic allegedly required in the construction of traditional drama was thought to be antithetical to women's nature (Thurner 17). On the other hand, there is the empirical fact that women were extremely productive authors of drama. In her seminal 1992 study, Susanne Kord counts hundreds of female German-language playwrights of the eighteenth and nineteenth centuries. And while many of these playwrights remained marginalized, a few of them did join the circle of the most successful dramatists of their generation. This is true for the German theatre landscape in general, and the Burgtheater also reflects this fact. Between 1814 and 1867, the Burgtheater introduced plays by eleven different

Fig. 5.1. Vienna, Old Burgtheater. Anonymous engraving of a painting ascribed to Eduard Gurk and Joseph Gurk, single sheet (no. 70) from the series "Wiens vorzüglichste Gebäude und Monumente" ("Vienna's Most Excellent Buildings and Monuments"), around 1825, KHM-Museumsverband, Theatermuseum Wien, ÖTM GS_GBM3883.

female playwrights.[10] This does not include the significant number of women who worked as translators for the theatre, nor the number of plays based on novels written by women. The women's rights activist Betty Paoli (1815–94), for instance, repeatedly and successfully translated for the Burgtheater.

The eleven female playwrights in the period from 1814 to 1867 were, taken together, responsible for seventy-four different plays in the Burgtheater repertoire. That means that, on average, there were one or two new plays by women per year during the directorships of Schreyvogel, Deinhardstein, Holbein, and Laube. Women, in other words, were regular contributors to the repertoire – but they still remained marginal. The seventy-four plays by women between 1814 to 1867 correspond to only about 7 per cent of the 1052 new productions over that same period.

In general, the Burgtheater's repertoire of female playwrights reflected the taste of the period more broadly. The three most popular female playwrights in the mid–nineteenth century – Johanna Franul von Weißenthurn (1772–1847), Amalie von Sachsen (1794–1870), and Charlotte Birch-Pfeiffer (1800–68) – were also the most successful women in the Burgtheater. Johanna Franul von Weißenthurn dominated during the time of Schreyvogel and Deinhardstein (twenty-five plays between 1815 and 1842); under Holbein, Amalie von Sachsen replaced Franul von Weißenthurn as the most popular female playwright (eleven plays between 1843 and 1846).[11] In the Laube years, Charlotte Birch-Pfeiffer saw the most productions (twenty-six plays between 1836 and 1867). The remaining eight female playwrights had only twelve plays to share among them.

It is instructive also to consider the age and national background of the female playwrights as well as the genres in which these playwrights wrote. What we find is that the female repertoire was overwhelmingly German, contemporary, and non-tragic. Of the eleven female playwrights, nine wrote their plays originally in German (the other two were French). Indeed, of the seventy-four plays, seventy (or 95 per cent) were originally German – noticeably more than the 63 per cent originally German plays in the Burgtheater repertoire as a whole. Moreover, all female playwrights were still alive when their plays were introduced. There were no women classics in the Burgtheater repertoire, and this period also did not produce any classics – almost without exception, these women are forgotten today and live on only as objects of (recent) scholarship.[12]

What stands out in terms of genre is that only one of the seventy-four plays was a tragedy: in 1814, the Burgtheater produced Franul von Weißenthurn's tragedy *Ruprecht, Graf von Horneck*, which was not a success; after just four performances it vanished again from the repertoire.[13] In other words, almost 99 per cent of the plays were dramas (*Schauspiele*) and comedies – more than in the repertoire overall, where "only" about 89 per cent of the plays were in non-tragic genres.

Finally, the success rate of female playwrights was lower than that of their male colleagues. One accepted indicator of a very successful plays appears to have been that it reached more than fifty performances.[14] Just over 12 per cent of all plays (by men, women, and anonymous authors) introduced between 1814 and 1867 eventually met that threshold.[15] Among the plays by women, by contrast, this was true for only under 7 per cent of plays.

What all of this points to is that female writing was not only marginalized in its share of the repertoire, but also deemed qualitatively different from the rest of the repertoire. It was clearly marked as much more ephemeral entertainment. As scholars have convincingly laid out, this characterization of women's writing for the theatre is best understood as an effect of the limited options women had for writing. If women were accepted as playwrights at all, they had to write in lighter entertainment genres. Politically engaged, or intellectually and aesthetically more ambitious drama was not accepted as a domain of female authorship. In that sense, writing as daringly and radically as Georg Büchner, who, in the 1830s, introduced the proletarian as a tragic hero and radically broke with existing conventions of dramatic structure, was the privilege of men.

Unfortunately, there are no systematic quantitative studies of nineteenth-century theatre repertoires, and so a direct comparison between the Burgtheater and other contemporary stages is not possible. But there is nevertheless good reason to assume that the Burgtheater was broadly representative of the wider trends in the history of theatre and literature. For instance, Susanne Kord counts only eighty-six tragedies among the roughly one thousand plays published by female playwrights in the eighteenth and nineteenth centuries (at the same time, women were very active as translators of tragedy; *Ein Blick* 93). The Burgtheater's apparently near-categorical vote against tragedies by women only heightens and reinforces the imbalance reflected in the general literary landscape of the period. Moreover, as already indicated, the three most popular playwrights in Burgtheater were also the three most popular playwrights overall. A glance at the court theatre in Weimar shows comparable numbers for these female playwrights: in Vienna, Johanna Franul von Weißenthurn, Amalie von Sachsen, and Charlotte Birch-Pfeiffer together wrote sixty-two new productions between 1814 and 1867. Similarly, in Weimar's court theatre, which performed on fewer days than the Burgtheater, these same three women were responsible for fifty-five new productions during this period.[16]

Negotiations of Women's Independence On and Off the Stage

Female playwrights of the mid–nineteenth century were predominately theatre practitioners: they wrote comedies and dramas that were acceptable to the theatres' guardians and that met the taste of contemporary audiences. The political, intellectual, and aesthetic diffidence of women's playwriting has been something of an embarrassment to critics who wanted to revitalize, against the sexist tendencies of conventional literary history, a lost tradition of women's writing – even if this diffidence is itself explicable as part of the unfavourable conditions for female writers. While some scholars have attempted to discover under the guise of political conformity a secret strand of subversion produced under difficult conditions (by paying attention to what women managed to say *in spite of everything*, to use Susanne Kord's phrasing),[17] others have insisted that women's dramatic productions corresponded categorically to the reigning bourgeois system of values.[18] As the following interpretations suggest, this latter assessment does, in some limited sense, correctly reflect mid-nineteenth-century women's writing for the theatre. Missing in this broad dismissal, however, is an awareness of the internal differentiation of what is conveniently, but reductively, identified as the "bourgeois system of values." This very system – if it was a system at all – was constantly in flux through debate, and such a dynamic debate can also be observed for the question of women's role in society, as the Burgtheater's many plays focused on marriage demonstrate.

At this point, one important caveat is necessary: it is not always very evident to what extent plays that appear to focus on marriage and the role of women in society were historically intended and perceived as contributions to a broader societal discussion of this matter. The social and political significance of the topic of marriage in dramatic plays is, paradoxically, both obvious and surprisingly difficult to gauge. Reading these plays as social commentary threatens to overlook the fact that writing on matters of marriage could also be the result of an abstention from political questions, even in a historical setting.[19] If the domestic sphere was chosen as the subject of a comedy this was possibly done to *avoid* politics, not to take a direct stance or to raise a contentious social or political debate.

Moreover – and in striking tension to the point just raised – the domestic sphere, was, since the mid–eighteenth century, a well-established allegorical sphere for the implicit discussion of political power structures when an explicit discussion was not allowed.[20] The use of the domestic sphere as a political allegory, however, also meant that the question of women's rights as such was sidelined. Both Halm's *Griseldis* and Bauernfeld's *Großjährig*, discussed in the previous chapter, are examples of such political allegories, in which the broader political meaning of women's obedience appears to override the gender politics that are the surface material of the play.

Finally, the social and political significance of the domestic plays is compromised by the very fact that they were indeed just that: theatrical plays, governed by – as well as consumed and judged according to – well-known generic conventions. Courtship and marriage are classic themes of German comedy since at least the Enlightenment and can be thought of not so much as the subject matter of the plays than as the structuring narrative pattern guiding the plays along an established arc of events (in a similar way in which murder can be the narrative vehicle rather than the subject matter of mystery novels). Even if the representation of marriage in the plays could be used as an indicator of changing underlying gender norms, these norms cannot easily be claimed to be the central concern of these plays. Instead, the rhetoric of female independence blends easily into standard comedic plots that are based on overcoming a series of obstacles to marriage. The politics of women's independence can, to some extent, be reduced to a function of such plots without any further intrinsic relevance.

For all of these reasons, it is difficult to study nineteenth-century plays on marriage as interventions in a contemporary debate on gender politics. And yet the connections between the plays and the debates over women's right to determine their own lives and over changing moral codes governing gender relations more broadly cannot be denied either. The theatre censors at least were keenly focused on any transgressions in this realm. Censorship on moral grounds was much more prevalent than censorship on state political or religious grounds (and morality here mostly referred to gender relations and the representation of sexuality). What is more, the censors were significantly stricter with female characters than with male characters (Kord, "The Curtain Never Rises" 360–1). In his oft-cited *Grundsätze der Zensur* (*Principles of Censorship*) from 1795, the Viennese censor Franz Karl Hägelin stipulated that it was permissible for male characters to engage in seduction but prohibited for female characters to respond positively to such attempts, even if this response was only pretended (361). Furthermore, there is a case from late eighteenth-century Vienna that indicates that the treatment of female insubordination could lead to the prohibition of the performance of a play.[21]

The censors' focus on codes of female conduct corresponded to a sustained public debate on the question of women's independence. Even though we commonly associate these debates with the second half of the nineteenth century, already the decades before mid-century saw a well-established discussion in Austria on women's roles.[22] This discussion was fueled in large part by the groundbreaking publication of Mary Wollstonecraft's *A Vindication of the Rights of Woman* (1792) in England as well as by the writings of Olympe de Gouges (1748–93) and George Sand (1804–76) in France.

The publications and protagonists of the Austrian debate over what would be later called the *Frauenfrage* ("women's question") were closely linked to the world of the playwrights, actors, and directors of the Burgtheater. Caroline Pichler, whose writing of historical novels transgressed established norms governing gender and genre, also had three of her plays performed in the Burgtheater.[23] Julie Rettich, the famous Burgtheater actress and lifelong friend and idol of Friedrich Halm, frequently spoke out against discrimination against women (Paoli 22–3). In the 1850s, Rettich even became one of the founders of the *Verein für Arbeitsschulen* ("Society for Labour Schools"), which was designed to provide young women from the lower strata of society with an education that would allow them to provide for themselves (Paoli 29). Most prominently, Betty Paoli, one of the leading voices in Austria's burgeoning women's movement, was a sought-after translator for the Burgtheater and a well-respected friend of Franz Grillparzer and Heinrich Laube. More generally, Grillparzer is known to have been deeply influenced by the women in his intellectual circles, including, in addition to Betty Paoli, Caroline Pichler and Marie von Ebner-Eschenbach.[24]

Within the spectrum of the early women's movement, Austrian women's public assertions on gender generally remained moderate. They mostly correspond to what Elke Frederiksen defines in her study of the later nineteenth-century German women's movement as the moderate bourgeois women's movement (*gemäßigte bürgerliche Frauenbewegung*), in contrast to the radical bourgeois women's movement (*radikale bürgerliche Frauenbewegung*) and the (Marxist) proletarian women's movement (*proletarische Frauenbewegung*). Austrian writers neither advocated for women's complete independence from men nor for the overhaul of the economy as a way to address gender inequality. Yet it is also important to be suspicious of the nature of such moderation. To some extent, the professed moderation could serve as a rhetorical door opener to otherwise controversial and unwanted debates. For as long as one can point to more radical positions than one's own, one's positions are legitimized as attempts to find a middle ground and to soften existing tensions in society. Whether more radical positions are actually being held anywhere is almost secondary (and all the better if they are not held, for then even the disavowal of them becomes a means to introduce them to society).

A good example for a strategic claim to moderation in contemporary Austrian writing off the stage can be found in an 1846 essay by Marie von Thurnberg – the essay, incidentally, was published by the same publishing house that also distributed Eduard von Bauernfeld's works: Anton Doll's Enkel. Thurnberg's essay *Gedanken einer Frau über die angeborenen Rechte des Frauengeschlechtes* (*A Woman's Thoughts on the Innate Rights of Women*) presents us with some of the principal questions concerning women's role in society as this topic was discussed at the time. At the outset of her essay, Thurnberg claims that the subject of women's abilities and ambitions "has almost become the question of our times" ("ist nun fast zur Zeitfrage geworden"; Thurnberg 1). Thurnberg positions herself in this debate by claiming that she will stake out a sensible middle ground between the reactionary voices and those that accord "too substantive rights" ("zu große Rechte"; 2) to women. Thurnberg urges men not to misinterpret her by confusing her demands with the "punishable disease of emancipation" ("strafbare Emanzipations-Sucht"; 150).

What this moderate position turns out to be for Thurnberg, as for other Austrian women writers in the nineteenth century, is a softening of the theses advanced by Mary Wollstonecraft in her *Vindication* at the end of the eighteenth century.[25] Like Wollstonecraft, Thurnberg demands a better education for women – but she omits Wollstonecraft's emphatic Enlightenment denunciation of all authority and obedience that is not built on reason. Instead of speaking about a world and gender order founded on reason, Thurnberg emphasizes the natural subservience of women to men and describes a woman's "main occupation, vocation, and pride" ("[i]hr Hauptgeschäft, – ihre Bestimmung, ihr Stolz"; Thurnberg 15) to be "a good housewife and mother" ("eine gute Hausfrau und Mutter"; 15). Moreover (and in a way that is again typical of contemporary women's writings), education is demanded largely as a tool for women to better fulfil the roles of mother and housewife (15, 22).

Despite these assurances, however, Thurnberg also discusses the option for women to remain unmarried and earn their living based on their own education. Thurnberg frames this option as a necessity: as wages were falling in this period in Austria and the cost of living was rising, traditional marriage and family life became unaffordable for many, and women had to be prepared to care for themselves. As a matter of fact, around the middle of the nineteenth century, Vienna had a particularly high share of unmarried women. At least according to one report, it housed more unmarried women than married women, which made it an anomaly among the large European cities of the time (Twellmann 28–9). For many of these unmarried women, the problem was not that they had to marry and give up their independence, but that they had no reasonable prospect of ever finding a husband – a social reality, incidentally, that is not accounted for in the Burgtheater's plays on women's role in society. It is for these women who are deprived of their "natural vocation" of fulfilling their duties in the household (and with that of a source of financial support) that independence is introduced as an option (Thurnberg 15).

It would be wrong to reduce Thurnberg's invocation of poverty and necessity to a strategic move alone, mentioned only in order to speak about a pathway to women's independence. The social problem of how to secure a living for unmarried women was real, and the foundation of schools for these women by Julie Rettich and others some years later attests to this reality. Nevertheless, the fact that at least under certain conditions, the question of how a woman may provide for herself could be raised signals an opening in the discourse whose importance extends beyond the concrete case of the women in precarious financial circumstances. As Thurnberg's essay illustrates, through various negations and indirect musings, the scandal of women's independence was being discussed in the period.

The concern over women's independence, which Thurnberg carefully introduces in her essay, also found an echo in contemporary Austrian fiction, notably in the story "Der Condor" (1840) by the quintessential nineteenth-century Austrian writer of fiction, Adalbert Stifter (who, incidentally, was another friend of the Burgtheater translator and women's rights advocate Betty Paoli). In "Der Condor," Stifter narrates a woman's daring decision to take part in a balloon flight. Cornelia's flight is framed as a disturbingly transgressive adventure that alienates the young heroine from her natural role as woman and ruins her relationship to her equally young, and somewhat insecure, lover, whose masculinity, it should be noted, seems to be as much in question as Cornelia's femininity.

At least on the surface, Stifter's story is more categorically dismissive than Thurnberg's essay of the idea "that a woman could declare herself free of the limits that austere men have imposed on her for millennia" ("daß auch ein Weib sich frei erklären könne von den willkürlichen Grenzen, die der harte Mann seit Jahrtausenden um sie gezogen hatte";

Stifter, *Studien* 8). Cornelia faints during the excursion and becomes seriously ill, while the two men whom she accompanies weather the flight apparently unaffected. Afterwards, she recognizes her mistaken overreaching of her powers and bares herself in all her weakness to her lover, which allows him in turn to enter the masculine role he previously had difficulties assuming – "in *one* minute he had become a man" ("in *einer* Minute war er ein Mann geworden"; 19). Yet their relationship is ruined and their paths in life diverge.

Stifter's story, critical as it may be of Cornelia's (literal) flight from her traditional place in society, is still an important indicator of the disturbances in traditional gender relations in the first of half of the nineteenth century. It is also interesting to note in this context that Stifter's text is likely based on Roswitha Kind's ballad *Die Luftschifferin* ("The Balloon Pilot"), which was published one year prior, in 1839 (Wozonig, "Freundschaft und Politik" 3–4). In Kind's ballad, too, a woman travels in a balloon, and here as well the journey is shown as perilous. However, Kind's poem grants noticeably more agency to the female balloonist. In contrast to Stifter's text, Kind's heroine ventures on her flight alone, and the outcome of her adventure is left tentatively open, even though a tragic ending is suggested.

The crucial point in comparing Stifter and Kind is not simply to present one of these texts as progressive and the other as reactionary. What makes the comparison between the two texts valuable is that it suggests a dynamic and nuanced spectrum along which writers positioned themselves in addressing the question of women's independence. The lesson to be learned here is neither that many publications were critical of women's questioning of reigning gender roles, nor that literature was a tool of subversion against these gender roles, but that contemporary moderate literature allowed for a considerable degree of uncertainty. There was, to say with only slight exaggeration, no one-sided bourgeois morality that these texts confirmed or transgressed. Instead, Stifter's and Kind's texts participate in an ongoing debate in which the reigning discourse on gender roles was kept open for transformation.

It is against the backdrop of these debates that the Burgtheater productions in the middle decades of the nineteenth century gain their significance. Even nuances and moderate variations become meaningful as indicators of an active discussion. Concretely, the most successful plays of the three most successful female playwrights in the mid-nineteenth century offer three distinct scenarios. While all show the eventual alignment of women's agency with obedience to husbands and fathers, they do so in very different ways, and they challenge established male authority to importantly varying degrees, from very little in the case of Amalie von Sachsen to very significantly in the case of Charlotte Birch-Pfeiffer. Amalie von Sachsen's *Der Majoratserbe* creates a system in which women's desire matches the demands of male authority; Johanna Franul von Weißenthurn develops in *Das letzte Mittel* a model for a middle ground between women's freedom and male authority; and Charlotte Birch-Pfeiffer's *Die Grille* imagines a world in which the eventual reconciliation heavily depends on the adjustment of traditional male authority. The general idea of a balance between freedom and obedience is thus concretized in three markedly different ways.

However, while it is insightful to thus see the range of positions in women's writing on Vienna's main stage, it is crucial also to understand the degree to which these positions related to those of popular male playwrights of the period. As we will see in the discussion of Roderich Benedix's *Wespe* and Eduard von Bauernfeld's *Bürgerlich* at the end of this chapter, women's writing on the stage of the Burgtheater departed from the conservative contemporary male voices (such as Benedix), but remained largely compatible with the more progressive male writers (such as Bauernfeld).

Amalie von Sachsen, *Der Majoratserbe*

Amalie, Princess of Saxony (1794–1870) stands out from among the three popular nineteenth-century female playwrights discussed in this chapter in that she was not a theatre professional.[26] Indeed, because the king of Saxony, Frederick Augustus (r. 1805–27), thought it unsuitable for a member of the royal family to appear as a playwright, she initially wrote merely for private performances. Only under Frederick Augustus's successor on the throne was she afforded more liberties, which led to a belated but all the more significant success. After Amalie's comedy *Lüge und Wahrheit* (*Lie and Truth*) was successfully produced at the court theatre in Berlin in 1833, she quickly rose to fame. In the following decade, her works were performed on virtually all German stages before vanishing again very quickly in the second half of the nineteenth century.

Amalie von Sachsen's astonishingly quick rise and fall on the German stage has led to some exaggerated claims. When the important nineteenth-century literary historian Karl Goedeke, for instance, maintained that Amalie von Sachsen's works "dominated the comedy repertoire" ("beherrschten das Lustspiel"; qtd. in Kord, *Ein Blick* 243) in the 1830s and 1840s, this cannot be taken quite literally. In this period, August von Kotzebue's comedies still enjoyed great popularity, and so did, at least in Austria, the comedies by Eduard von Bauernfeld. It should also be noted that, of the three great female playwrights of the mid–nineteenth century, Amalie von Sachsen was, at least in the Burgtheater, the least successful. Not only was she represented with fewer plays in the repertoire, but her plays also saw fewer performances. At twenty-seven performances between 1845 and 1877, *Der Majoratserbe* was already Amalie von Sachsen's most successful play in the Burgtheater (Rub 73).

Der Majoratserbe premiered in the Burgtheater in 1845, six years after its publication in book form and at a time when it had been established in other leading theatres (in Weimar, it had been on stage since 1838). The comedy's general plot line runs largely parallel to that of Bauernfeld's *Großjährig* (1846), discussed in the previous chapter. Again, the story centres on a young character who is faced with the imperative to marry. And while this order creates tensions between the authoritative father and the free-spirited young person at first, eventually the young person chooses of their own volition what they were initially ordered to do. As we have seen in the previous chapter, this is a clear emplotment of the nineteenth-century ideal of an alignment of obedience and freedom.

But let us begin by filling in this summary with some more concrete information. The Count of Lauerfeld has determined that his daughter, Bertha, an energetic and confident young woman, will marry the wealthy heir Count Paul von Scharfeneck. Bertha is abhorred by the seemingly squeamish and self-absorbed Paul. Especially the idea of being seen with Paul in public makes her shudder. "Heavens! This man is unpresentable," she exclaims ("O mein Himmel, den Mann könnte ich nirgends produciren"; Sachsen 77). Instead, Bertha wants to marry Paul's poor but brilliant cousin, Leo – but this goes against the wishes of her father. Yet as Bertha becomes better acquainted with Paul, she discovers in him a virtuous, generous, and unassuming man, whose foolish behaviour can largely be attributed to his insincere company (in awe of his wealth, no one has the heart to tell him just how badly he plays the violin, for example). The more spirited and entertaining Leo, by contrast, reveals himself to be rather backhanded and ungrateful. He seeks public attention by ridiculing his hapless cousin Paul, who is Leo's most loyal friend.

As this summary suggests, *Der Majoratserbe* presents us with a rather uncomplicated version of the reigning ideal of obedience. There appears to be very little of the ambivalence with which the alignment of obedience and free will is presented in *Großjährig*. The father's will, though initially questioned, reigns supreme and is shown to be in perfect correspondence with the daughter's matured understanding and agency.

Nevertheless, several elements in this play complicate this superficial reading and point to a slightly more subversive potential. First, the father's authority as such figures at no point as a very significant force in Bertha's thinking. The one seeming exception to this, when Bertha explicitly pledges her obedience to her father, actually further underscores this sidelining of paternal power. Bertha exclaims: "I will obey my father, obey him blindly. Whether I become happy or not – the world must praise me, and my consciousness must do so as well" ("Ich werde meinem Vater gehorchen, blindlings gehorchen, mag ich denn glücklich werden oder nicht, muß doch die Welt mich loben und auch mein Bewußtsein"; Sachsen 124). But this assertion comes only after she has already decided to marry Paul. As her words make clear, her obedience is also grounded less in the authority of the father per se than in the social approval of obedience. Even in considering obedience, Bertha is thus guided by the same vanity that characterized her throughout much of the play.

Moreover, Amalie von Sachsen chose to frame her seemingly conformist comedy around a widely discussed social, political, and legal complex. Paul's wealth is linked to the highly contested institution of entail laws (*Majorat* in German – hence the title). The reason why Paul is excessively wealthy while his cousin Leo is poor is that in the system of the *Majorat*, an estate is given undivided to the oldest heir. In the nineteenth century, the institution of the *Majorat* had become contentious, and it found prominent literary denouncement in E.T.A. Hoffmann's 1819 novella *Das Majorat*.[27] Like Hoffmann, Amalie von Sachsen shows the institution in a critical light. Her play suggests that a more equal distribution would have avoided the entire conflict of personalities, insofar as both cousins whom Bertha considers marrying at different points in the play would have likely not acquired their flaws, which are due to their excessive wealth and poverty, respectively. Both Leo's brilliant but poisoned sociability and Paul's foolishness are shown to be products of their economic status. As a consequence, the conflict between father and daughter would also have been avoided under these altered circumstances. Even if the critique of the institution of the entail laws was, by the 1830s, already fairly widespread (and the play's intervention in this debate thus relatively harmless), Amalie von Sachsen's critique invites a fundamental inquiry into the close ties between moral character and the unequal distribution of wealth. While such an inquiry does not pertain to gender relations directly, it generally encourages a reception of the play that is attuned to questions of social justice.

Both the discussion of legal and economic structures and Bertha's rather insincere invocation of filial obedience produce a tension to the conformist plot line of *Der Majoratserbe*. Still, compared to other plays produced in the Burgtheater during this time, Amalie von Sachsen's comedy remains subdued. Because the outcome of the play perfectly aligns Bertha's wishes with her father's demands, any real erosion of the father's authority is circumvented. The fact that the Burgtheater was willing to risk more subversive plays is well illustrated by Johanna Franul von Weißenthurn's comedy *Das letzte Mittel*, to which I turn next.

Johanna Franul von Weißenthurn, *Das letzte Mittel*

Johanna Franul von Weißenthurn entered the world of theatre when still very young. Born in 1772 as the daughter of an actor, she participated in her first ballet at age five. When she was fifteen, she gained an appointment as an actress at the court theatre in Munich. Two years later, in 1789, she joined Vienna's Burgtheater, where she remained employed until 1842, married to a respected civil servant in the city. Since 1796, Franul von Weißenthurn was also actively writing for the theatre.[28] Following the tastes of the period, her comedies and dramas (for these were the genres in she which wrote almost exclusively) were either in the Romantic style (that is, set in the Middle Ages or Early Modern period) or *Konversationsstücke* (in a contemporary setting).[29] Franul von Weißenthurn's track record as an actress and playwright is truly astounding. In total, the Burgtheater staged 912 performances of forty-eight plays by her. Napoleon, who saw her on stage in Vienna in 1809, was impressed enough to send her a gift of three thousand francs (Brümmer 207). Despite this remarkable success and long-lasting career as an actress and writer, however, Franul von Weißenthurn's accomplishments were sometimes belittled. Heinrich Laube writes of her as an insignificant actress and mediocre playwright (*Das Burgtheater* 89).

Yet even Laube names the comedy *Das letzte Mittel* as one of Franul von Weißenthurn's more valuable plays (*Das Burgtheater* 89). This play centres on a widowed baroness, Baronin Waldhüll, who enjoys great popularity in the upper circles of Vienna (or a city like Vienna, anyway, for the name of the city is never mentioned). Talented and beautiful, she enjoys the attention of various men. "You have legions of admirers" ("die Zahl Ihrer Anbeter heißt Legion"; Weißenthurn 79), she is told at one point – a, for the time, shocking line that appears to have been cut in some contemporary theatres, but not in the Burgtheater.[30] The baroness is resolved to marry Graf Sonnstett, a rather strict Northern man. This union, however, is endangered at the outset of the play when the baroness stays out until four in the morning, singing and dancing. While the baroness's many admirers are mesmerized by her presence during the long night out, the count, who was not present during the soirée, is dismayed at the news of his future wife's behaviour and promptly rushes into another marriage – a complication that the rest of the play sets out to resolve, leading to the eventual happy reconciliation of Baronin Waldhüll and Graf Sonnstett.

Das letzte Mittel is set up as a struggle for authority between two strong-willed lovers (that is, the baroness and the count). The baroness's clever waiting girl warns her mistress that in a marriage with the count, the baroness will get a "government" ("Regierung"; Weißenthurn 12), and she likens the count to a "Sultan" (12) – to which the baroness does not protest. The baroness herself, meanwhile, lives a life of unusual liberty and insists on her right to attract the attention of the men around her: "But why is he so odd?" she complains about Graf Sonnstett, "one can, after all, love only one man, and still be admired by a hundred other men" ("[W]arum ist er auch so Wunderlich, man kann ja wohl nur Einen lieben, und sich von hundert Andern bewundern lassen"; 13).

In the confrontation between the baroness's "libertinism" (judged by contemporary standards) and the count's stern patriarchal authority, the play provides a striking example of just how willing the Burgtheater was to put women's struggle for liberty on stage. To be sure, Franul von Weißenthurn, although intimately familiar with the theatre practice in Vienna, still exceeded in her printed play what could be said on stage in Vienna in the mid–nineteenth century (and perhaps she did so on purpose). When, for instance, the baroness claims programmatically near the outset of the play that the count's language was "too lordly for a time in which no one has a lord anymore" ("zu herrisch in einer Zeit, in der niemand einen Herrn mehr hat"; Weißenthurn 21), these lines were not actually uttered on stage.[31] And when another character claims at one point that no one believes in the concept of war [as] the peoples now live in peace ("Kein Mensch glaubt jetzt an dieses Wort, die Völker leben im Frieden"; 34), this too was cut as an apparently too sensitive statement. Direct political assertions like this could not easily be made. But where such explicitly political language was avoided, much could be said to question the established hierarchy between the sexes.

The Baronin Waldhüll is, of course, not simply a woman, but, more specifically, a widow – and a financially independent widow at that. The liberties that the baroness is afforded in the play are tied to this status. Although later in the nineteenth century the women's rights activist Hedwig Dohm famously identified widows as the group of women most strongly discriminated against in contemporary society,[32] at least wealthier widows could lead a comparatively self-determined life, because they stood under the authority of neither father nor husband.[33]

And yet, even if it were more acceptable for a wealthy widow to display the kind of independence that we witness in the character of Baronin Waldhüll in *Das letzte Mittel*, it is still remarkable that Franul von Weißenthurn focused on a widow as heroine in the first place. This was a rather untypical choice in the dramatic literature of the period, whose main archetype of the female lover was the unmarried young woman. Choosing a widow as main character afforded Franul von Weißenthurn the liberty to stage an otherwise unthinkable degree of female independence. Incidentally, Franul von Weißenthurn had, by the time that she wrote *Das letzte Mittel*, herself become a widow – a fact that likely was not lost on the Burgtheater audience. People in Vienna remained well aware of the principal events in the lives of the main Burgtheater personalities. The impression that Weißenthurn had created a character not too far from herself may have underscored a sense of endorsement for this character in the audience.[34]

Franul von Weißenthurn's portrayal of a character so confidently self-determined and assertive as the baroness undermines the prejudice against the Burgtheater as an institution unwilling to sanction anything but the most conservative of positions. As *Das letzte Mittel* demonstrates, the Burgtheater was also open to the performance of rather daring positions of female independence. And while the popularity of Weißenthurn's comedy alone does not allow us to conclude that the Burgtheater audience specifically applauded the display of freedom in this play, we can infer that such a display was not an obstacle to success.

To be sure, we cannot adequately judge this play simply by looking at the portrayal of the characters at the outset. The whole point of this comedy, one might say, is to show how these initial positions (of the libertine woman and august man) are negotiated and rewarded over the course of the action. Much of the play serves to chastise the initial haughty independence of the baroness. Soon enough, Baronin Waldhüll reveals how devastated she is at the loss of her prospective husband, and she plots to win him back. As the titular "last resort," she develops a scheme in which she pretends to marry another man, counting on the fact that the count's jealousy will lead him back to her. But once again, her hubris is corrected, and her intrigue yields the opposite result of what she had intended, further rushing the count's marriage with another woman. What turns out to be, in the end, the actual last resort that does allow her to win back the count, is an open declaration of her love – free of any of the cunning and clever speech that characterized her earlier.

This ending seems deeply problematic if one judges it by any standard of gender equality. Not only is the libertine woman subdued to marry the man whose patriarchal rigour she initially resented, but she is also reduced to the unsophisticated emotional existence that she was striving to escape from the outset. Yet we would do well not to place too much emphasis on the play's ending. Such a dismissal may appear counterintuitive, but just as a play cannot exclusively be read from the situation at the outset, it is also a mistake to judge it only by the results presented in the final scenes. First impressions leave a lasting impact on us: of a fictional character as much as of a person in real life. More to the point, literature, as Albrecht Koschorke argues in his seminal study of narrative, tries out and negotiates transgressions – and the mere display of these transgressions can be more important than their consequences (78). In the end, a literary work may choose to either approve and normalize these transgressions or to punish them, but that difference is not as significant as it may seem. Even if punished and censored, the very act of making the transgression explicit still signals an important opening in the discourse.

A closer look at the ending of *Das letzte Mittel*, however, also reveals that some transgressive elements are allowed to persist. For while the baroness admits her wrongdoing (in staying out so late at the party), she also insists that Sonnstett failed to reprimand her in a respectful manner. Even after confessing her love for him, she is ready to leave him because of his misstep:

> It may be that the applause of the world was too flattering for me, that I was too ready to display my talents, but this would have only merited a friendly reprimand, not this painful affront to my feelings. Where there is no respect, there is no love, no loyalty.
>
> Es mag seyn, daß mir der Beyfall der Welt zu schmeichelhaft war, daß ich zu nachgiebig war, meine Talente geltend zu machen, aber das hätte nur eine freundliche Zurechtweisung, nicht diese schmerzliche Verletzung meines Herzens verdient. Wo Achtung fehlt, ist keine Liebe, keine Treue [...]. (Weißenthurn 117)

In the Burgtheater, the baroness's indictment of Sonnstett, which extends even beyond the quoted passage, was significantly cut. The baroness was not allowed to make her principled speech about the limits of male authority. And yet, the central elements of her positions are still voiced. Much more laconically, she simply states: "Where there is no respect, there is no love, no loyalty" ("Wo Achtung fehlt, ist keine Liebe, keine Treue"; 117).

The count eventually does ask for forgiveness – and the baroness grants it, albeit only reluctantly, stating openly that she "should not" do so ("Ich sollte nicht"; Weißenthurn 120), before allowing her affection to get the better of her.[35] The baroness, in other words, does not simply yield to the count. Instead, both the count and the baroness have to move from their initial position to arrive at a middle ground: the count was right in disapproving of the baroness's libertine amusement, but he should have done so in a friendlier and more respectful manner.

This compromise is a rather "bad deal" for the baroness. She trades in her rights to live as she pleases for a nebulous notion of respect. She is willing to submit to the count's government as long as he still signals recognition – for without recognition (*Achtung*), as she urges, there is no love. Yet the fact remains that the future husband's initial demand is not met directly – instead, Franul von Weißenthurn's comedy negotiates and delimits a (future) husband's authority by outlining the conditions under which such authority can be wielded.

Charlotte Birch-Pfeiffer, *Die Grille*

As the cuts to *Das letzte Mittel* suggest, Franul von Weißenthurn already operated at the limits of what could be said on the Burgtheater stage. Still, there were plays in the mid-nineteenth-century Burgtheater in which an even more substantive infringement on male authority was tested. This is the case with Charlotte Birch-Pfeiffer's successful drama *Die Grille*, which premiered in 1857 and saw exceptional 123 performances until it was taken off the repertoire almost half a century later, in 1903.

Like Johanna Franul von Weißenthurn, Charlotte Birch-Pfeiffer started her career in the theatre as an actress, and like Franul von Weißenthurn she did so at a very young age. She first performed in the newly constructed Hoftheater am Isarthor in Munich in 1812, when she was only twelve years old. Subsequently, she held guest appointments in many important German-language theatres. In 1828, she began writing for the stage. An extremely prolific writer, Birch-Pfeiffer eventually produced a corpus of over one hundred plays.

In the middle decades of the nineteenth century, few authors, male or female, were more widely performed than Birch-Pfeiffer – although we should be careful here, too, to avoid false superlatives. While Birch-Pfeiffer was extremely successful, the notion that "[f]rom the 1830s through the 1850s her plays dominated the repertoire of the German theater each season" (Pritchett 13) is exaggerated, at least for the Burgtheater, where she had to contend with Eduard von Bauernfeld's popularity.

Birch-Pfeiffer was a theatre practitioner, writing primarily for performance on the large and small stages of her time, and not for publication in book form.[36] As a seasoned practitioner, Birch-Pfeiffer was well aware of the stringent censorship rules of the time, especially those governing in Vienna, where many of her plays were performed. But such awareness does not imply that her dramatic works were necessarily politically or morally conformist. For writers like Birch-Pfeiffer (or Franul von Weißenthurn or Bauernfeld), writing for performance and with the censors' rules in mind did not mean that they avoided all conflict. Self-censorship was not absolute. Instead, these writers carefully balanced just how much they might be able to pass by the censors. Often, they were erring on the side of transgression instead of conformity, and they dealt with the consequences, facing cuts to their plays (which was almost to be expected) or even seeing, at least temporarily, a play banned from performance. In a letter to the actor Emil Devrient, Birch-Pfeiffer complained that she managed to bring only one in eight plays through the Viennese censorship system (qtd. in Kord, *Ein Blick* 251) – a revealing statement, even if it cannot be taken literarily, given that Birch-Pfeiffer had twenty-five of her plays performed in the Burgtheater. Despite the interference by the censors, the texts that Birch-Pfeiffer managed to have performed remain remarkable and certainly go beyond what was being ventured in the plays by Amalie von Sachsen and Johanna Franul von Weißenthurn before her. This relative radicalism is certainly on display in Birch-Pfeiffer's most successful drama, *Die Grille*.

Like many of Birch-Pfeiffer's plays, *Grille* is based on a literary source – in this case George Sand's novel *La Petite Fadette* (1848; German translation 1849). While Birch-Pfeiffer's work on adaptations (rather than original plays) may have, in general, reduced her claims to genuine authorship in the minds of her contemporary audiences, at least in this case there was something rather bold and unusual in Birch-Pfeiffer's selection of her source. George Sand (1804–76) was Europe's most infamous female writer of the time – just as notorious politically, for being a sympathizer of the 1848 revolutionaries, as culturally and morally, for dressing in men's clothes and smoking cigars.

That said, the precise degree to which Sand's novel *Fadette* transgressed the prevailing norms in politics and gender relations has been the subject of some controversy in Sand scholarship.[37] On the surface, *Fadette* presents itself as a programmatic turn away from politics to focus instead on the simple life in the countryside. The novel focuses on a love story in southern France, and it makes very little mention of the political events that occur during the time in which the story is set, even though these include the French Revolution of 1789. In an 1851 preface to her novel, Sand emphatically claims that the duty of contemporary literature is to open a space beyond the political struggles of the day. In contrasting the contemporary writer's position with that of the great writers of the past who, like Dante, managed to capture the terror of their times in terrifying literary images of hell, Sand writes:

> The artist of our times [...] feels the imperative need of looking away, and of diverting his imagination, by turning toward an ideal of peace, of innocence, and of contemplation. It is his weakness that makes him do so, but he has no cause to blush for it because it is also his duty. In times when evil comes because men misunderstand and hate one another, it is the mission of the artist to praise sweetness, confidence, and friendship, and so to remind men, hardened or discouraged, that pure morals, tender sentiments, and primitive justice still exist, or at least can exist in this world. (Sand, *Fadette* [1895] 6)

Sand's emphatic disavowal of politics confronts us with considerable difficulty. On the one hand, one does well to be suspicious. If a writer says so explicitly that one should "look away" and "turn toward an ideal of peace, of innocence," the fictional idyll seems already overshadowed by the evil that it seeks to tune out. At the same time, one should be wary of any overly eager attempt to read against the grain. There is value in appreciating a text's surface meaning, and Sand's disavowal of politics appears to align well with the novel she prefaces. The plot of *Fadette* is removed from the direct political tensions that afflicted France in and around 1848 – and in the course of which Sand herself was faced with the threat of imprisonment. Politics, as a struggle over the distribution of power and wealth and, more broadly, over mechanisms of inclusion and exclusion, is, while not entirely absent from the novel, thematized only indirectly, through the calming pastoral prism of peasant life.

The titular heroine of Sand's novel is the ostracized young woman Fanchon Fadette, called "cricket" (in German, *Grille* – hence the title of Birch-Pfeiffer's play). Fanchon grows up with her grandmother, whom the village community sees as a witch. Fanchon's mother is absent: she has run away with a soldier. Fanchon herself is shunned by the village community, and her boy-like appearance significantly adds to her exclusion. Shockingly, however, two sons of one of the most respected families in the region, Landry and Sylvinet Barbeaud, fall in love with Fanchon. Much to the dismay of their parents, Landry is determined to marry Fanchon, and he carries this plan out against all resistance.

Finally, the reluctant father gives in, convinced by the credible testimonies of Fanchon's virtuous behaviour as well as by the surprising news of her considerable wealth.

Charlotte Birch-Pfeiffer's popular dramatization of Sand's work eliminates much of the remaining social and political provocation still found in the novel, and she softens the conflicts that characterize the original story. For instance, Birch-Pfeiffer cuts any discussion of the economic difficulties facing the Barbeaud family, and the psychologically intricate jealous conflict between the twin brothers is absent as well in Birch-Pfeiffer's play.

Such interventions were presumably necessary to grant the play its success – and a stunning success it unquestionably was, in the Burgtheater as well as beyond. Indeed, later nineteenth-century German and English translations of Sand's novel integrated the title of Birch-Pfeiffer's play (*Grille*) into their translated title of the novel, apparently to make the novel more widely recognizable (see Sand, *Grille*). The most curious anecdote to prove the popularity of Birch-Pfeiffer's drama, however, is that the Prussian king Frederick William IV (r. 1840–61) christened a steam yacht that he owned after the title of Birch-Pfeiffer's play, *Grille*.[38]

There is something odd and perplexing about the image of the Prussian king riding on a boat named – albeit indirectly – after the heroine in a novel of Europe's most infamous cigar-smoking feminist. Was there, after all, really nothing subversive about the rural idyll of Sand's novel *Fadette*, or at least of Birch-Pfeiffer's drama *Grille*? Despite all the cuts and harmonization that Birch-Pfeiffer applied to the original French novel, her play remains the story of a boyish social outcast who wins the love of a respected farmer's boy and thereby causes the father's authority to shatter. In Landry's struggle to marry Fanchon, not only does a son speaks out against his father, but, as Landry gains his mother's support, a wife also speaks out against her husband – until, eventually, the father and husband concedes.

Initially insisting that his son marry the daughter of a rich neighbouring farmer, Landry's father demands obedience: "You will obey, as you have done since you came into this world" ("Du wirst gehorchen, wie du es gethan, seit du auf der Welt bist"; Birch-Pfeiffer, *Grille* 74). But Landry does not obey. He insists on his will, and if harmony is eventually re-established in the family, this is because the father changes his position to agree with his son. Whether one goes so far as to read this struggle against the father allegorically in political terms,[39] or whether one reads this revolt more literally as expressive of a shift in family hierarchies, what remains true is that Birch-Pfeiffer's play significantly undermines established social structures and goes far beyond what other contemporary playwrights showed in the Burgtheater.

It is worth noting that we see here the son rebel, and not the daughter – and so this is not a story of female rebellion per se, even though this story of filial disobedience does also lead to a scene of marital unrest in which the wife successfully objects to her husband's position. Perhaps this same play could not have been performed in the Burgtheater if the gender roles had been reversed: that is, if it had been the story of a young woman rebelling against her parents to marry the male (and girlish) outcast. Showing a successfully rebellious son was, although largely without precedent, still more acceptable than showing a rebellious young woman. Even so, the boyish Fanchon is transgressive in her own right, as a heroic and wrongfully ostracized character who defies ruling gender norms. What is more, it is Fanchon's presence that incites the destabilization of the established hierarchy in the Barbeaud family. As Gretchen van Slyke argues with respect to the Fanchon of Sand's novel, Fanchon "quietly subvert[s] the patriarchal organization of her husband's family and plant[s] the seeds of a new social order" (van Slyke 3).

Even if, in a crucial scene, Fanchon seems to accept Landry's admonition to present herself in a more normatively female way, the character of Fanchon impresses herself both on Landry and on the audience as the clever and strong, spirited "tomboy" that she is at the beginning and as whom she appears in the play's title. Here, even more so than in many other cases, it seems justified to judge the play at least as much by its beginning as by its end. That is, even if the play can, to some extent, be read as just another variation on the theme of the unlikely and unwilling young woman being led to the altar, the great extent to which Fanchon's transgressive identity is stressed at the outset goes beyond the norm and impresses itself on the audience in its own right.

It will not come as a surprise that the Burgtheater did not quite stage *Grille* as it was printed. The surviving prompt book of the Burgtheater production gives us a good idea of the cuts that were made by the censors as well as by the Burgtheater itself.[40] In many cases, these cuts were motivated by considerations of political and moral decorum. When Fanchon praises Landry for taking up the cause of the "oppressed" ("Unterdrückten"; Birch-Pfeiffer, *Grille* 52) this line is struck out with the censors' red ink – even though Fanchon refers only to herself as being oppressed, and not to any politically oppressed group in contemporary society. And when Fanchon, disappointed by her own initial attempt to dress according to society's expectations, exclaims that she will "crawl back into my rags" ("ich will wieder in meine Lumpen kriechen"; 49), the red ink has firmly cut these words as well – presumably because of the all too vivid and unbecoming imagery. Perhaps the most extensive cuts, however, are in the scene in which the rich farmer's wife challenges her husband to accept Fanchon as his daughter-in-law. Interestingly, the Burgtheater even goes beyond what the censors removed. For instance, in another scene, Fanchon's explicit critique of Landry for neglecting his obedience to his father ("da du des Gehorsams gegen deinen Vater vergißt"; 90) is cut from the Burgtheater performance.[41]

Important as all these cuts are, they do not alter the core of the story about transgressive gender identity and filial disobedience. Here as elsewhere, the Burgtheater censors and practitioners are concerned with obviously political keywords and a direct affront to decorum. Words and passages that fall into these categories are cut, but the rest is left intact. As much as the censors deleted, enough dialogue is left even to convey the conflict between husband and wife over their son's marriage. Moreover, the censors' work shows some inconsistency: the word "rags" ("Lumpen") as a description of Fanchon's clothes, for instance, which we see cut at one point, is allowed on another occasion (see Birch-Pfeiffer, *Grille* 48).

More important than any cut to the text, in any case, is the fact that the story of resistance to authority is accompanied by numerous compensatory passages in which Fanchon's and Landry's obedience is emphasized (passages in which Birch-Pfeiffer could be relying on Sand's novel). At one point, Fanchon explicitly praises Landry as "an obedient son" ("ein gehorsamer Sohn"; Birch-Pfeiffer, *Grille* 66), and she tries to reinforce that obedient behaviour in him. When Landry wants to leave his parents and follow Fanchon to town, "she ordered him to stay and to be obedient, and only because of that, he did his duty" ("sie befahl ihm zu bleiben und gehorsam zu sein, nur darum that er seine Pflicht"; Birch-Pfeiffer, *Grille* 98). Fanchon herself also invokes her duty when she first turns down Landry's proposal (76).

It is striking just how frequent allusions to duty and obedience are in this drama, which is ostensibly so far removed from the conformist plays of the period. In contrast to many other plays, there is no easy synthesis between the characters' freedom and their obedience. And yet, an *uneasy* synthesis is nonetheless maintained, in which the shocking transgression of gender norms (Fanchon) and parental authority (Landry) is awkwardly balanced with the insistence that duty and obedience remain primary concerns for the protagonists.

Roderich Benedix, *Doctor Wespe*

The peculiar commitment to traditionally held values in plays that also undercut these values, which is on display in Birch-Pfeiffer's *Grille*, characterizes other works in the Burgtheater repertoire as well. This is best illustrated by a play that, as far as its explicit gender politics are concerned, is the polar opposite of Birch-Pfeiffer's drama, namely Roderich Benedix's notoriously conservative comedy *Doctor Wespe*.

The plot of *Wespe* follows a predictable conversion narrative, in which a young woman who is initially hostile to the idea of marriage eventually discards her unconventional leanings and accepts a husband. The young woman in question is Elisabeth, a wealthy banker's daughter and self-declared fighter for women's emancipation. At the outset of the play, she dresses in men's clothes, smokes cigars in front of a mirror, and fantasizes about her grand future as a liberator of all women – as if in critical allusion to the habits and (imagined) aspirations of the real-world George Sand.

Of all plays performed in the Burgtheater in the mid-nineteenth century, *Wespe* confronts the question of women's role in society most directly. It summons explicitly and extensively the burgeoning discourse on "emancipation" – a political buzzword that one does not otherwise find in the Burgtheater repertoire. At the same time, *Wespe* is, in its aggressive and patronizing dismissal of the women's rights movement a sexist and reactionary play that has rightly been cited in attempts to mark, by means of contrast, the progressive nature of women's writing of the time (Hes 38–9; Pritchett 39–40).

There is, in other words, in Benedix's play a tension – or a positive correlation – between the directness with which women's fight for independence is treated on the one hand, and the critical fervour with which this topic is being handled on the other hand. While one cannot possibly rescue Benedix's play from charges of sexism and reactionary gender politics, willingly or not Benedix reinforced with his play a debate on women's role in society that some factions preferred to see quelled altogether. A contemporary review of the Burgtheater production of *Wespe*, for instance, comments that the "distasteful doctrines of women's emancipation" ("abgeschmackten Doctrinen über Frauenemancipation"; F.W. 262) were not widespread enough to be a fitting and intelligible subject of comic correction. At least for this reviewer, the very treatment of the question of women's rights conjured a debate that one had better leave unacknowledged.

The paradoxical effect of *Wespe* promoting a debate on gender equality despite – and through – its conservative politics is further increased by a performative contradiction at the heart of this comedy. In what is perhaps the comedy's most memorable scene, situated at the precise centre of the play, the painter Honau – an ostensible spokesperson for the author – engages in a sword fight with Elisabeth.[42] Honau's goal in arranging the sword fight is to convince Elisabeth of the essential physical difference between men and women, which in turn serves to justify their different positions in society (confining women to the household and family while granting men a wider field of action abroad). Shortly into the first fencing session, Elisabeth has to admit her inability to keep up the fighting. She is overwhelmed not so much by Honau's superior technique as by the sheer physical exhaustion that results from holding the weighty weapon.

This is (literally) a rather heavy-handed display of women's alleged physical weakness and it stands, incidentally, in marked contrast to scenes of women-at-arms that the Burgtheater audience would have been familiar with from other plays and in which the women show much more talent and strength in handling their weapons. Spectators would likely have recalled at least Schiller's tragedy about the fifteenth-century female warrior Joan of Arc, *Die Jungfrau von Orleans* (*The Maid of Orléans*, performed successfully albeit heavily censored in the Burgtheater beginning in 1802).[43] Some audience members may also have attended Eduard von Bauernfeld's comedy *Die Geschwister von Nürnberg* (*The Nuremberg Siblings*), which features a scene in which a young princess wounds the leader of a band of robbers with her spear.[44]

Benedix chose not to follow the available precedents for a portrayal of female strength and used the trope of the woman-at-arms instead to highlight women's physical limitations. And yet this portrayal of weakness facilitated, on the level of the theatrical performance, a display of women's physical skilfulness. In a remarkable stage direction, it is explicitly noted that this scene is "written only for the actress" ("nur für die Schauspielerin geschrieben"; Benedix 73). The text further reads:

> For the skilled actress [literally, *Künstlerin* = female artist], it will be easy to display all sorts of naive grace in the physical fear of the exposed weapon. The actor [what is likely meant here is the actress] must necessarily be versed in fencing. It is also possible to replace the cut fencing with thrust fencing – however, as the rapier is heavier than the foil, the former gives the actress more occasion to show inaptitude and helplessness, which are calculated to create pleasure in this scene. Apart from that, the whole scene should not be drawn out; rather, it must pass by quickly.

> Es wird einer gewandten Künstlerin leicht sein, in der körperlichen Furcht vor der blanken Waffe alle mögliche naive Grazie zu zeigen. Der Darsteller muß notwendig mit der Waffenführung vertraut sein. Auch kann man leicht statt des Fechtens auf Hieb, das auf Stoß anbringen, obwol, da das Rappier schwerer als das Florett ist, jenes der Schauspielerin mehr Gelegenheit zu einer Ungeschicklichkeit und Unbehülflichkeit gibt, auf welche das Gefallen der Szene berechnet ist. Uebrigens darf die ganze Scene nicht gedehnt werden, sondern muß rasch vorübergehen. (Benedix 73)

The performative contradiction here arises, of course, from the fact that the very scene that, on the level of the plot, reveals women's natural limitations, showcases, on the level of the performance, the actress's physical aptitude – and, indeed, even her ability to wield the sword.[45] This performative contradiction is plain and explicit for the reader of the play – although it should be noted that Benedix's plays were meant largely for performance, not for reading. But even a slightly more thoughtful spectator among the theatre audience must have observed the contradiction of the actress performing such perfect and graceful impotence.

Again, we should not be too quick in reading Benedix's comedy against the grain as a secret harbinger of women's emancipation. The sword fight is followed by lengthy reasoning on women's distinct place in society, and this discourse conveys the play's central message, confirmed by the play's ending, in which Elisabeth dons women's clothes and abandons her resistance to marrying Honau. At the same time, it would also be naive to brush aside the prominently placed performative contradiction of the sword fight as a small inconsistency.

Indeed, the discussed performative contradiction is mirrored by another such ambiguity that is almost as important. Elisabeth's cousin, Thekla (perhaps not coincidentally the name one of Schiller's best-known female characters), dreams of becoming an actress. She, too, is cured of this unbecoming pretension by her future husband, and she accepts instead her role as housewife. However, because this cure from theatrical pretensions happens on the stage of a theatre, it is hard to imagine that this turn in the plot could be presented and perceived without some degree of irony. As a matter of fact, the entire play is framed by the discussion of a comedy competition in which the titular Doctor Wespe participates. And while at the outset Wespe cannot think of any plot around which to write his comedy, his friend Honau suggests, at the end, that the very events that transpired in the course of the play could serve as material for his comedy. If one thinks this hint through to its end (and one does not have to think very far for that), the very play that we have seen is already the play that Doctor Wespe will have written, and the Thekla who abandons the theatre, is already the actress playing Thekla. In this way, too, the strict pedagogical insistence that women abandon their far-flung aspirations is broken by a good measure of irony.

One may be tempted to find some solution to the contradiction on display between the reactionary nature of the explicit ideology of *Wespe* and the progressive essence conveyed in the performance of the play. Simply put, which of these two cultural and political tendencies dominates the play? But perhaps this question is ill conceived. It may be more useful to think of these two sides as necessarily coupled: like the dynamics analysed in Birch-Pfeiffer's *Grille,* the progressive elements need to be accompanied by more conservative statements – and, vice versa, the conservative statements would lose all their interest and justification if they were not presented against the backdrop of a more progressive discourse.

The point is not that it is impossible to define the cultural-political leanings of a play or that all plays in the Burgtheater worked through similar stagings of a fundamental conflict between progressive and reactionary tendencies. But these leanings come to the fore largely through the comparison of these plays with one another rather than through any truly unambiguous message in a given play. In that sense, *Wespe* remains one of the culturally conservative plays of the period, despite its own interior contradictions, because of the clearly perceptible distance at which it stands to the depiction of women in the popular plays by Amalie von Sachsen, Johanna Franul von Weißenthurn, and Charlotte Birch-Pfeiffer.

Eduard von Bauernfeld, *Bürgerlich und Romantisch*

As noted, there is good precedent for using *Wespe* as the reactionary backdrop against which the interventions of female playwrights of the period become visible in their relative progressiveness. However, despite the great popularity of Benedix's play, its conservative elements are not directly representative of the reigning bourgeois gender ideology of the period, or even of its representation in the productions of male playwrights in the Burgtheater. The greatest point to take away from the comparison between Benedix and his female colleagues is not the difference between male and female playwrights, but the heterogeneity of the bourgeois discourse on gender relations in general, as well as the fact that this heterogeneity was on prominent display on the stage of the Burgtheater. Even if it is surely no coincidence that we see the women – notwithstanding all their internal differentiation – promote a more progressive view than Benedix, the differences between the conservative and progressive voices do not fall squarely along gender lines. Once more, Eduard von Bauernfeld presents a more progressive side of the Burgtheater. Where Benedix constructs a social order in which men and women live together harmoniously to the extent that they accept their fundamental differences, Bauernfeld displays a more egalitarian view of gender relations.[46] This becomes clear when one studies one of Bauernfeld's greatest successes in the Burgtheater, the comedy *Bürgerlich und Romantisch*.

The comparison between Benedix's *Wespe* and Bauernfeld's *Bürgerlich* is all the more productive because the general plot of the two plays is similar. In Bauernfeld's play, we encounter again a young woman, Katharine von Rosen, who is infused with modern ideas of female independence and who envisions a life without marriage. Over the course of the play, Katharine encounters a man, Baron Ringelstern, who leads her to revise her opinions. By the end of the play, she abandons her old ideas and is now looking forward to the rest of her days in the company of her soon-to-be husband. This summary suggests that Bauernfeld's play is just as conservative as Benedix's, reinforcing marriage as the inescapable norm. The very name of Bauernfeld's heroine, which alludes to Katharina from Shakespeare's *The Taming of the Shrew* (which was very popular in Vienna), also invokes such a conservative paradigm.[47] And yet we witness in Benedix's and Bauernfeld's plays important differences in characterization and argumentation. These differences concern, in short, the relative sympathy with which the heroine's emancipatory aspirations are introduced; the precise rationale for women's inability to live independently; and the necessity for the young woman's suitor to give up some of his own pretensions of independence and strength.

The portrayal of Bauernfeld's heroine Katharine is sympathetic, and her freethinking is carefully justified as the result of her upbringing by her well-intentioned father as well as by her current situation. As the audience learns from Katharine herself, she lost her mother at a young age. From her widowed father, she received "a boy's education" ("die Erziehung eines Knaben"; Bauernfeld, *Gesammelte Schriften* 3: 193), allowing her to learn how to ride, swim, and climb. At age fifteen, her father died as well, and she was brought to an aunt whose very strict regimen led Katharine to seek refuge in books and artistic practice. This escape to the arts further divorced her from the real world and her place in it, and it instilled in her, we are told, unrealistic ideas about her future. Finally, when the aunt died too, Katharine had to defend her right to her own fortune against the greed of "evil relatives" ("böse Anverwandte";

3: 193). Eventually, she won the legal proceedings and the law courts declared her of age.[48] Even though there is a sense in all of this that Katharine's temerity and nonconformism are the unfortunate outcome of a hapless upbringing, the still largely sympathetic legitimization of Katherine's behaviour is strikingly different to Benedix's play: in *Wespe*, the heroine develops her dream of emancipation under the influence of the disingenuous and ill-conceived writings of a ridiculous journalist (the titular Doctor Wespe) who merely aims to please his audience.

The idea that Katharine's claims to female independence should be forgiven as a natural product of the influence of her social environment is further underscored by the way in which she is made to appear in the spa town in which the comedy is set. Upon her arrival, the owner of one of the spas addresses her as "madam" ("gnädige Frau"; Bauernfeld, *Gesammelte Schriften* 3: 192), thus indicating that she is – or was – married. Presumably because she is travelling alone, the other guests take her to be a widow, and she does not correct that impression, gratefully accepting the freedoms that this status affords her. If the play deems it necessary to explain Katharine's false pretensions to widowhood in such detail, this is to convey that she is as much pushed into the role of the free woman as she is actively pursuing it. And while Bauernfeld's strategy of portraying Katharine's liberal striving as an effect of family and social setting does little to defend such striving, it nevertheless makes it appear as something for which one cannot really blame Katharine herself. If it is an aberration, it is the aberration of either unhappy circumstance or social structure.

More important for the positive portrayal of the heroine in Bauernfeld's comedy, in any case, is the – in comparison to Benedix – less confrontational way in which she expresses her dream of independence. While Katharine's hopes are portrayed as naive, they were probably still meant to be likeable in all their naivety. Remarkably, the first lines that Katharine speaks in the play are a quote from Schiller's tragedy *Maria Stuart*: "Let me enjoy my freedom; let me be a child; be a child together with me" ("Laß mich der neuen Freiheit genießen,/Laß mich ein Kind sein, sei es mit"; Bauernfeld, *Gesammelte Schriften* 3: 152). In Schiller's play, Mary speaks these lines in a garden during a temporary release from her prison. In Bauernfeld's play, Mary's physical prison becomes a metaphor for the social confines of an unmarried woman in contemporary society. Given the great prestige that Schiller enjoyed in the mid-nineteenth century, and especially given that *Maria Stuart* was Schiller's most popular play in the Burgtheater,[49] the fact that Katharine expresses her feelings and aspirations by citing *Maria Stuart* can be assumed to elicit sympathy, even if the large number of literary references in the play more generally appear to have irritated parts of the audience.[50] At the very least, Katharine's quotation of Schiller creates a more positive effect than what we see in Benedix's *Doctor Wespe*, where the heroine self-indulgently poses in front of a mirror, dresses in men's clothing, smokes cigars, and rehearses the jargon from the newspapers.

To be sure, Katherine's Schillerian praise of freedom is not only overly enthusiastic given the social reality that Katherine faces, but, paradoxically, it also already foreshadows the very failure of Katharine's aspirations. In Schiller's play, Mary Stuart speaks these lines in a moment of what turns out to be false hope, shortly before the central and ill-fated meeting with Queen Elizabeth that seals her destiny. But it is uncertain whether Bauernfeld wanted the audience to even think that far – and, even if he wanted it, we do not know whether the historical audience realized that wish. Perhaps all that ever happened during the Burgtheater performances was that audiences appreciated in Katharine's lines the homage to one of their most admired plays and playwrights.[51]

What contributes most to the positive portrayal of Katharine is that she plans to enact her freedom in ways that are not only modest but also, even by historical standards, reasonable (which is, again, quite different from the more self-aggrandizing aspirations of Benedix's heroine). The central subject that is used to negotiate women's aspirations to independence in *Bürgerlich* concerns nothing more radical than the desire to take a walk alone on the promenade of the spa town:

> The sun shines for us all; birds sing, and flowers are fragrant for us all. Let us enjoy the beautiful springtime without any cares. Is it such a grand crime to take a walk without male company? Do I ask for more? And is it possible to ask for less?
>
> Diese Sonne lacht uns Allen, die Vöglein singen, Blumen und Blüten duften für Alle. Laß uns die schöne Frühlingszeit harmlos genießen. Ist es ein so großes Verbrechen, ohne männliche Begleitung spazieren zu gehen? Verlang' ich denn mehr? Und kann man weniger verlangen? (Bauernfeld, *Gesammelte Schriften* 3: 153)

Despite Katharine's assurances, however, it is a walk on the promenade that precipitates Katharine's failure in her striving for independence – or at least this is how Katherine's walk is later interpreted by Katharine's suitor, Baron Ringelstern: "You see, Miss, from what has happened, how difficult it is for a woman, despite all her wit and thoughtfulness, to get through the world *alone*" ("Sie sehen, mein Fräulein, aus dem, was vorfiel, wie schwer sich eine Dame, bei allem Geist und Witz, in der Welt *allein* behaupten kann"; Bauernfeld, *Gesammelte Schriften* 3: 211–12).

On some level, the logic of Bauernfeld's comedy appears to work in a similar manner to the sword fight in Benedix's play. Again, the heroine is confronted with her shortcomings, which force her to admit that her dreams of freedom and independence were illusory, born out of an incomplete understanding of herself and the world around her. However, a closer look at *Bürgerlich* makes clear that the situation here is more complex and that the fault sits much less clearly with the heroine. The problem with Katharine's walk is not her direct physical ability to venture on her outing but the gossiping response from the other spa members, which she underestimated. In other words, if a woman cannot take a walk by herself, this is the fault of the society that sits in judgment over so trivial a matter. More precisely still, what eventually turns Katharine's walk into a catastrophic event is not that she takes this walk alone, but that she takes it in the company of the *wrong* man – namely, the local spa officer Sittig, who is engaged to be married with another woman. To make matters even more confounding, the only reason why Katharine asks Sittig to accompany her on a walk that she originally intended to take alone, is that she is being harassed by her sudden new suitor, Baron Ringelstern. There is thus something ironic (or even cynical) about the fact that it is Baron Ringelstern who reveals to Katharine women's inability to live alone in the world. According to the logic of the events in the play, the only reason why Katharine cannot live alone in the world is Baron Ringelstern himself. If Ringelstern had not harassed Katharine, she would not have had to ask Sittig to accompany her, and, in turn, the spa community would have had no (or less) reason to gossip.

Even if this logic escaped the average spectator in the mid-nineteenth-century Burgtheater, it is evident in the play that women's reliance on men has less to do with any intrinsic shortcoming in women (as is suggested in the sword fight in Benedix's play), and more with the moral fabric of social reality. While the force of this moral fabric may be no less real than the alleged physical weakness of women on which Benedix focuses, it is nonetheless clear that the fault lies with society – and that in an ideal society, women could enjoy equal liberties to men.

All these important distinctions aside, it remains true for Bauernfeld's play as well that the young woman's struggle for independence ends when she realizes the necessity of male protection. Importantly, however, instead of "curing" women from their striving for independence by reinstating a traditional and strict gender divide of strong men and weak women, Bauernfeld matches the "taming" of the young rebellious woman (to cite again Shakespeare's popular paradigm) with the taming of her male counterpart. Baron Ringelstern, who speaks disdainfully of marriage at the outset of the play and who insists on the necessity for men to rule over women, is seen, at the end of the play, holding silk for his bride's needlework. What Bauernfeld envisions is a *moderation* (and levelling) of the genders. Indeed, the play opens with a political discussion about the disappearance of a *juste milieu*, and the plot of the play shows us, in ways that may be considered typically Bauernfeldian, the possible re-establishment of such moderation in all areas of life, including gender relations.[52]

Both because of this more conciliatory ending and because of the initially more sympathetic depiction of the rebellious young woman, Bauernfeld's play is much more akin to Johanna Franul von Weißenthurn's *Das letzte Mittel* than to Benedix's *Wespe*. That means that the positions on gender norms in the repertoire of the mid-nineteenth-century Burgtheater does not align neatly with the gender of the playwrights. To put it more carefully, Bauernfeld's play shows that it was possible for male playwrights of the period to side with the more progressive visions typically found in the works of female authors.

6 The Drama of National and Regional Belonging

Liberalism in the mid–nineteenth century was in large part a national liberalism (*Nationalliberalismus*), and in the Austrian context, such national liberalism could mean a double threat to the decidedly multinational Habsburg monarchy, both as liberalism and as nationalism.[1] When Austrian liberals emphasized a cultural and political belonging to a German nation, this potentially undermined the authority of the House of Habsburg, which, as became increasingly clear with Prussia's rise to power, would likely not play the central role in that nation. Open and direct political commitments to the German nation thus faced significant obstacles in the nineteenth-century Austrian political discourse. In this situation, the Burgtheater, originally founded as a *Nationaltheater*, played a crucial role for the discussion – and celebration – of a sense of belonging to the German *Kulturnation* in Vienna.

We possess a striking testimony of the Burgtheater's role as a place for the performance of a German national identity in an obituary that Betty Paoli wrote in 1866, on the occasion of the recent death of the most celebrated Burgtheater actress of the time, the German-born Julie Rettich.[2] How concretely Paoli thinks of this belonging to the German nation in the Austrian context – and of the Burgtheater's role in discussing this belonging – becomes clear when Paoli talks about Julie Rettich's enthusiastic reception in the Burgtheater in 1835, the year in which she was hired as a permanent member of the ensemble. Rettich came to Vienna with a proven track record of success: at the time, Rettich was employed at the court theatre in Dresden, under the important Romantic playwright Ludwig Tieck, and she had an alternative job offer from the court theatre in Berlin, the Burgtheater's main competitor as the leading German-language stage.

Yet, according to Paoli, Rettich's skill and renown alone do not quite explain the eagerness with which she was received in Vienna.

The excitement around her arrival should rather be understood in the context of the wider enthusiasm in and around the Burgtheater for all things German. The decisive passage from Paoli's biography is worth quoting in full:

> To get a clear sense of the enthusiasm that Julie's debut stirred, one must consider the importance that the Burgtheater had for Vienna during that period. This importance consisted not only in the exceptional talents that were at work here at the time, but also in the political conditions, which limited the public interest on this one point. Austria was separated from Germany as if there had been a Chinese Wall. This stage was the last, the only place of refuge for a German consciousness. For an overwhelming majority, the Burgtheater was the sole connection to the intellectual life of the German people. The supreme need [of the Austrians for a connection to the intellectual life of the German people], which cannot be extinguished by any pressure, was dependent on this stage alone, and, with glowing desire, it there sought its satisfaction.
>
> Um sich den Enthusiasmus, den Juliens Debüts hervorriefen, ganz zu vergegenwärtigen, muß man die Bedeutung erwägen, die das Burgtheater damals für Wien hatte. Sie lag nicht nur in den außerordentlichen Talenten, welche zu jener Zeit hier thätig waren, sondern auch in den politischen Verhältnissen, die das öffentliche Interesse auf diesen einen Punkt beschränkten. Wie durch eine chinesische Mauer war Österreich von Deutschland getrennt; die Bühne war die letzte, einzige Zufluchtsstätte deutschen Bewußtseins, für eine überwiegend große Mehrzahl der einzige Verband, in dem sie mit dem geistigen Leben des deutschen Volkes stand. Auf sie allein war das ideale Bedürfnis, das kein Druck ganz zu ertödten vermag, angewiesen, und mit glühendem Verlangen suchte es dort seine Befriedigung. (Paoli, *Julie Rettich* 18)

In the Austrian context, the Burgtheater was, or so Paoli claims, a sacred island: the only point of access to the intellectual life of the German people, which is imagined to be pulsating far away, beyond the wall of Austrian censorship.[3] The young actress Julie Rettich, newly arrived from the Protestant north, was – in Paoli's mind – an embodiment of that German spirit (or German mind).[4] Of course, Paoli's remarks refer most directly to the Burgtheater "back then" ("damals"), that is, prior to relative relaxation of censorship laws in 1848. After 1848, the Burgtheater was perhaps not quite as unique anymore as a venue for the performance of a German national identity. At the same time, and as we will see in more detail later on in this chapter, the Burgtheater also used 1848 as an opportunity to foreground its identity as an institution committed to a national project, and there was a patriotic wave in the repertoire in the aftermath of the March Revolution.

If Paoli speaks of the Burgtheater as the sole refuge of German consciousness and as the only connection to the intellectual life of the German people in the Austrian context, this is certainly not only because the Burgtheater housed a number of prominent actors and actresses from the north. But what precisely Paoli *does* have in mind is not all that clear. Paoli may refer to the Burgtheater as Vienna's main stage for the newly canonized national literature by Goethe, Schiller, Lessing, and Kleist. Less likely, Paoli's remarks might refer to the Burgtheater as an institution in which contemporary German playwrights were performed. In that respect, the Burgtheater was in very concrete ways a connection to the intellectual life of the German people. Watching popular comedies by August von Kotzebue, Roderich Benedix, Carl Töpfer, or Amalie von Sachsen, the audience of the Burgtheater could laugh and talk about the same things as their neighbours in the north. But all this still gives us an incomplete picture of the Burgtheater as an outpost of the German nation. For there was also a distinct tradition of very successful plays in which Austrian playwrights – Burgtheater playwrights, for all intents and purposes – contributed to the construction of a pan-German identity (with no specific reference to Austria). These playwrights wrote nostalgic pieces about key events in Germany's idealized past: from a battle against the Romans in antiquity, through the struggles of the Reformation and the peasant wars in the sixteenth century, to the Thirty Years' War of the seventeenth century. Through these plays, the Burgtheater served as the stage for a home-grown German nationalist discourse.

Friedrich Halm's tragedy *Der Fechter von Ravenna* (*The Swordsman of Ravenna*), is one of the best-known examples of this type of dramatic literature. Halm's play, which saw fifty-one performances in the Burgtheater between 1854 and 1889 (Rub 83), focuses on an episode in the orbit of the Germanic hero Arminius (or Hermann, in later German renderings). Famously, Arminius led Germanic tribes to a victory over the Romans in the Battle of the Teutoburg Forest widely in today's northern Germany during the reign of Emperor Augustus. The story of Arminius's fight against the Romans was a major inspiration for the German nationalist awakening in the nineteenth century and inspired a significant literary tradition. Heinrich von Kleist's 1808 drama *Die Hermannsschlacht* (*Hermann's Battle*) is today the most widely remembered example of this tradition (though in the nineteenth century, Kleist's play was not performed in the Burgtheater).

Halm's *Fechter* is set several years after the Battle of the Teutoburg Forest, after Arminius's assassination by fellow Germanic tribesmen. His wife, Thusnelda (played in the Burgtheater by Julie Rettich), is a Roman prisoner and their son, Thumelicus, is being trained in the city of Ravenna to become a Roman gladiator – he is the titular "Fechter von Ravenna." Thusnelda, who had been separated from her son, learns of Thumelicus's destiny shortly before his first fight in Rome. Committed to not let Arminius's memory and the pride of the German nation be debased by putting his son on display in the circus, Thusnelda kills Thumelicus before committing suicide herself. Thusnelda declares categorically, "my son shall not become Germany's disgrace" ("Die Schande Deutschlands wird mein Sohn nicht sein"; Halm, *Fechter* 104).[5] As the patriot and mother Thusnelda despairs to be forced to kill her son to preserve the dignity of the German nation, she calls for revenge against Roman tyranny that shall last "for centuries, millennia" ("Jahrhunderte, Jahrtausende hinaus"; 150). What is more, she envisions the ultimate victory of Germany not just over the Romans, but over the entire planet:

Victory, they rejoice, victory in Germanic tongues
And defeated by a Germanic sword,
And subject to the Germanic spirit,
I see the land, the ocean!
Yes, gods of the homeland, we are victorious, we are victorious,
And I see our oppressors in the dust,
I see them captured for a thousand years of servitude,
Grinding their teeth and creeping to our feet,
In vain they scream to seek your favour,
In vain they arm themselves –

Sieg, jubelt es, Sieg in germanischen Zungen
Und von germanischem Schwerte bezwungen,
Germanischem Geiste unterthan
Seh' ich die Erde, den Ocean!
Ja, Götter der Heimath, wir siegen, wir siegen,
Und unsere Bedränger seh' ich im Staub,
Seh' tausendjähriger Knechtschaft zum Raub
Sich knirschend zu unsern Füßen schmiegen,
Vergebens aufschreien zu eurer Huld,
Vergebens sich waffnend –

(Halm, *Fechter* 150–1)

Halm's image of a world lying defeated in dust during the one thousand-year rule of the Germanic gods is a striking example of the rabid nationalism to which the Burgtheater gave voice in the middle decades of the nineteenth century. However, his play is not directly representative of the discourse on German nationalism on that stage. It presents but one extreme voice in a variety of voices struggling to define a German national identity.

In the first part of this chapter, I take a closer look at two subtler cases of nationalist discourse, both introduced prior to the revolution of 1848: Johann Ludwig Deinhardstein's drama *Hans Sachs* (first performed in 1827) and Eduard von Bauernfeld's drama *Ein deutscher Krieger* (*A German Warrior*, first performed 1844). Both plays were just as successful as Halm's, while being much more conciliatory in tone.

One thing that the plays by Halm, Deinhardstein, and Bauernfeld have in common, however, is that they construct a German nation that is "extraterritorial": Halm's *Fechter*, Deinhardstein's *Hans Sachs*, and Bauernfeld's *Krieger* are all set outside the Austrian homelands. This significant pattern points to a distinctive feature of the German nationalist discourse as it emerged on the stage of the Burgtheater. In contrast to many other forms of nationalism, which are importantly tied the present land, the Austrian variety – or, more precisely, the Burgtheater variety – of German nationalism situated the German nation elsewhere.

Only relatively late and rather reluctantly did the Burgtheater also accommodate a discourse of nationalism that mobilized a sense of regional belonging, showcasing Austrian dialect and folklore. The Burgtheater's otherwise high-minded artistic and educational aspirations as well as its programmatic distinction from the suburban theatres, in which dialect and a manifestly Austrian tradition of comedy featured prominently, stood, for the most part, in the way of a clearer embrace of local custom and the regionalized discourse of *Heimat*, a term that will be discussed in more detail later on. The only broadly successful attempt to include a sense of regional pride in the celebration of nationhood occurred in 1848 with the staging of Alexander Baumann's comedy *Das Versprechen hinterm Herd* (*The Promise Behind the Hearth*).

In the second section of this chapter, I turn to Baumann's comedy to analyse how this dialect play could become a major success on that stage. One of the trends that was driving the success of Baumann's comedy was the contemporary interest in the new genre of the village story (*Dorfgeschichte*), a distinctly German phenomenon in the history of European realism. While literary realism in France and England focused largely on the growing urban centres (notably, London and Paris), German realists paid special attention to life in the countryside. The main

German writer of the realist village story was Berthold Auerbach, whose *Schwarzwälder Dorfgeschichten* (*Black Forest Village Stories*) were a great success since their first appearance in 1843. One of Auerbach's stories, "Die Frau Professorin" ("The Professor's Wife"), was turned into a drama by Charlotte Birch-Pfeiffer (*Dorf und Stadt* [*Village and Town*]), and when Birch-Pfeiffer's play premiered in the Burgtheater in 1847, it too became very popular. A brief survey of the period's (rural-themed) *Volksdrama* at the end of this chapter will demonstrate that the success of Birch-Pfeiffer's *Dorf und Stadt* was perhaps what most directly paved the way for the introduction of Baumann's play in the following year.

In sum, we see the Burgtheater in this chapter emerge as an institution in which one of the defining themes of nineteenth-century Austrian liberalism – namely, its embrace of German nationalism – was given significant room. This theme was debated with considerable variations, ranging from Halm's violent rhetoric of German world domination to the more moderate voices of Deinhardstein and Bauernfeld. Additionally, the largely extraterritorial construction of the German nation was at least occasionally joined by an attempt to include elements of an Austrian regional belonging into the broader notion of German nationalism.

While the Burgtheater was thus lending its stage to an extensive debate over competing versions of German nationalism, it also performed plays that appear to be at cross purposes with the celebration of German nationalism, be it extraterritorial or focused on a regional belonging to the Austrian homeland. For the image of the Burgtheater as an island of the German spirit and as an institution for pan-German solidarity glosses over the fact that the Burgtheater of the mid-nineteenth century simultaneously served, to some small degree, a very different end, namely the celebration of the Imperial House of Habsburg.

The commemoration of the Habsburg dynasty in Austrian theatre is today most commonly associated with Franz Grillparzer's historical plays, notably the tragedies *König Ottokars Glück und Ende* (*King Ottokar's Rise and Fall*; first performed 1825) and *Ein Bruderzwist in Habsburg* (*Fraternal Strife in Habsburg*).[6] However, as much as Grillparzer is remembered for these plays today, in the mid-nineteenth century they enjoyed limited popularity.[7] Of these two plays, only *Ottokar* was a major success on stage, with ninety-three performances between 1825 and 1912. Even in this case, the play's success can largely be attributed to the decades around 1900 – in the nearly fifty years between the premiere of *Ottokar* and Grillparzer's death in 1872, the tragedy saw only thirty-seven performances (Grillparzer, *Dramen* 859). *Bruderzwist* was even less successful, at only a modest sixteen performances. In the mid-nineteenth century, Grillparzer was much better known for his mythological or literarily-inspired Romantic plays. *Die Ahnfrau* (*The Ancestress*) reached 128 performances; *Sappho*, 135 performances; and *Der Traum ein Leben* (*Life is a Dream*), 139 performances (Rub 270). In other words, even Grillparzer was not primarily perceived as a Habsburg playwright on the Burgtheater stage. And there is no second writer of the period who produced truly successful plays on the subject of the Habsburgs for the Burgtheater.

The relative absence of Habsburg plays should not be misunderstood as necessarily and merely reflective of a lack of interest in – or enthusiasm for – the House of Habsburg. The Habsburg monarchy did enjoy considerable popularity among Austrian liberals in the mid–nineteenth century. But given the very close scrutiny by court and censors, staging even a celebratory play on Habsburg history bore more risk than rewards for the playwright. Grillparzer himself had to endure pushback from the censors for his Habsburg plays. The censors initially banned *Ottokar* in 1824, before authorizing its performance in the following year (Grillparzer, *Dramen* 859; see also ch. 2). In the end, it was safest to leave the subject of Habsburg history aside entirely. In whichever way one explains the relative lack of pronounced celebration of the Habsburgs and of a distinctly Austrian identity, this absence is a defining feature of the Burgtheater in the mid–nineteenth century.

If the few plays showcasing a distinct Habsburg identity did overall relatively little to counteract the image of the Burgtheater as an island for the "German national spirit" (as Betty Paoli wants us to see it), what does temper this image more significantly is that, throughout its entire history, the Burgtheater remained a decidedly international stage. As I discussed at greater length in chapter 3, in the European context, the Burgtheater's international repertoire is one of the crucial aspects that sets it apart from its European competitors, notably the Théâtre-Français in Paris. The Burgtheater was a place in which a distinctly German dramatic tradition thrived alongside the English, French, and Spanish classics. Moreover, despite all the critique of a French cultural hegemony, frequently voiced in German literature since at least the *Sturm und Drang* of the 1770s, the Burgtheater also continued to perform contemporary French conversation drama with great success.

Yet a closer look at the Burgtheater's international repertoire reveals an interesting nuance: at least on one occasion, a German adaptation of a foreign play served to advance the German nationalist discourse. When in 1826, the Burgtheater actor J.W. Lembert prepared a very successful German adaptation of the comédie-vaudeville *Vatel, Le petit fils d'un grand homme* (roughly, *Vatel, or The Little Grandson of a Grand Man*) by Scribe and Mazères for performance in the Burgtheater, the

German version quietly turned the French play into a typically anti-French comedy. In the French original, we see a vain male Parisian chef compete with an illiterate female cook of a less prestigious household. In the German version, Lembert's *Der Ehrgeiz in der Küche* (*Ambition in the Kitchen*), by contrast, the Parisian chef is transformed into a French emigrant whose excessive pride in French sophistication is exposed by his inferiority to the practical skills of a young female German cook of a middle-class household ("eine deutsch[e] Bürgersköchin"; Lembert 20), who reads German, but not French. In other words, what is in the French original primarily a comedy of class differences becomes in the German version a comedy of national differences, with clear sympathies for the simplicity of German manners and much derision for the pretentious sophistication of French manners.

The performative contradiction that is at play here, in which the satire of French influence came in the form of a popular play that was advertised as an adaptation from a leading French playwright, apparently went unnoticed – or at least this contradiction did not seem to create any significant tensions. Copying French drama and priding oneself in the superiority of German simplicity appears to have gone together rather unproblematically, at least in this case. And while this comedy may be an extreme case, it is symptomatic of a broader tendency in the mid-nineteenth-century Burgtheater to continue with an international repertoire while at the same time priding oneself as the stage for the celebration of a distinctly German identity.

The Drama of National Belonging

Johann Ludwig Deinhardstein's "dramatic poem" ("dramatisches Gedicht") *Hans Sachs* is in many ways the perfect embodiment of Betty Paoli's notion of the Burgtheater as the space for the performance of a German national identity that is located outside of Viennese and Austrian territory. The play focuses on one of the quintessential periods and places for the making of the German nation. It is set in Nuremberg in the early sixteenth century, a time when the prosperous city quickly adopted Martin Luther's Protestant Reformation, was home to the *Meistersinger* tradition, and housed some of Germany's most famous artists, including the painter Albrecht Dürer and the prolific writer (and cobbler) Hans Sachs.[8] At the centre of Deinhardstein's play is the young Hans Sachs himself. In the play, Sachs struggles to assert the value of his poetry, which breaks with the rules established by the *Meistersinger*, and he wishes to marry, despite his low social standing as a cobbler, the daughter of a prestigious and wealthy local goldsmith.

The nineteenth century discovered in the city of Nuremberg and in the period of the Reformation an important source of a German national heritage. The sixteenth century was imagined as a period in which a more distinct and distinguished German artistic and intellectual tradition emerged. This myth of a national awakening in the sixteenth century is prominently captured in the popular historiography of Gustav Freytag. In his biography of Martin Luther, first published in 1859 as part of his larger work *Bilder aus der deutschen Vergangenheit* (*Images from the German Past*), Freytag writes emphatically of this period:

> The period between 1500 and 1600 encompasses the greatest spiritual movement that has ever moved the innermost depths of a nation. This century has, as far human understanding can say, impressed its character on the German soul and character for all eternity.
>
> Der Zeitraum von 1500 bis 1600 umfaßt die größte geistige Bewegung, welche je eine Nation in den innersten Tiefen aufgewühlt hat. Für immer hat nach menschlichem Ermessen dies Jahrhundert dem Geist und Gemüth der Deutschen sein Gepräge aufgedrückt. (Freytag, *Doktor Luther* 1)

It was this fascination with Early Modernity as well as with the city of Nuremberg as one of the quintessential sites of Early Modern Germany that the Nazis tried to invoke in their Nuremberg rallies in the 1930s, famously captured in Leni Riefenstahl's 1935 propaganda film *Triumph des Willens* (*Triumph of the Will*). From Deinhardstein to Riefenstahl, Early Modern Nuremberg was a central element in Germany's imagination of a glorious national past. The historian Stephen Brockmann went so far as to dub Nuremberg Germany's "imaginary capital." By situating his play in Nuremberg, Deinhardstein activated a German nationalist discourse without directly discussing the politically contentious question of the formation of a German nation state. Indeed, the idea of "Germanness" is at no point explicitly mentioned in the play. Nuremberg remains the crucial synecdoche for an unspoken but nevertheless clear commitment to German greatness.

Deinhardstein's drama was *Nationaltheater*, and thus it was understood not only in the Burgtheater, where it was first performed and where it remained in the repertoire for forty-one years (until 1868; reaching a total of sixty-one performances), but also elsewhere (Rub 57). A year after its premiere in the Burgtheater, it had been introduced in twenty-eight additional theatres, as Deinhardstein boasts in the preface to the printed version of the play, which appeared in 1829 (ix). Today,

Deinhardstein's play is mostly forgotten. If it is cited at all, it is viewed largely as a precursor to Richard Wagner's opera *Die Meistersinger von Nürnberg* (1868). In its own time, however, Deinhardstein's play was widely known and almost universally celebrated. Upon its performance in Hamburg, a reviewer praised the play as a "true national poem" ("ächtes National-Gedicht"; D.V. 127), suited to found a "genuine national theatre" ("wahrhaft nationales Schauspiel"; 127) – a project that had first been attempted in the very city of Hamburg some sixty years earlier. For the production in Berlin's court theatre, the performance was accompanied by a reading of Goethe's poem "Hans Sachs." To mark the occasion, the almost eighty-year-old Goethe himself also wrote a new prologue for his poem.

The contemporary audience admired Deinhardstein's play, and it did so for the place and period that the play brought to life. In the play, Nuremberg is repeatedly praised as a space both of middle class success and of artistic greatness.[9] Indeed, the only regret that contemporary audiences apparently had was that the setting had not been introduced even more fully – a criticism against which Deinhardstein defended himself by reminding his audience that his play was meant for performance and that any additional attention paid to the scenic backdrop would have taken away from the development of the action and would thus have counteracted the play's goal to entertain (Deinhardstein x–xii).

The success of Deinhardstein's *Hans Sachs* was a product of the period's understanding of Early Modern Nuremberg as an epicentre of German greatness. Yet Deinhardstein's play is not without nuance, and there are a number of factors that attenuate the celebration of the German national past. Strikingly, the play includes no mention of Hans Sachs's most prominent German contemporary, Martin Luther. Luther, we should recall, was in the nineteenth century not only – and perhaps not even primarily – a religious figure, but also a figure associated with the beginning of German strength and independence. In this period, Luther's struggle with papal Rome was viewed as a fight against foreign influence more broadly. If the point of Deinhardstein's play was to invoke a glorious German past – and this was what contributed to its popularity with the audience – Luther would have been a logical figure to include. Since the historical Hans Sachs was an outspoken early follower of Luther, a reference to Luther would also have been easy to come by. But Deinhardstein abstained. The only hint in the direction of the famous reformer consists in the timing of the play, "around the year 1517" ("um das Jahr 1517"; Deinhardstein 2), which coincides with what is commonly regarded as the beginning of the Protestant Reformation (i.e., Martin Luther's posting of the Ninety-Five Theses against the sale of indulgences on the door of All Saints' Church of Wittenberg on 31 October 1517). The premiere of Deinhardstein's play in the Burgtheater on 4 October 1827 was close to the three hundred tenth anniversary of that event, and this was perhaps done intentionally. Thus far – and no further – Deinhardstein went. Deinhardstein, who would become director of the Burgtheater a few years later, in 1832, likely knew that any more explicit mention of Luther would have been difficult in Catholic Vienna.[10] The first appearance of Martin Luther in a play by one of the Burgtheater playwrights occurred only in 1850, during the brief relaxation of censorship rules, in Eduard von Bauernfeld's peasant war drama *Franz von Sickingen*.[11]

Deinhardstein not only cut references to Martin Luther and the Protestant Reformation, but he also combined the celebration of an extraterritorial German national identity in Nuremberg with a decidedly Austrian praise of the House of Habsburg. The second Habsburg emperor, Maximilian I, makes a somewhat surprising appearance as *deux ex machina* in the play's final two acts. Maximilian's wisdom and authority help settle the tensions disturbing the city and guarantee the play's good ending. Recognizing this blissful intervention, the play's final lines swear never-ending allegiance to the House of Habsburg, where all exclaim, "Hail Emperor Max!/Hail Habsburg! Hail forever!" ("Heil Kaiser Max!/Heil Habsburg! Heil für immer!"; Deinhardstein 123). Deinhardstein's *Hans Sachs*, one of the quintessential plays of the Burgtheater's characteristic extraterritorial nationalism, thus culminates in the celebration of the Austrian reigning family!

Despite this prominently placed reference to Maximilian I, the Habsburg family would have done well not to take the praise of their name too literally. There are good reasons to see it largely as a nod to the German literary canon and to a canonized ideal of individual agency, rather than to the Habsburgs as such. After all, Goethe's successful *Sturm und Drang* drama *Götz von Berlichingen* (1773) also includes positive references to Emperor Maximilian. And while the homage to Maximilian alone does not make the nod to Goethe's drama evident, the entire structure of this homage is similar. While Goethe's Götz fights fervently against the corrupt courts of the local princes, he remains committed to his loyalty to the emperor: Götz's rebellious freedom is presented as consistent with his simultaneous obedience to Maximilian. Deinhardstein's *Hans Sachs* follows the same logic. While Hans Sachs struggles with the narrow-minded and unfair citizens in Nuremberg, he never questions the goodness and authority of his *Kaiser*. Additionally, as in Goethe's play, the intermediate levels of authority are associated with the modern legal system. In Goethe's play, this system is embodied in the legal machinations at the princely court; in Deinhardstein's play, the legal system is embodied in Hans Sachs's fellow citizens, who invoke aesthetic laws to denigrate Sachs's superior poetry as well as secular laws (that is, Nuremberg city laws) to cast out Sachs as the undesired suitor of a rich goldsmith's daughter.

Because of these structural parallels, the praise of Maximilian in Deinhardstein's play points the audience to Goethe and to a canonized German construction of agency, consisting of a rejection of the modern legal bureaucracy and an emphatic celebration of individual freedom through the commitment to the supreme (but also mostly distant) emperor. There can be little doubt that the mid-nineteenth-century Burgtheater audience was nearly universally familiar with *Götz*. Goethe, together with Schiller (or at least closely after Schiller), was the most-recognized German writer of the period and thus required reading for anyone with an aspiration to literary and national education. In 1830, three years after the premiere of *Hans Sachs*, the Burgtheater also introduced Goethe's play to its own repertoire, in which it became, with 128 performances, a major success.

If the structural position of the Habsburg emperor evokes Goethe's *Götz*, the actual words spoken by Maximilian in Deinhardstein's play conjure another canonized German drama, namely Gotthold Ephraim Lessing's *Nathan der Weise* (*Nathan the Wise*), which was introduced in the Burgtheater in 1819 and saw an exceptional 165 performances between its debut and 1910. In solving the conflict between Hans Sachs and the burghers of Nuremberg, Emperor Maximilian seeks recourse to a parable of inheritance – the very ruse that Lessing's Nathan employs in the famous *Ringparabel* at the heart of *Nathan*.[12]

These allusions to the classics are a core feature of plays like Deinhardstein's *Hans Sachs*. They give substance to the later view of this dramatic literature as epigonic – and there is, in a sense, little one can say against such a charge when we look at Deinhardstein's play. And yet it is important to recognize that, in the Burgtheater as elsewhere, such borrowings were an important means for mid-nineteenth-century playwrights to construct a German cultural canon. It is, as we saw, likely that the contemporary audience would have recognized the spectre of *Götz* in *Hans Sachs*, and there can be virtually no doubt that it would have recalled the *Ringparabel* in Maximilian's words. Through these references, the audience was invited to experience its own national tradition as something to be imitated. The dismissal of authors like Deinhardstein, Bauernfeld, or Halm as epigonic overlooks the fact that their open borrowing from Lessing, Goethe, Schiller, and Kleist was crucial in *inventing* these earlier authors as exemplary artists and roots of any future literature.

To return to an earlier point, there is more than a tinge of irony in the fact that the Habsburg emperor Maximilian, seemingly introduced in the play as an antidote to any too-emphatic celebration of German nationalism, becomes, through the implicit references to Goethe and Lessing, part of a vehicle for the celebration of the German tradition. This is not to say that Deinhardstein's play carries some covert subversive message. There is no basis for believing that the loyal Deinhardstein – professor at the University of Vienna and on track to become head of the Burgtheater and, subsequently, the censorship office – sought to undermine Habsburg rule. For all intents and purposes, the Habsburg emperor is being praised in the play, and this praise carries over to Maximilian's reigning heirs in nineteenth-century Austria. At the same time, the praise of the Habsburgs clearly feeds into the celebration of German cultural heritage because, through the references to Goethe and Lessing, the Habsburg emperor himself reinforces the idea of German cultural greatness.[13]

Neither the omission of direct references to Luther nor the attention paid to the Habsburg emperor are able to take away from the play's celebration of the German *Kulturnation*. And yet something else did weaken the nationalist element of the drama. For in the context of Deinhardstein's larger dramatic oeuvre – and this was a context that would have been familiar to the Burgtheater audience, which had the opportunity to see no fewer than twenty-one of his plays between 1814 and 1888 (Rub 268) – *Hans Sachs* is recognizable as a typical Deinhardsteinian artist drama, in which questions of nationhood are secondary, at best.

In 1832, just a few years after the introduction of *Hans Sachs*, Deinhardstein's most successful play, the comedy *Garrick in Bristol*, premiered, and it is structurally similar to the earlier play about the Nuremberg poet. Again, a well-known artist is at the centre of the play, and again this artist struggles for recognition by his philistine contemporaries. Much earlier, in 1816, the Burgtheater had already performed another of Deinhardstein's artist dramas, the play *Boccaccio*, which remained, however, at only three performances, a disappointment. It is unlikely to have left much of an impression on the audience. Still, we have the succession of artist dramas: *Boccaccio* (1817), *Hans Sachs* (1827), and *Garrick* (1832). As this brief glance at Deinhardstein's dramatic work shows, Deinhardstein was clearly interested in the position of the artist, and this broader interest had relatively little to do with the specific concern with German heritage in *Hans Sachs*. Deinhardstein chose freely from among the canon of European art – and Hans Sachs's Early Modern Nuremberg is just one among many European locales in which Deinhardstein's drama of the artist could be played out. An audience familiar with Deinhardstein's oeuvre (such as the Burgtheater audience) would have had good reason to perceive the drama *Hans Sachs* not exclusively as *Nationaltheater*, but also as drama about the conflicts of the artist in modern society.

In the context of Deinhardstein's larger dramatic work, the celebration of the national past in *Hans Sachs* is shown to be perfectly compatible with the celebration of cultural achievements elsewhere. Deinhardstein's drama was thus far removed from the bloodthirsty nationalist fantasies of German world domination in Friedrich Halm's *Fechter*.

In Deinhardstein's case, the conciliatory or cosmopolitan aspects of his national pride become evident mainly for those who are familiar with his larger oeuvre. By contrast, in the work of another playwright of the period, Eduard von Bauernfeld's successful drama *Ein deutscher Krieger*, the attempt to reconcile the celebration of German culture with a recognition of other European cultures is an explicit topic. Paradoxically, however, not only are the conciliatory, cosmopolitan elements more explicit in Bauernfeld's play, but so is the patriotic language that they serve to counteract as well – and it is not entirely easy to determine whether the patriotic and nationalistic elements or the cosmopolitan elements prevail in the play as a whole.

Bauernfeld's *Krieger* focuses on a fictional episode at the end of the Thirty Years' War (1618–48). While much more gruesome – and potentially also much more divisive – than the topic of Early Modern Nuremberg in Deinhardstein's *Hans Sachs*, the Thirty Years' War was equally firmly established as a site for the construction of a German national identity. Most famously, this war provided the backdrop for Schiller's *Wallenstein* trilogy, but it was also the subject of popular novels of the period.[14] And while the *Wallenstein* trilogy could not be fully performed in the Burgtheater until 1848 – at which point it became a major success – the audience of Bauernfeld's *Krieger* would still have been at least rudimentarily familiar with Schiller's trilogy through reading.

It is not surprising that Bauernfeld's *Krieger* omits any allusion to the religious tensions between Catholics and Protestants, which were important to the Thirty Years' War. Like Deinhardstein almost twenty years before him, Bauernfeld knew that any comments that even remotely questioned the authority of the Catholic Church or religion would have caused problems with the censors.

Instead of speaking about religious frictions, Bauernfeld focuses his drama on the cultural and political tensions between Germany and France. In doing so, the plot borrows structural elements from classics of the previous generation, notably Heinrich von Kleist's 1810 drama *Prinz Friedrich von Homburg* as well as, once more, Goethe's *Götz* (both plays being very popular in the Burgtheater).[15] In Bauernfeld's drama, the colonel Götze (a namesake of Goethe's hero) successfully fights for the Saxon prince against the French. At the outset of the play, Götze has just conquered another village in the Alsace, and he is about to storm a French bastion. Importantly, Götze is in a militarily advantageous position and sure to win the bastion for his country and prince. But as he prepares for the attack, he receives an order to withdraw because a truce has been negotiated to end the war. He is thus faced with a conflict because the mandated obedience to the direct orders from his superiors is in tension with the duties that he perceives to have as a German patriot. The structure of this conflict clearly alludes to Kleist's *Prinz Friedrich*, in which the titular hero chooses to disobey his sovereign's commands in order to win him a battle.

In an important departure from Kleist, however, Bauernfeld's Götze is largely shown to disobey not so much the sovereign himself, who is in far-away Saxony, but his diplomatic middlemen. As a result, the Kleistian drama is supplemented with the theme of the fight against modern bureaucratic power below the level of the sovereign, with which the Burgtheater audience was familiar from Goethe's *Götz*.[16]

Bauernfeld's Götze, the titular "German warrior," who obeys his duty to the fatherland while disobeying the diplomatic middlemen confronting him with an unpatriotic command, becomes in the play the embodiment of German virtue. Throughout the play, Götze repeatedly voices his intense German patriotism. When his (generally benevolent) prince reproaches him of stubbornness towards the end of the play, Götze insists that he is not stubborn but only single-mindedly devoted to Germany: "I have but one thought in my head, and that is Germany, and for this one and only thought, I would have willingly sacrificed my head ten thousand times" ("Ich habe nur Einen Gedanken in dem meinigen [Kopf], der heißt Deutschland – und für den einzigen Gedanken hätt' ich gern meinen Kopf zehn tausend Mal her gegeben"; Bauernfeld, *Krieger* 144).

Moreover, in the central scene of the play, Götze gives an impassioned (and rather lengthy) speech on the essence of Germany, and the play switches for this speech from prose to verse. In Götze's oration, German greatness emerges from a symbiotic relationship between German land, German language, and Germany's "Ur-Volk" ("original people") (Bauernfeld, *Krieger* 82), which are safely united under Germany's great leader. This pure and productive Germany is described as "a bulwark of morality" ("der Sitte Bollwerk"; 83) and guarantor of all remaining European valour. If Germany goes down, all else will down with her:

> If Germany sinks, creative thought sinks as well;
> The creative Spirit will sink, and so will the arts and sciences,
> And the heart of the world – Europe will sink with Germany.

Mit Deutschland sinkt der zeugende Gedanke,
Der Geist, der schaffende, die Kunst, das Wissen,
Das Herz der Welt – Europa sinkt mit Deutschland. (83)

Götze directly contrasts the virile, healthy, and morally intact German force with French corruption and morbid artificiality.

Admittedly, the wording of Götze's speech that Bauernfeld chose for the print publication is more extreme than what he apparently thought possible for the purposes of performance. In the book version, the French language is described as – note the catachresis – a stillborn child borrowed from the Romans, "unfinished, indeterminate, therefore smooth and pliable" ("Unfertig, unbestimmt, d'rum glatt und schmiegsam"; Bauernfeld, *Krieger* 81). For performance, Bauernfeld specified that these lines should be cut (81). Yet even in the text meant for performance, the implicit and explicit contrast to the French is strong – especially when considering that Götze presents his praise of the German language to his main opponent, the powerful female French diplomat, Frau von La Roche, who acts in this encounter as the negotiator of the French bastion that Götze is about to attack. The extreme sentiments lost in the deleted passages are made up for by the fact that Götze addresses his praise of Germany directly to a Frenchwoman. Even when Frau von La Roche makes some conciliatory gesture in offering a handshake upon agreeing on the terms of surrender, Götze rejects the gesture, citing the unbridgeable divide between the Germans and the French: "German and French can never unite" ("Deutsch und französisch kann sich nie verbinden"; 88).

Incidentally, Götze's speech about German greatness evokes another prominent literary precedent. At least the Burgtheater's mid-nineteenth-century audience would likely have been reminded of the famous speech on Austria from the third act of Grillparzer's tragedy *Ottokar*. There are some direct parallels between the two speeches, especially in the allegory of age, in which different nations are associated with different human ages. Both Grillparzer's Austria and Bauernfeld's Germany are associated with a male youth ("Jüngling").[17] Yet Bauernfeld's allusion to the "Austria Speech" from *Ottokar* is ambiguous: it can be read both as reverence for the emerging Austrian dramatic tradition and, at the same time, as a brutal replacement of the Austrian patriotism that is associated with Grillparzer's play with a German patriotism.

The harshness of Götze's nationalist rhetoric, which appears to come rather close to the violent language of Halm's *Fechter*, should surprise us. After all, we have encountered Bauernfeld as politically progressive, and with a penchant for moderation. As noted in the discussion of *Bürgerlich* in the previous chapter, Bauernfeld's politics and poetics are those of the *juste milieu*, the "happy medium," balancing extremism of any kind. And yet, as we see in *Krieger*, when Bauernfeld addresses not abstract notions of liberalism (as in *Großjährig*) or gender roles (as in *Bürgerlich*), but German national identity, a much more radical tone makes itself felt.

It is important to note Bauernfeld's relative extremism in his nationalist language – even if the play eventually moves past it to arrive at a more conciliatory ending (so that the play does, after all, retain its difference to Halm's *Fechter*). Endings, as noted before, are not all that matters in a play. Although much of the narrative may be constructed to lead to a specific ending, the natural decline of an audience's attention span would suggest that the beginning and middle of a play create a more lasting impression. To put it more carefully, endings matter – but plays should not be reduced to them.

In this specific case, the ending of the play – the last of the three acts – is set in Saxony in the postwar era, where Götze, who awaits trial for his insubordination, and his opponent, Frau von La Roche, have found their new home. The old enmity between Götze and La Roche is all but forgotten and has given way to feelings of mutual respect and even love. In the closing scene of the play, La Roche reminds Götze once more of his verdict that "German and French can never unite" – to which Götze, now addressing his old opponent by her first name, responds: "Helen, can you forgive me these words?" ("Helene, könnt Ihr mir dies Wort vergeben?"; Bauernfeld, *Krieger* 150). As the curtain falls, we see Götze and La Roche approach each other, apparently preparing the union that Götze had earlier deemed impossible.

With its conciliatory ending, *Krieger* is structurally similar to *Bürgerlich*. Again, the play is based on a construction of opposites that are shown to be compatible – but compatible not so much as opposites, but compatible by their ability to move closer to each other. While Bauernfeld does not mean to undermine Götze's qualities entirely, he does have his main character give up qualities that characterize him at the beginning, notably his marked disdain for all things French or female. Seen from its appeasing ending, the play could be understood as cosmopolitan: the focus on Götze's hostile nationalist pride is replaced by a vision of love among both people and peoples. This ending in itself is unambiguous and there is no voice left to contest the reconciliation that characterizes the third and final act. Given the clear structural resonance of this ending with those of other plays by Bauernfeld, the audience would likely have been prepared for it and would have understood it as an expression of Bauernfeld's general world view. And yet the question remains whether this typically Bauernfeldian ending can really undo the outburst of nationalist pride that is given such a loud voice and central position in the play. Just as one cannot ever fully take back what one has said (but can only add to it), Bauernfeld's cosmopolitan ending cannot fully undo the chauvinist rhetoric that is, literally, at the centre of the play (even if such undoing was his intention). All cosmopolitanism notwithstanding, at least an echo of the nationalist craze remains lingering.

As we have seen throughout the three plays discussed in this chapter so far, the Burgtheater was an important stage for the debate over a German national identity. People came to the Burgtheater as "the only place of refuge for a German consciousness," as Betty Paoli describes it, and they were greeted with plays that presented a wide variety of suggestions for how this spirit was best to be understood, both within itself and with respect to the other European nations. The plays by Halm, Deinhardstein, and Bauernfeld give us a sense of the extent to which the Burgtheater could present either a conciliatory and cosmopolitan or, instead, a chauvinistic view of German national identity. However, the questions of belonging and of national identity are still incompletely captured in the plays discussed so far. What is missing here is the complex negotiation between regional and national belonging that defined much of the nineteenth century – in Vienna as well as in other parts of German-speaking Europe. Being German was navigated not only in the contrast to being French (or Italian or English), but also in relation to being Viennese, Swabian, Saxon, or Prussian. In the next section of this chapter, I turn to the question of how this navigation of regional belonging played out in the Burgtheater.

The Drama of Regional Belonging

In a German context, questions of regional belonging have long been discussed under the rubric of *Heimat* – a term whose sentimental charge and possible political implications are only insufficiently translated by its closest English equivalent, "homeland." Like the category of nationhood, the term *Heimat* saw a significant rise in interest in the nineteenth century, and the two terms share, to some extent, a common history, even though the precise relationship between these terms is still very much debated (see, for instance, Blickle 25–59).

As suggested at the outset of this chapter, the Burgtheater was in many ways ill-positioned to play a significant role in the discourse on *Heimat* as it was emerging in the nineteenth century. The Burgtheater's foundation as *Nationaltheater*, understood as an institution for transregional and relatively high-minded drama, as well as the Burgtheater's defining distinction from the dialect stages in Vienna, were significant obstacles to the inclusion of plays showcasing rural Austrian life and language. What is more, to the extent that the Burgtheater sought to define itself as a *German* theatre and as the main competitor to the court theatre in Berlin, any closer attention to a specifically Austrian locale might have been conceived as counterproductive.

Given all the obstacles that stood in the way of the performance of regional Austrian plays on Vienna's main stage, the evening of 9 December 1848, on which Alexander Baumann's short dialect play *Das Versprechen hinterm Herd* premiered, deserves to be remembered as one of the most important dates in the history of the Burgtheater. Now for the first time, a play was produced that drew heavily on Austrian dialect – a practice otherwise reserved for Vienna's less prestigious stages in the suburbs. In the Burgtheater itself, plays featuring Austrian dialect had not been performed for almost a century. In the mid–eighteenth century, dialect plays had been successful in the Burgtheater, but under the influence of the Enlightenment reformer Joseph von Sonnenfels, who came to that stage in the late 1760s, they had been banned (Lothar 18).

The exclusion of Viennese dialect plays, central to the establishment of the Burgtheater as *Nationaltheater*, was viewed critically by later generations. Writing in the late nineteenth century, the popular Austrian Burgtheater playwright and critic Rudolph Lothar, for instance, saw in Sonnenfels's act a fateful mistake by which the Burgtheater had cut off its ties to the lively local literary production and the soul of the Viennese *Volk*. Lothar is quick to point out that Sonnenfels, who worked against the local dialect plays, was the son of a Berlin rabbi and thus, he seems to imply, twice removed from the Austrian soul (Lothar 18). There is a great deal of nationalist essentialism and also antisemitism in Lothar's remarks (although the latter charge should be made with some caution because Lothar himself came from a Jewish family and even supported Zola in his intervention in the Dreyfus affair).[18] Lothar does capture a sentiment with which many later chroniclers of this stage in essence agree: namely that Vienna had a robust literary tradition of its own, but that this tradition was problematically pushed aside in favour of the adoration of a few classical German playwrights (Lessing, Goethe, Schiller, Kleist) and a lot of shallow reactionary entertainment.

Given the later scepticism towards the ban of dialect plays, it may not come as a surprise after all that Baumann's *Versprechen* was vastly successful. Between 1848 and 1863, this comedy saw an impressive eighty-five performances in the Burgtheater, and it was also staged in other leading German theatres, including Munich's Hof- und Nationaltheater. Incidentally, Baumann was not generally a writer of Austrian dialect drama. *Versprechen* was already Baumann's second play for the Burgtheater, but his first *Heimat*-play on that stage. In 1840, the Burgtheater had staged Baumann's comedy *Die beiden Ärzte* (*The Two Doctors*), but this play was still written in standard German, and it was set in a spa (*Badeort*), one of the favourite locales of contemporary German comedy.

At a modest nine performances, *Ärzte* was neither a complete failure nor very popular. With *Versprechen*, Baumann was testing new territory, and the impact was significant. *Versprechen* is considered to have done the same for drama that Berthold Auerbach's *Schwarzwälder Dorfgeschichten* did for prose, by establishing the theme of rural – and, particularly, peasant – life in contemporary German literature (Schmid 3).

The great success of Baumann's play in the Burgtheater does not imply that the use of dialect became universally accepted. Even over a decade later, in 1861, when Charlotte Birch-Pfeiffer's play *Der Goldbauer* (*The Gold Farmer*) was performed, which is set in the Bavarian countryside and also includes dialect (albeit in a much less pronounced way than *Versprechen*), a reviewer took offence at the language, which, they thought, was more fit for the suburban stages. The reviewer states harshly: "Finally, we have to categorically speak out against the performance of plays using dialect or, in any case, corrupt German in the Burgtheater. After all, we have the suburban stages for that" ("Schließlich müssen wir uns noch prinzipiell gegen die Aufführung von Stücken im Dialekt oder doch im verdorbenen Deutsch auf der Burgbühne aussprechen. Dazu sind ja die Vorstadtbühnen vorhanden"; "Wiener Wochenbericht" 220).

The sharp criticism of Birch-Pfeiffer's *Goldbauer* is in line with some of the earliest responses to Baumann's *Versprechen*. For while Baumann's comedy found a large and lasting following in the mid–nineteenth century, it was still controversial. Upon its first performance, the important Burgtheater playwright Friedrich Hebbel condemned not so much the play as such (about which he had little to say), as its inclusion into the repertoire of the Burgtheater. Hebbel viewed the production as sacrilegious: he compared the Burgtheater to a church and contrasted it to a beer house that, in this allegory, represents the suburban theatres. Baumann's play was for the beer house, not the church (Hebbel 236–8).[19] Incidentally, Hebbel was offended not only because of the use of dialect in the play, but also because of its inclusion of songs.[20] The Burgtheater was supposed to be a theatre for recitation, not song (240).

Hebbel's attack on the production of *Versprechen* was programmatic as much as it was personal. Hebbel himself had a new play performed in the Burgtheater in 1848, the bourgeois tragedy *Maria Magdalena*. Hebbel's play was the second play to be added to the repertoire after the March Revolution, directly after Heinrich Laube's roaring success, *Karlsschüler*, which focused on an episode in the life of the rebellious young Schiller. Just like Laube's daring drama, Hebbel's tragedy was clearly a post-revolutionary production: its radical critique of bourgeois morality went far beyond what was possible before the freedom of the press that came with the revolution of 1848.

Contemporary reviewers were fully aware of the radical innovation that Hebbel's play meant for the Burgtheater. Writing in 1848, the critic Sigmund Engländer states the importance of Hebbel's play in the following terms:

> The performance of *Maria Magdalena* in the Burgtheater, without the removal or alteration of a single passage, is a political event, a manifestation of the liberated people and it is here generally called an epoch-making event in the history of the Burgtheater.
>
> Die Aufführung der Maria Magdalena im Burgtheater, ohne daß eine Stelle dabei gestrichen oder verändert wurde, ist ein politisches Ereignis, eine Manifestation des frei gewordenen Volkes und wird hier allgemein als Epoche machend in der Geschichte des Burgtheaters bezeichnet. (Engländer 196)

If Hebbel's play was, as Engländer states, revolutionary for the Burgtheater, Baumann's play was certainly no less so. And perhaps Hebbel did realize that, and his violent reaction against Baumann's play may have been due to the fact that he understood that something very new was being tried out in the Burgtheater – only that it was not the kind of innovation that he wanted to see. What was at stake was the question of which direction the Burgtheater would take in its newfound freedom after the 1848 revolution.

Contrary to what Hebbel suggests, the Burgtheater's opening of doors to song and dialect should not be seen as simply a lowering of standards, done for commercial gain. Instead, the inclusion of Bauman's play forms part of the Burgtheater's reinvention as *Nationaltheater*, albeit in a sense different from what Joseph II had originally conceived. This reinvention also encompassed the name of the theatre itself: starting on 24 April 1848, the Burgtheater's daily bills no longer spoke of the "K.K. Hof-Burgtheater" ("Imperial and Royal Court-Castle Theatre") but of the "K.K. Hof- und Nationaltheater" ("Imperial and Royal Court- and National Theatre"). Starting the following day, female actors were also no longer listed with the French title of *demoiselle*, but with the German titles of *Frau* or *Fräulein* (depending on whether they were married or not). More importantly, the repertoire was heavily Germanized around this time. The years around 1848 see the highest concentration of newly introduced plays originally written in German. For the years between 1845 and 1850, the average share of newly introduced plays originally written in German sits at around 80 per cent (fig. 6.1). In 1848, German plays even make up 85 per cent of newly introduced plays. To put this into perspective, in the overall period between 1814 and 1867, German plays account, on average, for only 63 per cent of newly introduced plays.[21]

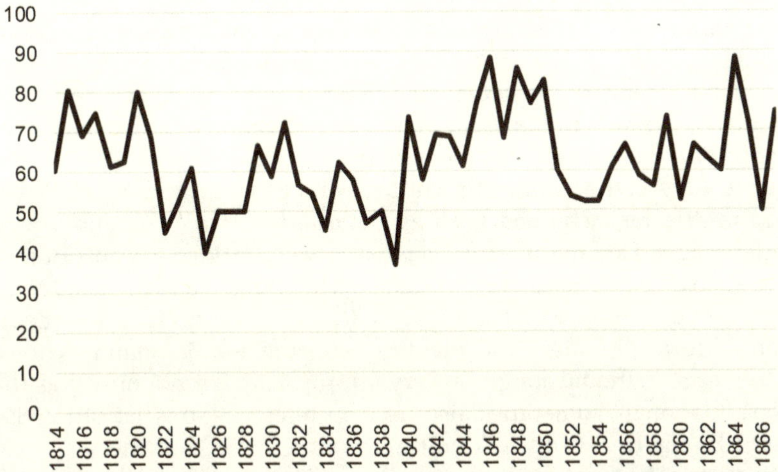

Fig. 6.1. Share of newly introduced plays originally written in German, 1814–67. Data based on the information in Rub.

The transition to dialect that came with Baumann's play was part of this new nationalization of the repertoire – and was also responsible for taking this nationalization one step further. It should also be emphasized in this context that Baumann's play is subtitled a "A Scene from the Austrian Alps with National Songs" ("Eine Scene aus den österreichischen Alpen mit Nationalgesängen"). It is thus precisely in the songs of the play – the very element against which Hebbel protested – that the "national" element, characteristic of the post-1848 Burgtheater, is most directly expressed. Like the use of dialect, the inclusion of songs served a political end, and not only the purpose of light entertainment.

In *Versprechen*, the songs are expressly marked as key elements. The play's main character is the financially comfortable traveller from Berlin, Arthur Stritzow. Stritzow speaks standard German and his fiancée is called Minna, in evocation of the Saxon Minna von Barnhelm from Lessing's canonical comedy of the same title. Stritzow actively seeks out "Nationalgesänge" on his journey through the Austrian Alps; he is a comical figure, the stereotyped urban outsider who falsely romanticizes life in the countryside. But behind this ridiculing portrayal, Stritzow plays an important role in legitimizing Austrian rural culture as an integral part of German national identity. Never before in the Burgtheater had the German spirit been sought in Austrian dialect songs.

The word "national" in the term "national songs" deserves some further commentary. At first sight, it may be considered surprising, or even confusing. After all, the dialect songs in question are decidedly regionalized, belonging to a rather small portion of what might constitute the nation. As we saw in the earlier parts of this chapter, in the context of Vienna and the Burgtheater, the nation is usually kept distinct from the specifically Austrian linguistic, cultural, and geographical realm. When the Burgtheater fashioned itself as *Nationaltheater* in 1776, and when, decades later, Deinhardstein's *Hans Sachs* was heralded as contributing to the project of *Nationaltheater*, what was intended was a form of literature and performance that could serve to unite the nation under a common cultural discourse and identity. Nonetheless, Baumann's choice of the term "national songs" is very appropriate. For not only was the word "national" sometimes also used in reference to what otherwise might be referred to as folk culture around 1848,[22] but the play also actively tries to construct a union between the regional and the national, between the Austrian and the German. It is, in other words, the ultimate point of Baumann's play that the "Nationalgesang" (in the sense of a popular regional dialect song) is a *national* song (in the sense of a song that is expressive of the alleged original culture of the Germans).

Baumann develops this union between the regional and the national by gradually deconstructing the opposition that is posited between Stritzow and his Austrian hosts at the outset of the play. In this deconstruction of the cultural boundary, Baumann produces a remarkable variation of a larger trend in the German pastoral of the 1840s. As Elystan Griffiths explains in his study on the history of the German pastoral, mid-nineteenth-century writers broadly began to undermine the alleged innocence and otherworldly idyll of the pastoral realm. The "Pastoral in the Age of Capital," as Griffiths titles his chapter on the mid–nineteenth century, shows the rural world to be driven by the same capitalist logic from which middle-class city dwellers sought to escape. This new trend, Griffiths notes, also included the popular Viennese playwright Johann Nepomuk Nestroy (1801–62), the star of Vienna's suburban theatre scene. In his 1844 comedy *Der Zerrissene* (*A Man Full of Nothing*), Nestroy reveals the old images of pastoral idyll to be little else than "the projections of an urban mindset" (Griffiths 196).

The interesting – and, dare we say, surprisingly ingenious – spin of Baumann's play on this wider trend in the mid-nineteenth-century pastoral consists in the fact that the blurring of boundaries between the pastoral and the urban – or the regional and the national – is presented as largely positive. The worlds of Stritzow and his Austrian alpine hosts can be happily reconciled only because they are ruled by the same laws.

In the north as well as in the south, in the big city as well as in the remote Alps, what reigns is the power of money and the power of law, but also the power of love and of the pleasure of song. Were it not for these universal patterns, *Versprechen* would not arrive at its happy ending.

Initially, to be sure, Stritzow is disappointed when he finds that the Alpine world is not all that different from the northern urban realm that he sought to escape. Greed and disappointed romantic hopes, Stritzow realizes, destroy the happiness of the rural population as well. For as it turns out, his host, the innkeeper Quantner, prohibits his son, Loisl, from marrying the poor cowgirl Nandl, who lives, idyllically but penniless, in one of Quantner's huts high up in the mountains. The initially disappointing commonalities between the urban and the rural, however, eventually pave the way for the happy ending. It is precisely the parallel between the pastoral world and his own that allows Stritzow to become fully integrated in the pastoral realm, which at the outset he could only longingly watch as an outside witness, eager to be allowed to participate in the imagined amusements of the Alpine lands.

Stritzow's integration into the Alpine world happens in connection with the titular "promise behind the hearth." The sequence of events concerned with that promise is quickly summarized. One day, the innkeeper Quantner visits Nandl and discusses her plans to marry. Quantner would like to see Nandl marry as soon as possible because that would alleviate his concerns about the romance between Nandl and his son, whom he wants to see tied to someone significantly wealthier. To Quantner's great surprise, Nandl announces that she has found someone she might marry, and she reminds Quantner of his promise that she may make a request of him when she marries. Quantner immediately renews his promise and is surprised when all that Nandl asks of him is to keep what she has behind the hearth in her hut. He agrees to her seemingly modest request, and, at her urging, he gives his promise in writing. What Quantner does not know – but the audience does – is that behind the hearth no one but Quantner's son Loisl lies in hiding. Unwittingly, Quantner thus agrees to the marriage he came to prevent. Stritzow, too, hides elsewhere in the background: Loisl had taken Stritzow up to Nandl's hut, and Stritzow is thus the crucial witness to this scene.

When the real state of affairs is revealed to Quantner, he wants to break his promise and tear up the written contract. In this moment, however, Stritzow appears on the scene and makes his witness status a decisive factor in the course of events. Claiming his authority as a lawyer ("Jurist"; Baumann, *Versprechen* 15), Stritzow convinces Quantner that the courts will uphold the latter's promise to Nandl, and that he will be sent to prison if he fails to consent to the marriage. Additionally – and to counteract any remaining ill will on Quantner's part – Stritzow promises to give "the beautiful shepherd girl" ("der holden Schäferin"; 15) the round sum of one hundred talers so that she is, as Stritzow asserts, "no longer poor" ("nicht mehr arm"; 15).

The fact that the modern systems of money and law govern the supposedly remote pastoral Austrian realm proves in Baumann's play to be rather fortuitous: this is what assures the happy ending. Fittingly, in the final song of the play, Stritzow is also no longer a mere listener, but now participates with his own stanza. In contrast to his fellow characters on stage, Stritzow sings his stanza in standard German and not in dialect, but he too closes his stanza with the yodel "halodie!" (16).

While not all differences between the rural and the pastoral have vanished, the two realms can be successfully reconciled. This reconciliation has important implications for the construction of national identity in this play. For Stritzow embodies not only the urban, but as a Berliner, he is a citizen of the Prussian German North, and, speaking standard German (without, incidentally, any shade of Berlin's urban dialect), he is also an embodiment of the extraterritorial Germanness that usually characterizes representations of German identity on the Burgtheater stage. The rural Austrian realm is, for the first time perhaps in literary history, constructed both as an object of desire and as fundamentally akin to the wider German identity. If *Versprechen* presents an idyll, as we may expect of traditional pastoral, this is not so much the idyll of the remote, original *Heimat* – a perfect, uncompromised world far from civilization – but instead, an idyll of the ultimate reconciliation of a regionalized Austrian identity and a larger German identity.

In discussing the significance of Baumann's play, it is important also to keep in mind the curious position of the Burgtheater audience. On the one hand, the audience is clearly invited to see the action unfold through Stritzow's eyes. The play opens and closes with Stritzow's speech (and song), and we are largely presented with the rural world by exploring it together with Stritzow on stage. The Viennese Burgtheater audience would thus have been led to identify with the (geographically remote) Berlin urbanite on his journey through the exotic land of the spectators' own (geographically close) Alpine sphere – and one can only assume that the Burgtheater audience felt comfortable enough in this position of the German outsider. At the same time, the heavy dialect used in this play required an audience familiar with the rural Austrian variants of German. The comic effect of the play relies at least in part on an audience that understands dialect more readily than Stritzow and thus can laugh about his difficulties in communication. Rather than just embodying Strizow's perspective, in other words, the Viennese Burgtheater audience united in itself the two extreme sides of the cultural spectrum that the play shows to be compatible. Baumann's play strongly validated the Viennese audience as a cultural bridge, holding the various ends of German culture together.

While Baumann's *Versprechen* enjoyed great success in the Burgtheater, dialect plays remained outliers in the repertoire. Two years later, in 1850, the Burgtheater introduced another dialect play by Baumann. Baumann's new play, *Der Freiherr als Wildschütz* (*The Baron as Poacher*), was written as an afterpiece (*Nachspiel*) to *Versprechen*, but it saw a relatively disappointing seven performances before it was given up three years later (Rub 78). In subsequent years, Baumann continued writing plays in standard German. The year 1853, for instance, saw the premiere of his farce *Die Engländerin* (*The English Lady*), which, however, was even less successful. After the obligatory three performances, it disappeared from the repertoire (Rub 81). Perhaps the only interesting point to note about *Die Engländerin* is that it contains some English dialogue – as far as I can see, this is another innovation in the Burgtheater repertoire at that time, and it is indicative of the fact that Baumann was, to some extent, simply interested in experimenting with linguistic variation in theatre, be it in the form of Alpine dialects or in the form of foreign language.

In saying that dialect was, with few exceptions, banned from the Burgtheater and pushed aside as a marker of the suburban theatres, it is important to keep in mind that dialect actually "plagued" the Burgtheater for much of the period here under consideration. While the Burgtheater might have disdained plays with scripted dialect, and while there exists a considerable discourse and mythmaking around the cultivation of a supposedly dialect-free *Burgtheaterdeutsch* ("Burgtheater German"), the truth of the matter is that many of the actors on Vienna's main stage had speech marked by a range of different dialects.[23] Lessing, who visited the Burgtheater in 1775 (before what is now often considered the theatre's official foundation in 1776), critically remarked upon this perceived weakness (Lothar 30). Despite repeated efforts to "cleanse" the Burgtheater of dialect, the problem stayed with this institution for many decades to come.

The attempt to cultivate a stage language free of dialect had already begun with Joseph II's foundation of the Burgtheater as *Nationaltheater* in 1776 (Peter 18). Several decades later, Joseph Schreyvogel (in office, 1814–32) also worked in this direction by seeking to hire actors whose speech was free of dialect (Klingenberg 43). His efforts appear to have been crowned with only limited success. Heinrich Laube, who directed the Burgtheater much later, from 1849 to 1867, found the problem still troubling enough to hire a language teacher to instruct the actors in standard German (60).

The vehement rejection of dialect plays, in other words, occurred on a stage that was far from living up to its ideal of presenting a national theatre in a supra-regional German variety. If Baumann's *Versprechen* was able to create such controversy, it was perhaps also because of the Burgtheater's very uneasy relationship to the dialect that was spoken on its stage on a much more regular basis than is usually acknowledged.

While plays written in dialect remained a controversial exception in the mid-nineteenth-century Burgtheater, the same cannot be said of plays set in areas where one would expect dialect to be spoken, that is, the rural and remote areas of Austrian and German lands. Plays situated in the countryside (but scripted mostly in standard German) as well as plays contrasting the countryside with life in the city were among the most popular in the Burgtheater, and they were sometimes published with a distinct genre specification as *Volksdrama, Volksschauspiel* ("folk drama"), or *Bauernstück* ("peasant drama"). While these plays avoided dialect (or used it only very sparingly in select interjections or forms of address), they are characterized by a simple idiom that, in its plainness, does seek to approximate the rural milieu. The *Volksdrama* constituted an important alternative not only to the classical repertoire but, more directly, also to the equally popular contemporary *Konversationsstück* (conversation play), which was usually set in an urban environment (without exploring urban life as such in much detail) and that relied on witty and fast-paced dialogue.

The degree to which the *Volksdrama* explicitly thematized the countryside as an important site of German (or Austrian) belonging varied significantly from play to play. Three particularly successful folk plays – Ernst Raupach's *Der Mülller und sein Kind* (*The Miller and His Child*), Salomon Hermann Mosenthal's *Deborah*, and Charlotte Birch-Pfeiffer's *Dorf und Stadt* – illustrate this range. While the rural largely remains an atmospheric backdrop in the plays by Mosenthal and especially Raupach, it is the focal point of Birch-Pfeiffer's play. Because of this focus on the rural and other facets of the play, Birch-Pfeiffer's *Dorf*, which premiered in the Burgtheater in 1847, is the closest precursor to Baumann's 1848 comedy *Versprechen*.

The most popular *Volksdrama* in the mid–nineteenth century was Ernst Raupach's drama *Müller*, which first appeared in the Burgtheater in 1830 and saw, up to 1897, an exceptional 120 performances. In Raupach's drama, the rural setting contributes significantly to the melancholic tone of the gothic story, which is set in the relatively distant past of the early eighteenth century, in a village in (Protestant) Silesia. Raupach's drama can be categorized under the rubric "mourning obedience," in the way in which I discussed this category in chapter 4. It presents a story in which obedience is marked as a virtue of the past and, as such, both idealized and simultaneously shown to have tragic shortcomings.

Müller tells the story of a wealthy miller's young daughter, Marie, who obediently accepts her father's harsh prohibition to marry the penniless young man, Konrad, with whom she is in love. The despairing Konrad visits, on Christmas Eve, the local graveyard, following the superstition that on that night, one can see the people who will die in the coming year. In the graveyard, Konrad believes that he sees both the miller and Marie. Konrad divulges what he has seen – though initially mentioning only the sight of the miller. Subsequently the miller indeed dies, at least in part because of the fright that Konrad's announcement causes to him. The dying miller resents Konrad for his revelation, and so does his daughter, who also dies, a little while after her father. Shortly before her death, however, Marie forgives Konrad, after her pastor has allowed her to do so. The curtain falls as Konrad plays, in fulfilment of Marie's last wish, the melody to the song "What God Does Is Done for the Best!" ("Was Gott thut – das ist wohlgethan!"; Raupach 119–20).

The rural setting of *Müller* underscores the sense that we are seeing an old world order, in which there still existed an exemplary obedience, but where people were also subject to an unrelenting authority that, too, is marked as an element of times gone by. Importantly, there is no explicit discussion of the countryside as such in Raupach's play. The countryside simply features as a synecdoche for a time gone by, without any very specific links to the homeland of the Viennese audience of the Burgtheater (who inhabit both a geographically as well as culturally-religiously separate sphere).

There were relatively few plays that presented an explicitly Austrian countryside in the Burgtheater. By far the most popular of these, the Austrian playwright Salomon Hermann Mosenthal's *Volksschauspiel* and melodrama *Deborah* (1849), had a markedly delayed start on Vienna's main stage. This delay, however, appears to have less to do with the play's setting in the Austrian *Heimat* (it is set in a Styrian village around the year 1780), than with the fact that it exposes the antisemitism in that village community.

Deborah premiered in the Stadttheater Hamburg in 1849, and over the following decades it became a major success not only on various German-language stages, but, through translations and adaptations, also in London, New York, and elsewhere. As Jonathan Hess, the leading expert on this play, writes, "Mosenthal was the only German dramatist of his era who managed to write a play that became a true international sensation" (30). Hess contends that it was in particular the overt (and melodramatic) condemnation of antisemitism that sat well with nineteenth-century liberal audiences around the world – although there is certainly room to argue that the play's success was also due to the fact that, in its very philosemitism, it allowed a range of stereotypes about Jews to persist.[24]

In Vienna, *Deborah* was first produced in 1849 – not in the Burgtheater, though, but in the Theater an der Wien, where it was "frequently performed" ("vielfach wiederholt wurde"; Mosenthal, "Skizze" 136). In the Burgtheater, the newly appointed director Heinrich Laube advocated for its performance as well, but initially he was met with resistance. While it is not entirely clear who precisely vetoed the production in the Burgtheater, Laube reports a conversation with Count Moritz von Dietrichstein, the recently retired *Oberstkämmerer*, in which the latter dismissed Mosenthal's play as a *"Judenstück"* ("Jew piece") and apparently found the contentious problem of antisemitism unfit for the Burgtheater (Laube, *Das Burgtheater* 401).[25] Only in 1864 was Laube eventually able to produce the play in the Burgtheater, and, over the next thirty-two years, *Deborah* saw a total of fifty-six performances on that stage.

Setting the controversy over the treatment of the Jewish subject matter in Mosenthal's play aside, and focusing instead on the depiction of rural life in *Deborah*, we see, in comparison to Raupach's *Müller*, a more explicit treatment of the rural as a space that exists distinct from urban or foreign spheres. Through the Jewish characters in the play – refugees in transit to America – a range of foreign places are positioned in contrast to the Styrian countryside, and there are also some passing references to the local urban centre of Graz as a place of liberal modern learning. Yet the countryside remains in *Deborah*, too, overwhelmingly an atmospheric backdrop to the action, important more for the stage effects of the play than for the play's plot development.

A decidedly more explicit focus on the countryside can be found in another popular work of the period, Charlotte Birch-Pfeiffer's drama *Dorf*, which saw 117 performances in the Burgtheater between 1847 and 1901. While *Dorf* is set outside Austria, in a village in the Black Forest as well as in an unnamed town in that region, the play is, through its central opposition of urban and rural life as well as through the tentative introduction of dialect and song, the closest precursor to Alexander Baumann's *Versprechen*, which entered the Burgtheater's repertoire the following year. Moreover, Birch-Pfeiffer's drama is based on one of the most popular of the Black Forest stories by Berthold Auerbach (Aurnhammer and Detering 176), which, as noted before, have been compared to Baumann's *Versprechen*.

Allegedly, the popular Burgtheater actress Luise Neumann had approached several writers, including Mosenthal and the former Burgtheater director Franz Ignaz von Holbein, to write a play based on Auerbach's recently published story "Die Frau Professorin" (1846) – but only Birch-Pfeiffer accepted the challenge (Bettelheim-Gabillon 173). Auerbach, incidentally, was enraged over Birch-Pfeiffer's appropriation of his story, and the ensuing debate over intellectual property caused a big uproar in the German press.[26]

Birch-Pfeiffer's play saw its first production in the Hoftheater Berlin in 1847, before it was also produced in the Burgtheater in the same year, with Neumann in the central role of the farmer's innocent daughter Lorle (or Leonore, as she is called when she moves to town). If Neumann's memoires are to be trusted, the initial reaction in the Burgtheater upon witnessing a play that included roles in scripted dialect was utter silence. As the curtain fell, neither applause nor signs of displeasure were to be heard (Bettelheim-Gabillon 173). Only upon repeat performances in the following year – not coincidentally, perhaps, the revolutionary year 1848, with its increased emphasis on German drama – the play was finally enthusiastically received to become a mainstay in the repertoire for decades to come (173).

Birch-Pfeiffer was the first playwright to have included dialect in a play performed in the Burgtheater since its foundation in 1776. In the print version of her drama, Birch-Pfeiffer explicitly asked for the use of dialect on stage, although her vision of dialect remains relatively mild, affecting only a handful of words (glossed with footnotes in the print edition) and a general guideline to adapt the pronunciation in some respects.[27] In this measured imitation of dialect, Birch-Pfeiffer followed Auerbach, who had also decided that only essential features of regional variants were to be retained in his stories (Aurnhammer and Detering 174). Notwithstanding this relative mildness of the dialect, especially when compared to Baumann's *Versprechen*, and even though the dialect in *Dorf* is Swabian (rather than of any Austrian variety), Birch-Pfeiffer's drama appears to have paved the way for Baumann's play. Without the precedent of Birch-Pfeiffer as an established playwright, Baumann might not have dared to write a dialect play, and the Burgtheater might not have been willing to produce it. Still, the loud public outcries after the premiere of *Versprechen* also make clear that *Dorf* did not achieve the normalization of dialect on the Burgtheater stage.

Beyond the relative emphasis on dialect, *Dorf* and *Versprechen* differ in the way in which they navigate the compatibility of rural and urban life, though in both cases, this problem features very prominently both as a topic of dialogue and as a structural element of the plot. Essentially, *Dorf* remains significantly more sceptical of such a cultural union. In *Dorf*, Birch-Pfeiffer presents the rural sphere as one that is almost completely cut off from urban life, and a return to the authenticity of rural life is possible only at a significant cost for the disappointed urbanites.

Birch-Pfeiffer's *Dorf* tells the story of the established painter (and townsman) Reinhold who, on his journeys, falls in love with the daughter of a wealthy innkeeper in the countryside. Setting aside warnings that people from village and town are not suitable for one another, Reinhold and Lorle marry and move back to the town in which Reinhold had previously lived and where he has now been offered a lucrative post as gallery director and professor (the town in question being the unnamed capital of a small principality).[28] Once in town, the relationship between Reinhold and Lorle soon deteriorates. Lorle has difficulties adjusting to the refined manners of the urbanites, and she is now also met with her husband's rigid expectations to fit in. Strikingly, he complains, among other things, about her all-too-natural manner of walking – much to Reinhold's chagrin, Lorle always puts her heel down first (Birch-Pfeiffer, *Dorf* 69). In the end, crushed both by her own unhappiness and the visible distress of her husband, Lorle resolves to leave town and to move back to her native village. Hearing this, Reinhold belatedly understands his mistakes and sees (again) Lorle's true value. He resolves to ask for his dismissal and vows to join Lorle on her return to the village.

The reunion of husband and wife at the end of Birch-Pfeiffer's drama is without precedent in Auerbach's story: in "Die Frau Professorin," Lorle returns alone to her village while the desperate Reinhold flees to Rome. However, the seemingly more conciliatory ending in *Dorf* does little to assuage the cultural conflict between the urban and the rural that is at the heart of the play. Not only is the conflict laid out in significantly more detail than the rushed reunion at the end and thus impresses itself more clearly on the play's audience, but also, more importantly, the very ending can be understood to further underscore the incompatibility of rural and urban life. The life together for husband and wife is made possible only by Reinhold's sacrifice of his high position (and income) in town. There is thus not the happy insight we find in Baumann's play about the compatibility of the urban and the rural. Even though we are invited to picture Reinhold and Lorle living together happily ever after, the cost at which this happiness comes clearly highlights the perilous nature of their union.[29]

The limitations set on the union between the urban and rural spheres also has implications for the *Heimat* discourse in Birch-Pfeiffer's play. If we are meant to identify *Heimat* with the rural in *Dorf*, then a return to *Heimat* is not possible – or possible only at such a high price that, for all intents and purposes, it must remain a fantasy. As discussed, this view of *Heimat* is markedly different from Baumann's *Versprechen*.

To conclude, we see a significant range in how *Heimat* is presented through the rural in the popular plays in the Burgtheater. As the genre for the debate on *Heimat* in the Burgtheater repertoire, *Volksdrama* stands in competition not only with the equally popular urban *Konversationsstück* as well as with the classical repertoire: even within the *Volksdrama*, there is a meaningful internal differentiation. These differences concern both the question of dialect use and the way in which the rural world of *Heimat* is discussed. Some plays, like Raupachs's *Müller* and, to a lesser extent, Mosenthal's *Deborah* treat the rural as a world within itself, cut off culturally from the urban, and also cut off historically from the present, so that it remains an object of nostalgic longing (tinged again with varying degrees of negative aspects). Other plays, like those of Birch-Pfeiffer and Baumann do show the rural life of *Heimat* as a condition of the present and as a *potential* alternative to urban life. But here again, the extent to which the idealized sphere of the rural really is a viable option for contemporary urban society is very differently answered from play to play. What all of this amounts to is that the Burgtheater was certainly open to the contemporary discourse about *Heimat*, but that this very discourse remained strikingly heterogenous and controversial. Both the degree to which the rural life was imitated in drama and the extent to which a return to a rural *Heimat* was thought possible differed appreciably.

Conclusion: The Mid-Nineteenth-Century Burgtheater as a Case Study

The Burgtheater of the mid–nineteenth century has traditionally been viewed as an artistically refined but largely apolitical institution that, under the pressure of the contemporary censorship system, concerned itself with lightweight entertainment for the aristocracy. As I argued at length in this book, this image is in need of revision. At least under Joseph Schreyvogel and Heinrich Laube, the Burgtheater was led by known liberals of the period. Moreover, the Burgtheater hosted an audience that reached significantly beyond the aristocracy and the wealthiest bourgeoisie. Most importantly, the Burgtheater provided a stage for debate on a number of crucial themes of great social and political concern, notably the meaning of individual liberty, the role of women in society, and the status of the German nation in the Austrian context.

This study treated these three topics separately to clearly lay out the range of positions that the audience was exposed to in each case. In reality, of course, these topics often overlapped and reinforced one another. It is not without significance, for instance, that two of the four plays discussed in the chapter on freedom and obedience centre on female characters. Even though the importance of Griseldis in Halm's eponymous play or of Cordelia in Shakespeare's *Lear* extends beyond the specificity of female agency to address more universal concerns, the fact that these characters are women matters. The construction of ideal modes of freedom and obedience through the female characters both relied on an existing understanding of gender roles and also defined these gender roles in return. In a different manner, questions of gender continue to resurface in the discourse on nationhood, albeit in strikingly diverse ways. For instance, the patriot's free submission to the fatherland could be cast either as a female virtue (as we saw in Halm's *Fechter*) or, quite to the contrary, as a sign of male strength (as we saw in Bauernfeld's *Krieger*).

One of the benefits, however, of treating the repertoire under distinct thematic rubrics is that this procedure allows us to better compare how the various discourses were handled in the Burgtheater. While I emphasized throughout the book the significant range in the positions on each of the topics discussed, we can now also reflect more clearly on the interestingly varying scope of this range. The widest range of positions existed in the abstract discussion of freedom and obedience. All the ambiguities of the individual plays notwithstanding, in the contrast between Shakespeare and Grillparzer as well as between Halm and Bauernfeld, clear alternatives emerge. Obedience is held up either as a positive alternative to a reliance on affective relationships (Shakespeare) or, quite to the contrary, it is revealed to come at too high a price for precisely these affective relationships (Grillparzer). Similarly, the synthesis between obedience and freedom is displayed either as an ideal model of modern agency (Halm), or, quite to the contrary, it is ridiculed as mere camouflage of the old authoritarian system (Bauernfeld).

In the negotiation of German national identity and German nationalism, the difference between the various positions is already less pronounced. To be sure, here too we saw significant variance between the aggressive chauvinism of Halm's *Fechter* and the decidedly more conciliatory nationalism in the plays by Deinhardstein and Bauernfeld. But the general commitment to German nationalism was a universal hallmark of at least the popular Burgtheater playwrights of the period, if not of the repertoire as a whole. The treatment of the related topic of the local *Heimat* supports this impression of a more modest diversity of positions in a different way. Admittedly, there is a tension between the Burgtheater's general lack of interest in its own regional *Heimat* on the one hand, and the great popularity of Alexander Baumann's Austrian dialect play *Versprechen* on the other. Yet by and large, Baumann's play remained an exception, and on the topic of dialect and *Heimat*, my claim about the diversity of the Burgtheater repertoire relies heavily on the inclusion of Baumann's comedy and a few other exceptional plays.

Relatively speaking the least variety can be observed in the debate over women's role in society. Instead of clear categorical alternatives, we are confronted largely with differences in tone and nuance. Meaningful as these differences may be, they fall short of the oppositions that characterize the debate on liberty and even the debate on nationalism. As the contrast between Benedix's *Wespe* and Bauernfeld's *Bürgerlich* reveals, plays of the period show varying levels of sympathy for women's emancipatory ideals. In the end, however, it is impressed on the audience that these ideals have to be given up by the female characters – either completely or in exchange for a relatively modest concession on the part of the male characters.

In sum, the more concretely the discussed topics touched on the lived reality of the Burgtheater's audience, the narrower the range of positions became. For the average spectator in the Burgtheater in the middle decades of the nineteenth century, women's claims to independence had a much more direct relevance in their day-to-day lives than the question of national identity. And both of these topics were more vividly felt than the relatively abstract debate over the adaptability of obedience to modern notions of freedom. The fact that the Burgtheater's repertoire was more homogeneous where issues of concrete social relevance were concerned is important to consider because it qualifies the overall claim in this book about the great heterogeneity of the debates in the Burgtheater. Where it really mattered, the debate became more limited. And yet this critical insight should not really surprise us – after all, it is easier to be more speculative where less is at stake. More importantly, this point does not invalidate the observation that there was a diversity of positions for all topics here discussed, including women's role in society – and that debate on these topics was thus shown to be possible. Once more, the insistence that debate was possible and that a variety of viewpoints could be presented is perhaps more significant than the radicality of any individual position. For once a debate was initiated, it could also extend beyond the precise viewpoints promulgated on stage.

On the remaining pages, I revisit key points of this study in broader terms, with the goal not simply to summarize these points, but to spell out their implications for future work in four different areas: first, the larger history of the Burgtheater; second, the history of Austrian liberalism; third, the project of comparative repertoire studies; and fourth, the theory of the politics of art. All of these four areas are ripe for a major reassessment, and the best possible outcome for this present book would be to serve as a case study towards such a reassessment.

1. Towards a New History of the Burgtheater

This book focused on the roughly fifty-year period from 1814 to 1867, in which the Burgtheater rose to become the most prestigious German-language stage. While this period was crucial in establishing the Burgtheater as an institution of leading artistic significance, it is not directly representative of the Burgtheater's history more broadly. In each period of Austria's history, and under each political regime, the Burgtheater's substance changed.

The period between 1814 and 1867, from the end of the Napoleonic Wars to Austria's first lasting constitution, was characterized by a relatively stable conservative regime.[1] As such, it is different both from the years of enlightened absolutism under Joseph II that led to the foundation of the modern Burgtheater in 1776, as well as from the more liberal years after the abolishment of (most) censorship following the constitution of 1867. Between 1814 and 1867, the Burgtheater had to contend with a strict but not downright hostile regime, and it found ways to provide both entertainment and material for political debate under these circumstances.

In the twentieth century, Austria saw several much more fundamental political shifts that in turn each changed the framework within which a leading state theatre could operate: the end of the Habsburg monarchy and beginning of the First Republic in 1919; the period of Austro-Fascism (1934–8); the years of Austria's incorporation into the "Third Reich" following the Anschluss of 1938; and, finally, the foundation of the second republic in 1955. In recent decades, the Burgtheater's problematic support of the politics of Austro-Fascism and of the Third Reich have especially become the subject of a more sustained scholarly and artistic debate. Most notable in these efforts is Elfriede Jelinek's 1985 farce *Burgtheater: Posse mit Gesang* (*Burgtheater: Farce with Songs*), which focuses on a group of famous Burgtheater actors during the Nazi period (Zangl 281). Under Claus Peymann's directorship (1986–9), the Burgtheater itself managed to play an important role in Austria's gradual reckoning with its Nazi past, especially through the production of Thomas Bernhard's play *Heldenplatz* in 1988, which revolves around the cheering welcome that Hitler received upon his arrival in newly annexed Austria in March 1938 (conspicuously, however, Jelinek's *Burgtheater* still awaits performance on Vienna's main stage).[2]

In more recent years, the Burgtheater has followed and defined important cultural and political trends, lending its stage to an artistic program well beyond traditional European drama. Under Nikolaus Bachler's directorship (1999–2008), for instance, the Burgtheater saw Christoph Schlingensief's infamous postmodern multimedia spectacle *Area 7* (in 2006), the important Austrian avant-garde artist Hermann Nitsch's eight-hour-long bloody and ritualistic *Orgien Mysterien Theater* (in 2005), and a concert by the iconic German punk rock band Die toten Hosen (also in 2005).[3]

From the time of Bachler's departure from the Burgtheater in 2008 to the moment in which I finish this manuscript (in summer 2022), the Burgtheater has had three new directors, including its first female director (Karin Bergmann, 2014–19), each with their own vision and each working in a different political, cultural, and, indeed, public health environment. While these few highlights can indicate some of the diverse paths that the Burgtheater has taken in its almost 250-year history since its reconceptualization by Joseph II in 1776, the time has come for a new, comprehensive history of the Burgtheater that is written in a manner cognizant of the approach taken in this book. Rather than just highlighting leading personalities and important productions, such a history should make the repertoire visible in its whole breadth and seek to explain how and why this relative breadth changed over time. Such a work would provide a valuable case study in our understanding of the history of modern theatre while also providing new insights into broader cultural shifts in the scope of the political debates in Austrian history.

2. Towards a Reassessment of Austrian Liberalism

Over the past decades, nineteenth-century Austrian liberalism has been the subject of several excellent monographs (see for instance, Judson, *Exclusive Revolutionaries*; Kwan). By and large, however, these studies approach liberalism as a political movement in a relatively narrow sense. The history of liberalism in this type of reading focuses on the struggle for a constitution, individual rights, and a centralized state, as well as on the question of how this struggle unfolded under the conditions of rising nationalism throughout the Habsburg Empire. While these are undoubtedly central concerns of Austrian liberalism in the nineteenth century, what is sidelined here is the broader cultural context in which – and alongside which – the political liberalism emerged.

Paying attention to liberalism's cultural context means, first, expanding the source material to better include the robust debates that occurred directly as well as indirectly through literature, theatre, and other arts. In much of the historical scholarship, there continues to be a mismatch between the important status of the arts in nineteenth-century intellectual life and their relative neglect by today's scholars (outside of literary studies and art history, of course). In this book, I have looked at the debates in one particularly prominent theatre of the period, but there would still be much more to discover and to understand through a comprehensive comparative approach that reaches across the various theatres and the very significant literary production of the period. However, more than merely expanding the corpus relevant to the study of liberalism, a cultural contextualization of liberalism's history should also expand our notion of liberalism's scope, which includes a number of fields that are not as overtly political as the fight for a constitution. To stick to the examples developed in this book, a cultural history of liberalism should retrace how liberals pictured (and narrated) human freedom in action, and how they imagined human freedom across gender lines. Especially the notion of gender is noticeably absent from some of the most impressive recent books on liberalism – even though a cursory glance at theatre repertoires suggests that it is in the context of gender that notions of liberty were very frequently debated.

3. Towards Comparative Repertoire Studies

Our ability to understand the Burgtheater is limited by the fact that we are not fully able to compare its relative polyphony to that of other contemporary theatres. Ideally, we would be able to state how the Burgtheater compares to other leading court theatres of the period, including the court theatre in Weimar and the court theatre in Berlin. Likewise, we would gain much from establishing in precise terms how the variety of offerings in the Burgtheater compares to that of Vienna's suburban theatres in the nineteenth century.

In answering these questions, we could draw on the contemporary discussion of these theatres as well as on the existing theatre scholarship of the twentieth and twenty-first centuries (even though the body of work on individual theatres remains relatively limited). But answering these questions more comprehensively also requires a systematic and detailed analysis of the repertoire and daily playbills for these various theatres – a truly Herculean effort that is still to be completed and that no single scholar can accomplish alone. It is my hope that some of this research will be carried out in the years to come, and that the present book can provide one possible paradigm for it.

Such work has been a long time coming. Already in 1955, the theatre historian Heinz Kindermann called for "a history of the repertoires of our entire old continent" ("Spielplangeschichte unseres ganzen alten Kontinents"; "Notwendigkeit" 166). Kindermann, who wrote under the shadow of the First and Second World Wars and of the most brutal nationalism (in which Kindermann himself was involved to a troubling degree; see Pilger), expected that a study of repertoire would reveal the significant extent to which the various European traditions had been intertwined for centuries. Since Kindermann's call to action almost seventy years ago, relatively little work has been produced to approximate such a comprehensive European history of repertoire. Now, with major digitization efforts under way at various leading institutions in Europe (notably at Weimar's court theatre and Paris's Théâtre-Français), the conditions are uniquely favourable for such an endeavour.[4]

4. Towards a Reconceptualization of the Politics of Art

The project of studying the politics of the Burgtheater by focusing on the range of positions represented within the repertoire – rather than on the radicality or transgressiveness of any single position – has broader implications for our thinking about the politics of art. Ideally, what I would like to see emerging from this book are discussions and investigations – both theoretical and empirical in nature – that seek to assess artistic diversity as a political category in a variety of contexts in which the mode of reception encourages comparison between different works. Obvious examples are museums and exhibition spaces, where we experience works literally hanging side by side. But a similar case could also be made for publishing houses, bookstores, libraries, broadcasting stations, journals of literary criticism, and school curricula. In all these different venues, there is great promise in looking not only at what works were included or excluded in different periods, but also at what the relative range of positions was that was allowed. This type of analysis could be much better attuned to the politics of more moderate or politically controlled spaces, as we have seen in the case of the Burgtheater in this book. In this analysis, spaces that are forced (or even inclined) to exclude some extreme voices may still turn out to have been robust platforms for debate by virtue of the variety of voices that they did admit.

The point in this is not to deny the relevance of radical politics or of the institutions that made it their mission to amplify such radicality, even at the cost of diversity. Certainly, the outcome of such an analysis could not be that, for instance, subversive publishing houses that distributed radically democratic literature throughout German lands in the aftermath of the French Revolution should now be judged politically less meaningful because they did not also print literature in favour of the Ancien Régime.[5] Even so, as a metric to complement conventionally held views of what counts as politically relevant art, the study of the internal differentiation of a corpus does appear very promising. This relevance extends both to our understanding of individual institutions (of theatres, museums, publishing houses, etc.) and to our understanding of broader historical processes. Indeed, we may find that when it comes to the range of ideas represented in one platform, there is, even and especially for us today in our highly polarized media environments, still much to admire in the large court theatres of the mid–nineteenth century.

Notes

Introduction: Reassessing the Mid-Nineteenth-Century Burgtheater

1 Freytag writes: "A German drama must enjoy the good fortune to succeed in eight to ten larger theatres across the various parts of Germany before its performance in the remaining theatres can be regarded as a matter of course. While the prestige of a play that emerges from Vienna's Burgtheater determines, more or less, what will happen in the other theatres of the [Austrian] Empire, already the Berliner Hoftheater has a much smaller circle of influence" ("Ein deutsches Drama muß das Glück haben, bei acht bis zehn größern Theatern in den verschiedenen Theilen Deutschlands Erfolge zu erlangen, bevor sein Lauf über die übrigen als gesichert betrachtet werden kann. Während das Renomee eines Theaterstücks, welches von der Wiener Burg ausgeht, so ziemlich die übrigen Theater des Kaiserstaates bestimmt, hat schon das Berliner Hoftheater einen viel kleineren Kreis, in dem es den Ton angibt [...]"; Freytag, *Die Technik des Dramas* 304–5).

2 Among these works stand out especially the many publications on Viennese theatre history by Franz Hadamowsky, notably *Wien. Theatergeschichte* (1994). Strikingly, among Hadamowsky's many publications, there is not a single book devoted solely to the Burgtheater. Among the few twentieth- and twenty-first-century monographs on the Burgtheater are Klaus Dermutz's *Das Burgtheater und die Wiener Identität 1888–2002* (2010) as well as Heinz Kindermann's two highly ideological studies from the period of national socialism (*Der Lebensraum* [1939] and *Das Burgtheater* [1944]).

3 Link's book, however, consists mostly in a collection of archival materials and provides relatively little analysis.

4 The only monograph that focuses specifically on this period is Annmarie Stauss's specialized (German-language) study *Schauspiel und Nationale Frage* (2011).
5 Not all of the four men actually carried the title of *Direktor*. For more detail on the organizational structure of the Burgtheater, see chapter 2.
6 See, for instance, the (otherwise) formidable studies *The Habsburgs* by Martyn C. Rady (2020) and *The Habsburg Empire* by Pieter M. Judson (2016).
7 Klingenberg's book generally resonates with the accounts of other scholars (see, for instance, Koll).
8 Unless otherwise noted, all translations are my own.
9 For an account of the importance of clubs (*Vereine*) to the political sphere in Austria, see especially Pieter Judson's 1996 history of Austrian liberalism, *Exclusive Revolutionaries*. Judson pays little attention to the theatre as another important platform for contemporary liberalism. Jonathan Kwan's *Liberalism and the Habsburg Monarchy, 1861–1895* (2013) also mentions theatre only in passing.
10 In speaking here and below of "Burgtheater playwrights," I refer to contemporary writers who resided in or around Vienna and whose plays were regularly performed in the Burgtheater. Principal among these are Eduard von Bauernfeld, Franz Grillparzer, Friedrich Halm, and Johanna Franul von Weißenthurn. Importantly, these writers typically had additional ties to the Burgtheater. Franul von Weißenthurn was a long-time actor while simultaneously being a playwright. Bauernfeld and Halm are known to have advised Franz Holbein, and perhaps other directors, on the repertoire (see ch. 2). Halm also became the Burgtheater's director from 1867 to 1868. In Grillparzer's case, the status of a Burgtheater playwright was made more official when, in 1825, he was given an annual salary of two thousand guldens for five years – in return, Grillparzer had to offer all his dramatic works first to the Burgtheater (Wlassack 140–1). There were of course many other popular playwrights whose works were performed in the Burgtheater who did not reside in Vienna and for whom the Burgtheater was not the primary stage. For an extensive discussion of the repertoire and its contributors, see chapters 2 and 3.
11 In his autobiography, *Aus Alt- und Neu-Wien*, Eduard von Bauernfeld gives a lively account of the interaction that he and Grillparzer had with the leading liberals of the period (*Gesammelte Schriften* 12: 129–55).
12 On the importance of self-censorship in German playwriting around 1800, see Bachleitner's "Die Dialektik von Gehorsam."
13 The following brief account of these scandals and riots follows Booth (308–9, 311–13, 324).

14 Austria banned both French and German printed editions of *Hernani* in 1830 (the German edition had appeared in Darmstadt). More precisely, the Austrian prohibitions were in the category *erga schedam* (roughly, "with special permission"), thus allowing some restricted groups access to the texts.

15 A prominent possible exception is Beaumarchais's comedy *Le barbier de Séville* (The Barber of Seville, 1775), which had been produced in the Burgtheater, albeit several decades earlier (it saw twenty-one performances between 1776 and 1781; Rub 2).

16 The lines that caused this outburst of indignation run: "Don't forsake the oldest ancestor for some other ancestor; [don't forsake] him who was there before even the sun was there, him who formed mean [*niedern*] dust in his own image. The face of humanity [*des Menschen Antlitz*] is his coat of arms" ("Gib nicht für einen Ahn, so alt er ist, Den ersten auf, den ält'sten aller Ahnen, Ihn, der da war, eh' noch die Sonne war, Der niedern Staub geformt nach seinem Bild. Des Menschen Antlitz ist sein Wappenbild"; qtd. in "Wiens poetische Federn und Schwingen" 187.)

17 This, at least, is the account provided in Heinrich Laube's history of the Burgtheater (*Das Burgtheater* 138–40).

18 See the entry on Siegmund Engländer in the *Österreichisches Biographisches Lexikon*.

19 See also chapter 5.

20 More positively, Leopold made the Burgtheater actors pensioned state employees, equal to the Habsburg bureaucracy's civil servants (Klingenberg 28).

21 For a record of the performances of Euripides at the court theatre in Weimar, see the database *Theater und Musik in Weimar 1754–1990.*

22 A major milestone on the way to the 1867 constitution was the so-called February Patent (*Februarpatent*) of 1861.

23 Notably, the new freedom of the press did not extend to the theatres, which continued to be governed by the censorship system declared in the 1850 *Theaterordnung*. Officially, this system of theatre censorship was only abolished in 1926. In practice, however, theatre censorship declined significantly after 1867, and even more so after 1918 (Yates, *Theatre in Vienna* 42–8).

24 Klingenberg's *Das gefesselte Burgtheater* is the clearest example of this trend, but, to a lesser extent, the charge may even be laid against Yates's *Theatre in Vienna*.

25 These dates follow Susanne Kord, *Ein Blick hinter die Kulissen* (361). As Kord also notes, there is some disagreement over these dates.

26 While the works of female playwrights of the period have found some attention in two groundbreaking monographs by Susanne Kord from

the 1990s (*Ein Blick hinter die Kulissen* [1992] and *Sich einen Namen machen* [1996]), they are still absent from the major investigations into the Burgtheater. However, it is especially in the context of the Burgtheater's broad and varied repertoire that it becomes possible to appreciate the importance of the female playwrights.

1. What Makes a Theatre Politically Significant?

1 Even around the middle of the nineteenth century, about half of the population, especially the lower classes, did not consume any kind of literature, although most of them were able to read (Ehlert 339).

2 Recent scholarship has pointed out that there is only limited evidence for the conventionally claimed exclusion of women and slaves in Greek theatre (see Critchley 53–6).

3 The following brief survey of eighteenth-century German drama and theatres adopts a passage from my introduction to the special issue of *Oxford German Studies*, "The Drama of Obedience," co-authored with Elystan Griffiths (Wagner and Griffiths).

4 The population of today's territory of Vienna grew from about 231,000 in 1800 to about 1,675,000 in 1900. These numbers follow the information on the webpage "Bevölkerung." On the shifting ratio between theatre seats and population in Vienna, see Bachleitner's *Die literarische Zensur* (258).

5 See the discussion of the repertoire in chapter 2.

6 Examples include Eduard Devrient's *Geschichte der deutschen Schauspielkunst* (1848) and Heinrich Laube's histories of the Burgtheater (*Das Burgtheater*, 1868) and of the North German Theatre (*Das norddeutsche Theater*, 1872).

7 While the theory of tragedy outweighed the discussion of comedy, there was, as Philipp Böttcher convincingly showed, also a more substantial body of work on the comic genre in the nineteenth century than has traditionally been claimed (45–81).

8 The same could also be argued for other important works on drama from the period, notably Hermann Hettner's influential 1852 study *Das moderne Drama*.

9 Only four canonical playwrights of previous generations (Shakespeare, Lessing, Goethe, and Schiller) had more frequently performed plays in the nineteenth-century Burgtheater. However, even taking these classical playwrights into account, Freytag's *Die Journalisten* remains the most popular *comedy* of the period (see the statistical overview in Rub 265–305).

10 Interestingly, Wagner's criticisms of mid-nineteenth-century theatre in general essentially echo the criticisms often made against the

Burgtheater in particular, notably its exclusivity and its emphasis on light entertainment.

11 On Wagner's often overlooked revolutionary politics, see Berry.

12 Incidentally, Wagner's mythical vision of the *Volk's* self-recognition in theatre bears some resemblance to the otherwise quite different contemporaneous poetics of realist drama, advocated by Hermann Hettner, Gustav Freytag, and others. The proponents of realism also called for a greater use of the theatre to present the audience with an image of itself, albeit with decidedly more emphasis on the social fabric of reality (see, for instance, Hettner, *Das moderne Drama* [1852], and more broadly the recent survey of the realist dramatic poetics in Böttcher 45–81).

13 On Goodlad's project, see Pfister (59–60).

14 See, for example, Goodlad (143). The same metric could, of course, be used for any work of literature (including novels and poems), but the question of the extent to which a work perpetuates existing social and moral systems appears to be particularly relevant for (theatrically performed) drama because the audience gathers here as a collective and thus also has to navigate as a collective how to respond to potential transgressions.

15 The Burgtheater was closed for holidays and during parts of the summer. In the mid–nineteenth century, there were performances on roughly 300 to 320 days out of the year. For a detailed breakdown, see the record of daily playbills at "Jahresauswahl."

16 See, for instance, the analysis of plays by Deinhardstein and Bauernfeld in chapter 6.

17 A rare exception to this pattern is Eduard von Bauernfeld's drama *Franz von Sickingen,* which critically discusses the Catholic Church as a political actor. However, the play was performed only in 1850, during the brief pause in theatre censorship in the direct aftermath of the 1848 revolution.

18 René Wellek defines Bakhtin's concept of polyphony in the following terms: "Bakhtin asserts that Dostoevsky created a totally new kind of novel he calls 'polyphonic': i.e., it consists of independent voices which are fully equal, become subjects of their own right and do not serve the ideological position of the author" (32). The applicability of Bakhtin's concept of polyphony to Dostoevsky's novels has been questioned repeatedly. See Wellek (33) and Zhongwen (787–9).

19 See especially Critchley (48–52). As if in direct (albeit unavowed) contestation of Bakhtin's claim, Critchley also emphasizes "polyphony" in tragedy (57–62). Critchley, however, does not explicitly reference Bakhtin.

20 In the nineteenth-century Burgtheater, *Maria Stuart* was Schiller's most successful play, and one of the most popular productions overall. On the production of *Maria Stuart* in the Burgtheater, see also chapter 3.

2. Making the Burgtheater Repertoire

1 Heinz Kindermann's foundational 1955 article on the importance of repertoire research continues to be an important reference. Kindermann also points to some agents who do not receive much discussion in my study – notably the stage designer, who, at least in baroque theatre had a significant authority over the selection of plays ("Notwendigkeit und Aufgaben" 162). In the nineteenth-century Burgtheater, stage designers do not appear to have had a major influence on decisions concerning the repertoire. In recent years, some scholars have investigated the process of repertoire-making in the context of contemporary German theatres (Schmidt; Cossel). However, the findings from these studies have limited bearing on the mid–nineteenth century because, as Thomas Schmidt notes, the structure of today's theatres goes back to innovations of the late nineteenth and early twentieth centuries. Among the main differences between contemporary theatre and that of the mid–nineteenth century are the abolition of aristocratic courts as sponsors of theatre production, the greater of authority of the theatre director (*Intendant*) and stage director (*Regisseur*) in today's theatres, and the greater independence from ticket sales through increased public funding.

2 These numbers are based on an analysis of the daily playbills of the Burgtheater ("Jahresauswahl"). The ratio between old and new plays shifts slightly if one adds to the twenty-six plays introduced in 1842 those seven plays that were introduced in 1841 after 3 April (when Holbein was appointed) and that were still performed in 1842. By that measure, slightly under one quarter of all plays performed in 1842 had been introduced under Holbein's leadership. Additionally, a handful of plays, though previously introduced to the repertoire, were advertised on the playbills as "neu in Szene gesetzt" (newly produced).

3 For instance, nine years later, in 1851, during the second full year of Heinrich Laube's tenure, the Burgtheater performed 139 different plays.

4 I use the term stage director (*Regisseur*) here in distinction from the theatre director (*Direktor*).

5 Susanne Kord's suggestion that the Burgtheater directors, notably Heinrich Laube, were "without real powers" ("ohne reale Befugnisse"; Kord, *Ein Blick* 25) is in need of qualification. While the directors' powers were limited, the directors remained the single-most important agents in the Burgtheater.

6 It was stipulated that the director did not have the power to appoint new actors without the court's approval (Wlassack 207). However, Holbein, and later also Laube, were allowed to hire actors provisionally, on one-year terms (207, 235).

7 On the influence of Schröder's acting style, see Yates's *Theatre in Vienna* (20).
8 On the transformations of the Burgtheater's style after the move to its new building in 1888 more broadly, see Dermutz.
9 Bauernfeld's success extended beyond Austria to other leading German theatres, but in much less pronounced form. While the Burgtheater produced forty-eight of his plays in a total of 1126 performances, Weimar's court theatre, for instance, produced only fourteen plays in a total of 110 performances. It should be noted that Bauernfeld did not write in dialect and that, in many of his plays, the Austrian context is not very prominent. Bauernfeld's underwhelming success outside Austria thus cannot be explained by framing him as a regional writer in terms of either language or content matter.
10 The actors, to be sure, did not choose the roles themselves; instead, the casting was the task of the theatre directors.
11 On the system of the *Wöchner*, see Lothar (28–9).
12 In 1797, the Burgtheater's lessee, Baron Braun, claimed that the number of annual submissions was between seventy and eighty plays (Hadamowsky 324).
13 Many larger state-sponsored theatres in German-speaking Europe today perform on one or more smaller stages in addition to their main stage. Across these various stages, the number of new plays per year is often roughly similar to that introduced in the Burgtheater (on the repertoires of contemporary German state-sponsored theatres, see Schmidt).
14 Handke's play was scheduled to premiere at the Burgtheater in February 2021. Its original production was at the Salzburg Festival in summer 2020.
15 For the Burgtheater's 2020/1 season, see "Premierenübersicht."
16 See the statistical record in Rub (265–305).
17 See the statistical record in Rub (283–97).
18 The premiere in Weimar's court theatre (on 6 March 1841) was even half a year earlier than in the Burgtheater (on 28 September 1841).
19 Susanne Kord shows more broadly to what extent nineteenth-century German theatres were dependent on the productivity of popular playwrights (Kord, *Ein Blick* 24–5).
20 Bauernfeld's opera libretto *Der Graf von Gleichen*, which discusses a story of bigamy in the aristocracy, was banned in 1826 (Bachleitner, *Die literarische Zensur* 256). His drama *Franz von Sickingen*, which premiered in the Burgtheater in 1850, towards the end of the freedom from censorship in the wake of the 1848 revolution, was subsequently put aside (Bauernfeld, *Gesammelte Schriften* 6: 223). Moreover, on three occasions Bauernfeld was confronted with bans from the censors for his poems and essays. The details are recorded in the database "Komparatistik Wien Zensurdatenbank."

21 An older system based on success, according to which the gross income of the third performance went to the playwright, had been discontinued in 1789 (Wlassack 208).
22 My examples are taken from Bachleitner, "Die Dialektik von Gehorsam." Bachleitner also points to the complete databank of all prohibited books in Austria between 1750 and 1848 ("Komparatistik Wien Zensurdatenbank").
23 "Komparatistik Wien Zensurdatenbank."
24 Bachleitner notes this explicitly for drama of the late eighteenth century ("Die Dialektik von Gehorsam"), which saw admittedly fewer prohibitions than the period after the *Karlsbader Beschlüsse* ("Carlsbad Decrees") of 1819. However, the large increase in prohibitions after 1819 affected especially journalistic writing (Bachleitner, *Die literarische Zensur* 170). Moreover, there were, at least in print publications of the 1830s and 1840s, still about six to eight times as many books published as banned. For the 1820s, the ratio of accepted plays to banned plays is lower than that (see the statistics on the prohibition of print publications in Bachleitner, *Die literarische Zensur* 161–2).
25 On self-censorship in the Burgtheater, see Bachleitner's *Die literarische Zensur* (241).
26 This arrangement ended in 1867, when the Burgtheater was moved from the portfolio of the *Oberstkämmerer* to that of the *Obersthofmeister*, a court office similar in rank to the *Oberstkämmerer* (Wlassack 275).
27 From 1826 to 1835, Count Czernin was at once *Direktor* and, in his capacity as *Oberstkämmerer*, also *Oberster Hoftheaterdirektor*.
28 Chapter 4 turns to this case in more detail.
29 For a historically comprehensive overview of the Burgtheater audience beyond the period here under investigation, see Margret Dietrich's 1976 two-volume study, *Das Burgtheater und sein Publikum*.
30 This division, as a general distinction between commercial and court theatres, is claimed by Kord (*Ein Blick* 24).
31 Hadamowsky (328–9) provides a detailed breakdown for the years 1817–18.
32 For the season 2004/5, the Burgtheater reported ticket sales amounting to 5.57 million Euros, while receiving 43.73 million Euros in subsidies. When these numbers were reported, the artistic directors complained that an increase of subsidies was overdue and that it was challenging to maintain the theatre's work with the existing level of support. See "Burgtheater."
33 State-owned theatres in Germany rely on ticket sales for, on average, 15 to 20 per cent of their costs, with high-profile theatres (comparable to the Burgtheater) raising only 15 per cent through the box office. With ticket sales amounting to 27 per cent of its costs, the Thaliatheater in Hamburg is the commercially most successful *Staatstheater* ("state theatre"). A few

smaller public stages produce more income through ticket sales, with the Theater Fürth (40 per cent) being at the top (Schmidt 44).

34 Simon Williams writes that, once inside the Burgtheater, everyone had the sense of "being a personal guest of the Emperor" (Williams, "Shakespeare at the Burgtheater" 22; see also Williams, *Shakespeare on the German Stage* 109). For a sceptical review of Williams's claim, see Bachleitner's "Die Dialektik von Gehorsam."

35 Most notable among the scholarly discussion is Dietrich's *Das Burgtheater und sein Publikum.*

36 See the Burgtheater's posted announcement of 1 September 1851 ("Theaterzettel" [1851]).

37 The argument has been made that the very reasonable prices of some of the more modest seats, which also lagged the general inflation of the period, were deliberately kept in place to attract the poorer parts of the Viennese population (Stauss 18–19). Moreover, in his ideologically charged 1939 book on the Burgtheater, the theatre historian Heinz Kindermann claimed (without, however, providing any evidence) that, up until the end of the First World War, there had been a long tradition of "students standing next to young workers with enthusiasm for the arts" in the cheap seats of the fourth gallery ("Wenigstens auf dem Stehplatz der vierten Gallerie des Burgtheaters stand seit langem schon der Student neben dem kunstbegeisterten jungen Arbeiter"; Kindermann, *Der Lebensraum* 6). See also Kindermann's *Das Burgtheater* (13).

38 In chapter 6, I discuss two of the plays that are especially highlighted here among the popular pieces: Charlotte Birch-Pfeiffer's *Dorf und Stadt* (*Village and Town*) and Alexander Baumann's *Versprechen hinterm Herd* (*The Promise Behind the Hearth*).

39 There is no discussion of those occupying the open seats in the fourth gallery – but presumably those would have received a discussion similar to that of the "zweites Parterre."

40 The only shortcoming of this part of the audience, the author notes, is that it was too indulgent of the exaggerated acting style of which some of the performers were guilty ("Das Burgtheaterpublikum II" 178).

41 Otto Rub lists for Gutzkow eleven plays with a total of 355 performances between 1840 to 1912 (270). *Uriel Acosta* alone saw 114 performances.

42 Rub (73); for a detailed discussion of this play, see chapter 6.

43 On the power of the critics in the Burgtheater, see Klingenberg (59).

44 The following account relies on Lothar Kahn's 1975 biographical article on Saphir.

45 Of these six works, four received the strict verdict *damnatur*, while the two others received the slightly milder *erga schedam*, which allowed the

books to be purchased by "very reliable citizens" ("sehr verlässlichen Bürgern"). Information from the database found at "Komparatistik Wien Zensurdatenbank."

46 For an example of such a direct influence, see the discussion of Charlotte Birch-Pfeiffer's *Dorf und Stadt* (*Village and Town*) in chapter 6.

47 On the limited possibility to address matters of religion in the Burgtheater, see also the discussion of Deinhardstein's *Hans Sachs* and Bauernfeld's *Ein deutscher Krieger* (*A German Warrior*) in chapter 6.

3. The Scope of the Burgtheater Repertoire

1 To be sure, as I argued elsewhere (Wagner, "Ad fontes?"), the positivistic philological work in which Halm was engaged as a librarian was not entirely free of tension with his pursuits as a writer.

2 In 1827, Wenzel Klicpera's comedy *Die Zwillinge* (*The Twins*) was performed in a translation by Grammerstätter. *Die Zwillinge* was discontinued after the obligatory three performances (Rub 57). Otto Rub lists Therese von Artner (whose drama *Stille Größe* [*Quiet Greatness*] was performed in 1821) as a Hungarian playwright (51). However, the Hungarian-born Artner wrote her plays in German.

3 Plautus's comedy *The Casket* (*Das Kästchen*; orig. *Cistellaria*), which had been introduced in 1801, fared even worse: it saw only one performance (Rub 30).

4 The information is based on statistics provided by Rub (297–303). The two Spanish playwrights are Don Juan Manuel Diana and Jose de Lara, each of whom was represented by only one play (202–3). By comparison, Schreyvogel introduced no new Spanish playwrights; Deinhardstein introduced two, and Holbein, one (202–3). Among the Italian playwrights, only Deinhardstein introduced two new playwrights. Schreyvogel and Holbein also did not introduce any new Italian playwrights. The very popular comic playwrights Carlo Goldoni and Carlo Gozzi had already been introduced in 1776 and 1777, respectively (301–2). For English playwrights, the record is as follows: Schreyvogel introduced three new authors; Deinhardstein, two; and Holbein, one (297–300).

5 For French playwrights, the breakdown is as follows: under Schreyvogel, twenty new playwrights were introduced; under Deinhardstein eleven; under Holbein five; and, as noted, under Laube, thirty-nine (Rub 283–97).

6 These statistics are based on the survey of the repertoire in Rub.

7 Schiller's *Wallenstein* trilogy had previously been performed in two different abbreviated versions (Wlassack 172).

8 Kotzebue retained after his brief tenure a pension of one thousand guldens annually in return for submitting all his new plays to the Burgtheater (Yates, *Theatre in Vienna* 20).

9 Not mentioned here are those writers who largely appeared in the repertoire as translators. Most notable among these is the Viennese author Franz August von Kurländer (1777–1836), who contributed sixty-three translations and who was of great importance for the introduction of a wide range of French entertainment (Wlassack 188). I also do not include here those playwrights whose productivity falls largely outside the time span that I am concerned with in this book.

10 For an example of a play that suggests, in the print version, cuts for the performance, see for instance Eduard von Bauernfeld's *Ein deutscher Krieger* (esp. 81–3). See also Alexander Baumann's *Das Versprechen hinterm Herd* (3–4).

11 For instance, in the six years between 1837 and 1843 (the time of Charlotte Birch-Pfeiffer's directorship in Zurich), there were only twenty-nine performances of plays by Schiller, ten by Shakespeare, seven by Kleist, five by Goethe, and two by Lessing (Caduff 100).

12 The actors' ability to circumvent censorship has been mentioned in the case of Shakespeare's *King Lear*. In the Burgtheater performances before 1851, King Lear was not allowed to die, but the actors "still generally hinted at the tragic outcome" ("den tragischen Ausgang anzudeuten pflegten"; "Sudermanns neueste Dramen" 38).

13 To put this into perspective, *Götz* premiered at the court theatre in Karlsruhe already a decade earlier, in 1820 (Haass 37). At the court theatre in Weimar, *Götz* was introduced as early as 1804 (*Theater und Musik in Weimar 1754–1990*).

14 There is no specific mention of *Götz von Berlichingen* in the censorship records (as captured in "Komparatistik Wien Zensurdatenbank") until 1840, although it may have been affected by some prohibitions of early collected works editions (from 1775, 1779, and 1800). Several of Goethe's works, most notably his successful first novel, *Die Leiden des jungen Werthers* (*The Sorrows of Young Werther*), had initially been banned by the Austrian censors. At least the *Werther* ban, however, was lifted in 1786 (Bachleitner, *Die literarische Zensur* 67). By the time that the 1828 Cotta edition of Goethe's works appeared, only one volume (volume 13) of the fifty-five volumes was marked *erga schedam*. This was not the volume containing *Götz von Berlichingen*. For an overview of the Austrian censorship of Goethe, see Bachleitner's *Die literarische Zensur* (305–10).

15 The rest of the performances are made up of several less-common genres.

16 The precise difference in the average number of tragedies performed may be somewhat higher than here suggested: we do not have playbills for the years from 1816 to 1820, and in the Schreyvogel era, tragedy was, generally, more frequently performed.

17 In 1848, tragedy was performed on sixteen evenings; in 1855, on seventeen evenings. One also has to consider that the Hoftheater Karlsruhe, in contrast to the mid-nineteenth-century Burgtheater, accommodated not only spoken drama, but, to a lesser extent, also opera. On the theatre in Karlsruhe, see Haass.

4. Mourning and Reforming Obedience

1 Sand's thoughts had, allegedly, been shaped by Follen, and this led to a new scrutiny of university teaching and of all publications as potential sources of agitation.
2 Ernst Raupach's popular drama *Der Müller und sein Kind* (*The Miller and His Child*, first performed in the Burgtheater in 1830) falls under the rubric of what I discuss in this chapter as an – albeit ambivalent – "mourning of obedience" (I briefly discuss Raupach's play in ch. 6). There are many plays that could be categorized, in the sense of this chapter, as "reforming obedience," in that they discuss the possible alignment of obedience with the agency of modern subjects. In another publication, I have made this case for Friedrich Halm's *Verbot und Befehl* (*Prohibition and Command*), which premiered in the Burgtheater in 1848 (Wagner, "Zur Gehorsamskritik"). The same could also be argued for August von Kotzebue's successful comedy *Das Taschenbuch* (*The Paperback*, first performed in the Burgtheater in 1817) and, with qualifications, for his farce *Pagenstreiche* (*Tricks of a Page*) (first performed in the Burgtheater in 1817). In general, the question of an alignment of obedience and freedom is a major concern in many comedies focused on marriage – see, for instance, the discussion of Amalie von Sachsen's comedy *Der Majoratserbe* (*The Tenant in Tail*, first performed in the Burgtheater in 1845) in chapter 5.
3 Stifter, let it be noted, mentions neither the Burgtheater, nor Schreyvogel, or the leading actor Anschütz explicitly, but to contemporary audiences, the reference would have been unmistakable.
4 Quotations are from the English original. In the cases quoted here and later, the text prepared by Schreyvogel for the Burgtheater does not differ decisively. For the German text, see Shakespeare, *König Lear* (7).
5 Critics have sometimes described Cordelia as disobedient, and this makes sense insofar as she refuses to comply with her father's immediate wishes. However, more generally speaking, Cordelia insists that her bond with Lear should be defined by obedience rather than affection. For a discussion of Cordelia's disobedience, see Dodd.
6 Only when Heinrich Laube updated the production in 1851 was Lear allowed to die (Großegger 234).
7 For further reasons for caution in this respect, see Prutti (386).

8 See, for instance, Lorenz (148–61). Lorenz, however, is more concerned with the critique of monarchy in the play than with a critique of Bancbanus, whom she continues to laud – albeit not for his obedience, but for his abstention from violence and intrigue.

9 The authenticity of Grillparzer's peculiar anecdote remains open to doubt. At least in the case of *König Ottokars Glück und Ende*, Grillparzer has been shown to significantly misrepresent the activities of the censors in his autobiography (see Heady 118–19).

10 Bauernfeld's 1846 comedy *Großjährig* (*The Age of Majority*), discussed further later in this chapter, is as another example of this trend. In his study of the Austrian censorship system, Bachleitner points to a longer history of ambiguous and inconsistent censorship in the Burgtheater, dating back at least to Joseph II, who both praised and prohibited Wagner's *Sturm und Drang* play *Die Zwillinge* (*The Twins*) after it had been performed in the Burgtheater (Bachleitner, *Die literarische Zensur* 451).

11 This section draws on two previous articles of mine: Wagner, "Navigating and Owning Obedience" and Wagner, "Zur Gehorsamskritik."

12 See, for instance, Sonnenfels's praise of liberty as an effect of bureaucratic service (see Heindl 95–6). For an early Enlightenment literary rendering of this idea, see also my article on Daniel Defoe's novel *A Journal of the Plague Year* (1722) (Wagner, "Defoe"). According to Koselleck's famous analysis in *Kritik und Krise* (*Critique and Crisis*), this sentiment is even older, dating back to the resolution of European religious wars in the absolutist states of the seventeenth century. As Koselleck argues, the Enlightenment subsequently lost the appreciation of the freedoms afforded by the absolutist states and thus eventually relapsed into civil war.

13 On Hegel's concept of freedom, see Patten.

14 Grillparzer's notion of the "heroism of duty," cited earlier, already points us in this direction. For Grillparzer, there was, as he explains with reference to the tensions in the Vendée in the years after 1789, as much to admire in the commitment to the established ideals of the *ancien régime* as in the revolutionary fight for a republic (Grillparzer, *Selbstbiographie* 182).

15 In a note dated 16 September 1836, the actor Carl Ludwig Costenoble calls *Griseldis* the most commercially successful play in the Burgtheater at that time (294). At least part of the success in the Burgtheater has to be attributed to the main actress, Julie Rettich (Wagner, "Navigating and Owning Obedience").

16 There was no need for Halm to specifically cut the final concession from Petrarch's story, in which Griseldis asks to spare the new wife the same harsh treatment, because Halm cuts this entire scene.

17 For a detailed reading of this play, see Wagner, "Zur Gehorsamskritik."

18 Halm himself later complained, when he wrote the dedicatory poem for the printed publication of *Verbot*, that in the revolutionary zeal no one paid attention to his comedy (Halm, *Werke* 6: 5).

5. Performing the Women's Movement

1 A rare exception to this is Charlotte Birch-Pfeiffer's historical drama *Elisabeth* about the historical English queen Elizabeth I (Birch-Pfeiffer's play was published under the pseudonym Franz Fels in 1840; it was performed in the Burgtheater four times in March 1842; Rub 71). As both Gaby Pailer and Viviane Jasmin Meierdreeß recently pointed out, Birch-Pfeiffer breaks with Schiller's critical depiction of the unmarried queen in his play *Maria Stuart* by presenting Elisabeth's independence in much more positive terms (Pailer 89–92; Meierdreeß 105).

2 At fifty-nine performances, *Das letzte Mittel* was one of the playwright's greatest successes in the Burgtheater. More precisely, it was the greatest success among the plays introduced during the period here under consideration (1814–67). Three of her earlier plays were even more frequently performed: *Der Wald bei Hermannstadt* (117 performances), *Ein Haus zu verkaufen* (sixty-nine performances), and *Die beschämte Eifersucht* (sixty-two performances) (Rub 282).

3 *Die Grille* appeared under the genre specification "ländliches Charakterbild" ("rural character study").

4 On Birch-Pfeiffer's work as theatre director, see Caduff.

5 The numbers are based on the list of actors in Rub 223–30. There is some imprecision in these numbers because Rub only names the year, but not the precise dates on which actors were employed. My calculations do not take into account the appearance of visiting actors, which, however, remained numerically negligible in most years.

6 In the early nineteenth century, the Burgtheater specified that the maximum annual salary for male actors be 2,500 guldens while that for female actors was set at 2,000 guldens (Wlassack 111). Similar codified differences in the remuneration of male and female actors were in place in many contemporary theatres (Kord, *Ein Blick* 36). However, in 1822, the highest salaries were actually paid to female actors: Sophie Schröder and Wilhelmine Schröder-Devrient each received 5,000 guldens, more than the 4,600 guldens paid to the male actor and stage director Siegfried Eckhardt Koch (Wlassack 157).

7 On the role of the *Regisseure*, see chapter 2.

8 On the actress in nineteenth-century German-language theatres as an important subject in contemporary debates on gender relations, see most recently Jackson.

9 Susanne Kord claims for eighteenth- and nineteenth-century German-language theatres in general that "the female audience usually outnumbered the male audience" ("das weibliche Publikum in der Regel stärker vertreten war als das männliche"; Kord, *Ein Blick* 37). For the mid-nineteenth-century Burgtheater, I am not aware of data confirming a female majority in the audience, and there is reason to be sceptical of this (see the account of the audience in ch. 2).

10 The female playwrights are Caroline Pichler, Therese von Artner, Helmina von Chézy, Johanna Franul von Weißenthurn, Emilie von Binzer (pseudonym Ernst Ritter), Amalie von Sachsen, Pauline Werner (pseudonym A.P.), Caroline Bertron, Delphine de Girardin, Marie von Ebner-Eschenbach, Charlotte Birch-Pfeiffer (sometimes under the pseudonym Willibald Waldherr).

11 Franul von Weißenthurn's success in the Burgtheater began significantly before the period on which this study focuses. In total, she had forty-eight plays in the repertoire and reached 912 performances. Based on the number of performances, only ten playwrights were more successful in the Burgtheater in the long nineteenth century: Franz Grillparzer (fifteen plays; 985 performances), Eduard von Bauernfeld (forty-eight; 1,126), August Wilhelm Schlegel (twelve; 1,143), Heinrich Laube (twenty-five; 1,149), August Wilhelm Iffland (thirty-nine; 1,329), Friedrich Schröder (fifty-four; 1,412), Eugène Scribe and his workshop (seventy; 1,690); Friedrich Schiller (nineteen; 1,911), William Shakespeare (twenty-seven; 2,177), and August Kotzebue (one hundred fourteen; 3,872). These numbers are based on Rub, who covers the period from 8 April 1776 to 1 January 1913.

12 Of course, many of the popular male writers of the period fell into neglect as well. To what extent the oblivion into which the formerly popular female playwrights have sunk can be attributed to gender directly is therefore not easy to determine.

13 Reportedly, Franul von Weißenthurn's tragedy was criticized for its baseless plot, improbable situations, and indistinct characters – in other words, for elements that are, at least on the surface, unrelated to the female author's choice of the genre (Bergmann 20).

14 This is the metric that Otto Rub applies in his statistical review of the Burgtheater.

15 This number is calculated based on the data provided in Rub.

16 The data for the Burgtheater is based on Rub; the data for the court theatre in Weimar is based on the entries in the database *Theater und Musik in Weimar 1754–1990*.

17 "An attempt should be made at least to question the concessions [in women's plays] made to patriarchal political and social conditions, and

one should try to read what is being said in spite of everything" ("[D]er Versuch sollte gemacht werden, die Zugeständnisse an patriarchalische politische und soziale Zustände zumindest anzuzweifeln, und zu lesen, was trotzdem gesagt wird"; Kord, *Ein Blick* 41).

18 For an overview of this debate, see Thurner (19–21).

19 While most female writers of the period abstained from treating political questions in either a contemporary or a historical setting, an important exception can be found in the works of Caroline Pichler (1769–1843). Pichler's novels and plays did cover Austrian political history, and this choice has sometimes been described as one of the most transgressive features of Pichler's writing (see Becker-Cantarino; Robertson).

20 For an extensive discussion of the family as an allegory of political change in a range of eighteenth-century dramatic genres well beyond the bourgeois tragedy alone, see Weiershausen. For the implicit political importance of women's domestic plays specifically, see Kord's *Ein Blick* (42). For the Vormärz tendency of discussing politics through the representation of personal relationships, see Kleinwort (169). For the problematic unwillingness to look beyond the topic of marriage in women writers, see Bohm (130).

21 Susanne Kord provides the example of Joseph von Sonnenfels's recommendation to prevent performance of the Viennese playwright Bernardon's play *Die Zauber-Insul* (*The Enchanted Island*, 1770) (Kord, "The Curtain Never Rises" 361–2).

22 This is notably the case for the struggle for women's participation in politics: the beginning of the Austrian suffrage movement is traced to the 1848 revolution (Bader-Zaar 191). On the women's movement in Austria at the end of the nineteenth century, see Anderson. The period leading up to the 1848 revolution is, at least briefly, covered in Gabriella Hauch's study *Frau Biedermeier auf den Barrikaden* (1990).

23 Of these three plays, the most successful work was the tragedy *Heinrich von Hohenstaufen, König der Deutschen*, which saw twenty-seven performances between 1813 and 1818 (Rub 43). Pichler, incidentally, is the only female playwright of the period who wrote predominately tragic works – two of her three plays performed in the Burgtheater were tragedies.

24 Grillparzer's close ties to the important female Viennese intellectuals of his time, and the impact that these interactions had on the depiction of women in Grillparzer's plays are the subject of Matthew McCarthy-Rechowicz's study *Franz Grillparzer's Dramatic Heroines* (2018).

25 Betty Paoli, for instance, makes similar arguments in her 1885 essay *Die Wandlungen der Frauenfrage* (*The Evolution of the Women's Question*). On Paoli's navigation of Wollstonecraft, see Wozonig, "Moral, Leidenschaft

und Brotberuf." There is a longer tradition of a moderate reception of Wollstonecraft in Germany, dating back to the first German translation by Johann Christoph Salzmann in 1793/4 (Botting 514–15).

26 The biographical information on Amalie von Sachsen follows Kord, *Ein Blick* (243–4).

27 On the institution of the *Majorat*, especially in the context of Hoffmann's story, see König.

28 The biographical information on Johanna Franul von Weißenthurn follows Kord, *Ein Blick* (271–2).

29 The same divide also characterizes, for instance, Bauernfeld's dramatic work.

30 In the copy used for Burgtheater productions, this line is left intact (Weißenthurn 79). This copy has been digitized by the Austrian National Library (and can be accessed through that library's online catalogue). In a copy owned by Carl Friedrich Wittmann (1839–1903), director of the theatre of Helgoland from 1876 to 1896, the same line is cut. Wittmann's copy has also been digitized by the Austrian National Library.

31 This passage is cut from the copy used in the Burgtheater (see note 30). As handwritten notes testify, the copy was used from 1855 onward. The cuts likely do not stem from the censors, but from practitioners in the theatre itself. Interestingly, in Wittmann's copy of the play (see note 30), the line is left intact, suggesting that not all contemporary theatres felt it necessary to cut the line.

32 See especially Hedwig Dohm's novel *Werde, die Du bist* (*Become Who You Are*, 1894).

33 On the exceptional status of widows both in German social history and in literature, see, for instance, Arnd Bohm's exploration of Luise Gottsched's 1745 comedy *Das Testament* (131).

34 Franul von Weißenthurn did not play the role of the widow herself. This role was left to the actress Julie Löwe. Franul von Weißenthurn filled a minor role in the play. Of course, the choice of her role may not have been made by Franul von Weißenthurn herself, but by the stage director or by the theatre secretary, Joseph Schreyvogel.

35 The baroness states: "I should not [forgive you], but the intercession of this kind woman as well as the advocate who pleads your case in my heart will likely eventually win this trial" ("Ich sollte nicht, aber die Fürsprache dieser gütigen Frau, und der Sachwalter, der in meinem Herzen für Sie spricht, werden am Ende wohl den Prozeß gewinnen"; Weißenthurn 120).

36 To be clear, her works were published in print as well, often upon their first release on stage, and then again in her *Gesammelte Dramatische Werke* (*Collected Dramatic Works*), which span an impressive twenty-three volumes.

37 This controversy is captured by Gretchen van Slyke in her English edition of Sand's novel (van Slyke), and I draw here on van Slyke's expertise.
38 See "Die Jubiläumsfeier der Charlotte Birch-Pfeiffer" (280).
39 The case for such an allegorical reading is less strong than in the case of Bauernfeld's comedy *Großjährig*. As in Bauernfeld's play, however, the generational conflict is carried out at the threshold of majority: by the fifth act, Landry refers to himself as now of full legal age ("mündig"; Birch-Pfeiffer, *Grille* 104). The term "majority" invokes social and legal categories of freedom and independence.
40 This prompt book has been digitized by the Austrian National Library (Birch-Pfeiffer, *Grille; mit theilweiser Benutzung*).
41 This appears to be an act of self-censorship because in the Burgtheater's prompt book (see note 40), this line is struck through with black ink, not with the red ink typically used by the censors.
42 That scene is the fourth of seven in the third act of this five-act comedy.
43 On the censorship of Schiller's *Die Jungfrau von Orleans* in the Burgtheater, see Yates's *Theatre in Vienna* (32).
44 *Die Geschwister von Nürnberg* premiered in May 1840, but it was not a success. After only four performances, it was taken off the repertoire a month after its first appearance on stage. Heinrich von Kleist's *Penthesilea* (1808), today perhaps the best-known German play of a woman-at-arms, was not performed in the nineteenth-century Burgtheater, but part of the audience might have known that play through print versions (although the print version was also banned; see Bachleitner, *Die literarische Zensur* 314–16). On women-at-arms in German-language literature, see Koser.
45 Benedix's wording in the stage directions is slightly ambiguous. It is not entirely clear whether he means that the actor or the actress must be well versed in fencing, but the latter appears more likely because the stage directions here focus on the behaviour of the actress.
46 To be sure, Honau's claims concerning the hierarchy between men and women are not entirely consistent. In a contradictory – or at least paradoxical – statement, he claims that women's position "is not a subordinate one [...] just because it is in some respect the second position" ("Diese Stelle ist darum noch keine untergeordnete [...], weil sie in mancher Beziehung die zweite ist"; Benedix 44).
47 *The Taming of the Shrew* premiered in the Burgtheater in Deinhardstein's translation (as *Die Widerspenstige*) in 1838. From then until 1912, it was performed 158 times, which made it Shakespeare's second-most popular comedy in the nineteenth-century Burgtheater (Rub 67). Only *Much Ado About Nothing* (in German, *Viel Lärm um nichts*) was slightly more popular (163 performances across three different translations between 1793 and 1901; Rub 80).

48 The term and motif of being "großjährig" (Bauernfeld, *Gesammelte Schriften* 3: 194) thus appears here once more in Bauernfeld's dramatic work (see ch. 4).

49 The popularity of *Maria Stuart* extended beyond the performance of Schiller's tragedy itself to plays that dealt with the same subject matter, notably Charlotte Birch-Pfeiffer's historical drama *Elisabeth*. On the reception of Schiller's *Maria Stuart*, see also *The Queen's Two Bodies*, edited by Elena Agazzi, Gesa Dane, and Gaby Pailer.

50 In a review for Moritz Gottlieb Saphir's newspaper *Der Humorist*, the literary references in *Bürgerlich* are denounced as a "bad German habit" ("deutsche Unart"; Rdtz 398).

51 The reception documents for this play are sparse, and to my knowledge, do not comment on this point.

52 Steiner stresses the search for a "middle ground" as a defining feature of Bauernfeld's work (183). Incidentally, the literary historian Klaus Ehlert analysed German literature of the mid–nineteenth century more broadly under the rubric of a "literary *juste milieu*" ("literarischen Juste-milieu"; 300).

6. The Drama of National and Regional Belonging

1 On the history of Austria's liberalism and its increasing embrace of nationalism in the second half of the nineteenth century, see Judson, *Exclusive Revolutionaries*. More recently, Jonathan Kwan (2013) argued that liberalism's ties to German nationalism were, at least in middle of the nineteenth century, less pronounced than previously assumed. The full embrace of a German nationalism came, Kwan argues, only in the final decades of the nineteenth century, when liberalism was already on the retreat. The readings in this chapter, however, suggest that nationalism was an important topic in the middle decades of the nineteenth century, even if its manifestations varied significantly.

2 As noted in chapter 2, Rettich had risen to fame, in part, for her work as lead actress in Friedrich Halm's major plays, from his 1835 *Griseldis* to his 1854 *Der Fechter von Ravenna* (*The Swordsman of Ravenna*).

3 Paoli's statements, incidentally, found a remarkable and troubling echo in Heinz Kindermann's 1939 essay *Der Lebensraum des Burgtheaters* (*The Sphere of the Burgtheater*), in which Kindermann also emphasizes the Burgtheater's important role in creating, among the audience, a sense of belonging to the German nation (5–6; see also Kindermann, *Das Burgtheater* 12).

4 When Paoli writes of the "geistigen Leben des deutschen Volkes," the adjective "geistig" in conjunction with the qualifier "deutsch" can invoke

an emphatic notion of a "German spirit" or slightly less charged ideas of a "German mind" or even a "German esprit."

5 This line is repeated with minimal variation shortly afterwards (Halm, *Fechter* 117).

6 Grillparzer's representation of the Habsburg Empire has been the subject of an extensive body of scholarship, and there is some disagreement over the extent to which Grillparzer's celebration of the empire – also as an alternative to the rise of German nationalism – is accompanied by a critical awareness of the empire's shortcomings. The debate is summarized in Roe 76–112.

7 The iconic status that Grillparzer's plays earned in the twentieth century is perhaps best illustrated by the fact that the Burgtheater celebrated its reopening after the Second World War (in 1955) with a new production of *König Ottokar*.

8 Sachs is also a major figure in the history of German drama. His 208 plays with many worldly (rather than spiritual) subjects contributed to the secularization of German theatre (Beutin 82–3). However, Sachs's contributions to drama are not the focus of Deinhardstein's play.

9 The speech of the emperor's "First Servant" ("Erster Kämmerling") at the opening of Act 3 is a case in point (Deinhardstein 66–7).

10 Deinhardstein was apparently so thoroughly attuned to the work of the censors that, starting in 1829, he began working for the censorship office himself.

11 Bauernfeld's historical drama *Franz von Sickingen*, in which Luther appears as a *deus ex machina* to solve the conflict between the rebellious knight Franz von Sickingen and the powerful Archbishop of Trier, Richard von Greifenklau, saw nine performances between February and October 1850 (Rub 77). As Emperor Franz Joseph began to walk back the liberties granted in the immediate aftermath of the 1848 revolution, the play was put aside (Bauernfeld, *Gesammelte Schriften* 6: 223).

12 With the use of the parable, Emperor Maximilian tries to establish that Hans Sachs is the rightful husband of the rich goldsmith's daughter (Deinhardstein 116–18). In Deinhardstein's drama, the parable is thus not used in the context of a debate over religion, as is the case in Lessing's play.

13 As a main subject, Emperor Maximilian seems to have attracted relatively little attention. While Deinhardstein's next play, *Erzherzog Maximilians Brautzug* (*Archduke Maximilian's Wedding*, which premiered in the Burgtheater in 1829) was dedicated to the Habsburg emperor, it saw only seven performances (Rub 59).

14 As I have discussed elsewhere, the Burgtheater playwright Friedrich Halm based his pen name (his real name was Eligius von Münch-Bellinghausen)

on one of the contemporary novels on the Thirty Years' War, Karl Hold's *Anton Halm und sein Schützling* (1826; see Wagner and Slipp).

15 Kleist's *Prinz Friedrich* was first performed in the Burgtheater in 1821, under the title *Die Schlacht bei Fehrbellin* (*The Battle at Fehrbellin*). The censors had rejected the original main title; only in 1860 did the Burgtheater start to advertise the play as *Prinz v. Homburg*. Between 1821 and 1912, Kleist's drama saw forty-four performances in the Burgtheater (Rub 51).

16 The fact that, in Bauernfeld's play, the prince embodies the highest level of authority, and not the middleman, as in other plays of the period, including Goethe's *Götz* and Bauernfeld's own *Franz von Sickingen*, is of secondary importance. What matters more is the structural differentiation between two levels of authority and the associated commitment to the higher level of authority at the expense of the lower level.

17 Otherwise, the two allegories are rather different. In Grillparzer's play, the youth Austria is the happy medium between the child Italy and the man Germany; in Bauernfeld's play, the healthy youth Germany is poised to overcome the sickly "Roman Europe" ("römischen Europa"; Bauernfeld, *Krieger* 88).

18 The antisemitism in the discussion of Sonnenfels's influence recurs, even more clearly, in Heinz Kindermann's 1939 essay *Der Lebensraum*. In Kindermann's narrative, the "baptized Jew" ("getauft[e] Jud[e]," 8) Sonnenfels is critically depicted as being engaged in a "battle against everything grounded in the *Volk*" ("Kampf gegen alles Volksverbundene," 8; see also Kindermann, *Das Burgtheater* 25–8).

19 The comparison of the Burgtheater to a church or temple appears elsewhere as well. Bauernfeld, for instance, uses a similar metaphor in his discussion of *Versprechen* – albeit with some irony and with considerably more respect for Baumann's play: "With Baumann's in its own way rather excellent *Versprechen hinterm Herd*, the temple [i.e., the Burgtheater] later lost its chastity" ("Mit dem an und für sich vortrefflichen *Versprechen hinterm Herd* hatte der Tempel in der Folge seine Keuschheit eingebüßt"; Bauernfeld, *Gesammelte Schriften* 12: 166).

20 While song was generally shunned in the Burgtheater, music more broadly appears to have been occasionally present on that stage in the mid-nineteenth century. Heinrich Laube's 1851 production of Shakespeare's *Coriolanus*, for instance, was supplemented by music by Beethoven (Wlassack 242) – presumably the *Coriolan Overture* (1807), originally written not for Shakespeare's play, but for Heinrich Joseph von Collin's *Coriolan*, which had premiered in the Burgtheater in 1802 (Collin [1772–1811] was a successful Burgtheater playwright in the early years of the nineteenth century).

21 The average share of originally German-language plays is even lower, of course, if we do not include the peak years of 1845–50.

22 Otto Holzapfel writes: "national was, at the time, the fashionable term for regional, local [*heimatlichen*] references" ("National war damals das Mode-Stichwort fur den regionalen, heimatlichen Bezug"; 161).

23 On the difficulty of substantiating and defining the term *Burgtheaterdeutsch*, see Peter.

24 Hess acknowledges the problematic depiction of Jews in Mosenthal's play, but he urges readers nevertheless to take the play's philosemitism seriously as the positive sentiment that it is on the surface.

25 Because Dietrichstein was no longer in charge of the Burgtheater at this time, he would not have been authorized to reject the play. Mosenthal himself corroborates that Laube advocated for the production in the Burgtheater, but Mosenthal, too, fails to mention who precisely spoke out against the play (Mosenthal, "Skizze" 136). In any case, Hess's claim that *Deborah* was rejected by the Burgtheater director "who refused to even consider producing what he dismissed as Mosenthal's *Judenstück* until 1864" (Hess 30) appears to be wrong or, at least, imprecise.

26 Somewhat hyperbolically, the debate over Birch-Pfeiffer's appropriation of Auerbach's story has been called the most important discussion in Germany prior to the revolution of 1848 (Aurnhammer and Detering 190).

27 In a note to the printed edition, Birch-Pfeiffer specifies: "The roles of Lorle, of Lindenwirth [Lorle's father], of Christoph Balders [a local farmer], and Bärbel [Lindenwirth's cousin – another character from the village] will definitely have to be spoken in dialect, which is, in part, already suggested [in the script]. The main aspect of the Swabian dialect, however, always remains: every ['s' in an] 'st' has to be pronounced as an 'sch' [compare English 'sh,' as in 'shoe'] [...], but the same is not done for the 's' without 't'; this 's' always remains the High German 's' [examples include sounds like 'glass' in English] [...]. At the end of words that terminate in 'en,' the 'n' always has to be dropped: for example 'haben' [to have] is pronounced 'habe,' 'leben' [to live] is pronounced 'lebe,' 'geben' [to give] is pronounced 'gebe,' etc." ("Die Rollen des Lorle, Lindenwirths, Christoph Balders und der Bärbel müssen durchaus im Dialect gesprochen werden, der theilweise schon angedeutet ist. Die Hauptsache im schwäbischen Dialect aber bleibt immer: daß jedes st – wie sch – ausgesprochen wird, wie ischt, – bischt – hascht – etc. – nie aber dem S – ohne T – das ch beigesetzt werden, das bleibt immer das hochdeutsche: S wie z.B. Bas – Glas – naß – Roß – blaß – etc. Am Schluß der Worte die mit: en – endigen, ist stets das N – wegzulassen, z.B. haben – heißt habe – leben: lebe – geben: gebe etc."; Birch-Pfeiffer, *Dorf* 103.)

28 While the precise location would not have been of great concern to the Viennese audience, one might think of Karlsruhe, the historical capital of the Grand Duchy of Baden.

29 Of course, in Baumann's play, the harmony between the urban and rural is partially possible because there is no mention of a marriage between the urban outsider and a village person. But this limitation is not explicitly thematized as such in Baumann's play: for all that the play tells us, the initial assumption of a deep divide between country and town turns out to be unfounded.

Conclusion: The Mid-Nineteenth-Century Burgtheater as a Case Study

1 The upheaval of 1848 constitutes, of course, a significant exception.

2 Jelinek's *Burgtheater* premiered in Bonn in 1985; its first performance in Austria occurred in 2005, in Graz's Theater im Bahnhof (see Fiddler 229–30). For an overview of the Burgtheater's productions between 1976 and 2009, see Fundulus.

3 Christoph Schlingensief's *Area 7* was performed in January 2006 (Schlingensief returned to the Burgtheater in 2009 with the show *Mea Culpa*). The Hermann Nitsch performance of 19 November 2005 ran under the title *Das Orgien-Mysterien Theater. 122. Aktion*. The concert by *Die Toten Hosen* was performed on 1 and 2 September 2005, under the title *Nur zu Besuch: Unplugged im Wiener Burgtheater*.

4 For the Parisian theatre, see *Registres de la Comédie-Française*. For the court theatre in Weimar, see *Theater und Musik in Weimar 1754–1990*. The theatre playbills have also been digitized for Vienna's court opera alongside those of the Burgtheater ("Theaterzettel" [1787–1898]). See also the digitized playbills for the Hoftheater Karlsruhe on the website *5 Titel*.

5 On the history and politics of publishing houses of radically democratic German publishers in the nineteenth century, see Sangmeister.

Works Cited

9 Titel in Theaterzettel [9 Titles in Playbills]. Badische Landes-Bibliothek, https://digital.blb-karlsruhe.de/blb/theaterzettel/topic/view/2949538. Accessed 4 Mar. 2023.

Agazzi, Elena, et al., editors. *The Queen's Two Bodies: Maria Stuart und Elisabeth I. von Schiller bis Jelinek*, special issue of *Jahrbuch für internationale Germanistik*, series A, vol. 143, 2021.

Alewyn, Richard. *Probleme und Gestalten: Essays*. Insel-Verlag, 1974.

Anderson, Harriet. *Utopian Feminism: Women's Movements in Fin-de-Siècle Vienna*. Yale UP, 1992.

Anschütz, Heinrich. *Erinnerungen aus dessen Leben und Wirken, nach eigenhändigen Aufzeichnungen und mündlichen Mittheilungen*. Leopold Sommer, 1866.

Aurnhammer, Achim, and Nicolas Detering. "Berthold Auerbachs *Frau Professorin*: Revisionen und Rezeptionen von Charlotte Birch-Pfeiffer bis Gottfried Keller." *Berthold Auerbach (1812–1882): Werk und Wirkung*, edited by Jesko Reiling, Universitätsverlag Winter, 2012, pp. 173–220.

Bachleitner, Norbert. "Die Dialektik von Gehorsam und Aufbegehren im Drama und auf den Bühnen des späten 18. Jahrhunderts." *The Drama of Obedience*, special issue of *Oxford German Studies*, edited by Martin Wagner and Elystan Griffiths, vol. 50, no. 3, 2021, pp. 285–304. *Taylor & Francis Online*, https://doi.org/10.1080/00787191.2021.1958569.

– *Die literarische Zensur in Österreich von 1751 bis 1848*. Böhlau, 2017.

Bader-Zaar, Brigitta. "Gaining the Vote in a World in Transition: Female Suffrage in Austria." *The Struggle for Female Suffrage in Europe: Voting to Become Citizens*, edited by Blanca Rodríguez-Ruiz and Ruth Rubio-Marín, Brill, 2012, pp. 191–206.

Bakhtin, Mikhail. *Problems of Dostoevsky's Poetics*, edited and translated by Caryl Emerson. U of Minnesota P, 1984.

Bauernfeld, Eduard von. *Ein deutscher Krieger: Schauspiel in drei Aufzügen*. Anton Doll's Enkel, 1847.

– *Gesammelte Schriften*. Wilhelm Braumüller, 1871–3. 12 vols.

Baumann, Alexander. *Die beiden Ärzte: Original-Lustspiel in drei Aufzügen. Beiträge für das deutsche Theater*, Ghelen, 1849, pp. 103–66.

– *Das Versprechen hinterm Herd: Eine Scene aus den österreichischen Alpen mit Nationalgesängen*. 2nd ed., Wallishausser, 1872.

Becker-Cantarino, Barbara. "Caroline Pichler und die Frauendichtung." *Australian Women Writers*, special issue of *Modern Austrian Literature*, vol. 12, nos. 3/4, 1979, pp. 1–23. EBSCOhost Academic Search Complete.

Benedix, Roderich. *Doctor Wespe: Lustspiel in 5 Acten*. Beckeresche Buchhandlung, 1844.

Bergmann, J.H. *Jahrbuch der Zeitgeschichte: Eine Uebersicht der merkwürdigsten neuesten Ereignisse in Natur, Leben, Staat, Kirche, Wissenschaft und Kunst*. Vol. 1, pt. 1, J.G. Calve, 1820.

Bernhard, Thomas. *Heldenplatz*. Suhrkamp, 1995.

Berry, Mark. "Richard Wagner and the Politics of Music-Drama." *The Historical Journal*, vol. 47, no. 3, Sept. 2004, pp. 663–83. *Cambridge Core*, https://doi.org/10.1017/S0018246X04003905.

Bettelheim-Gabillon, Helene. "Erinnerungen von Louise Gräfin Schönfeldt-Neumann: Fortsetzung." *Österreichische Rundschau*, vol. 5, 1905–6, pp. 167–80.

Beutin, Wolfgang. "Humanismus und Reformation." Beutin et al., *Deutsche Literaturgeschichte*, pp. 59–102.

Beutin, Wolfgang, et al., editors. *Deutsche Literaturgeschichte: Von den Anfängen bis zur Gegenwart*. 9th ed., Metzler, 2019.

"Bevölkerung." *Wien Geschichte Wiki*, Stadt Wien, 21 Jan. 2021, https://www.geschichtewiki.wien.gv.at/Bev%C3%B6lkerung.

Birch-Pfeiffer, Charlotte. *Dorf und Stadt: Schauspiel in zwei Abtheilungen und fünf Akten mit freier Benutzung der Auerbachischen Erzählung: "Die Frau Professorin."* Sturm und Koppe, 1847.

– *Gesammelte dramatische Werke*. Philipp Reclam, 1863–80.

– *Die Grille: Ländliches Charakterbild in fünf Akten*. Gubitz, 1856.

– *Die Grille. Ländliches Charakterbild in fünf Akten; mit theilweiser Benutzung einer Erzählung von G. Sand*. Gubitz, 1856. Austrian National Library, https://digital.onb.ac.at/OnbViewer/viewer.faces?doc=ABO_%2BZ252123108.

Blickle, Peter. *Heimat: A Critical Theory of the German Idea of Homeland*. Camden House, 2002.

Boa, Elizabeth, and Rachel Palfreyman. *Heimat: A German Dream: Regional Loyalties and National Identity in German Culture, 1890–1990*. Oxford UP, 2000.

Bohm, Arnd. "Authority and Authorship in Luise Adelgunde Gottsched's *Das Testament*." *Lessing Yearbook*, vol. 18, 1986, pp. 129–40.

Booth, Michael R. "Nineteenth-Century Theatre." Brown, *Oxford Illustrated History*, pp. 299–340.

Böttcher, Philipp. *Gustav Freytag – Konstellationen des Realismus*. De Gruyter, 2018.

Botting, Eileen Hunt. "Wollstonecraft in Europe, 1792–1904: A Revisionist Reception History." *History of European Ideas*, vol. 39, no. 4, 2013, pp. 503–27. *Taylor & Francis Online*, https://doi.org/10.1080/01916599.2012.725668.

Brockmann, Stephen. *Nuremberg: The Imaginary Capital*. Camden House, 2006.

Brown, John Russell, editor. *The Oxford Illustrated History of Theatre*. Oxford UP, 1995.

Brümmer, Franz. *Deutsches Dichter-Lexikon*. Verlag der Krüll'schen Buchhandlung, 1876.

"Das Burgtheaterpublikum." *Recensionen und Mittheilungen über Theater und Musik*, vol. 7, no. 11, 17 Mar. 1861, pp. 161–2.

"Das Burgtheaterpublikum II." *Recensionen und Mittheilungen über Theater und Musik*, vol. 7, no. 12, 24 Mar. 1861, pp. 177–8.

"Burgtheater: Rekordeinnahmen und Steigerung der Besucherzahl." *Der Standard*, 16 Feb. 2006, https://www.derstandard.at/story/2334378/burgtheater-rekordeinnahmen-und-steigerung-der-besucherzahl.

Caduff, Corina. "Charlotte Birch-Pfeiffer: Direktorin des Zürcher Theaters von 1837 bis 1843." *Und schrieb und schrieb wie ein Tiger aus dem Busch: Über Schriftstellerinnen in der deutschsprachigen Schweiz*, edited by Elizabeth Ryter et al., Limmat, 1994.

Carlson, Marvin. *The Haunted Stage: The Theatre as Memory Machine*. U of Michigan P, 2001.

Cavell, Stanley. *Must We Mean What We Say? A Book of Essays*. Updated ed., Cambridge UP, 2002.

Cossel, Friederike von. *Entscheidungsfindung im Kulturbetrieb am Beispiel der Spielplangestaltung im Theater*. Rainer Hampp, 2011.

Costenoble, Carl Ludwig. *Aus dem Burgtheater: 1818–1837. Tagebuchblätter*. Carl Konegen, 1889.

Critchley, Simon. *Tragedy, the Greeks, and Us*. Vintage, 2020.

Deinhardstein, Johann Ludwig. *Hans Sachs: Dramatisches Gedicht in vier Acten*. Carl Armbruster, 1829.

Dermutz, Klaus. *Das Burgtheater und die Wiener Identität: Kontinuität und Krisen 1888–2009*. Bibliothek der Provinz, 2010.

Devrient, Eduard. *Geschichte der deutschen Schauspielkunst*. I.I. Weber, 1848–74. 5 vols.

Dietrich, Margret. *Das Burgtheater und sein Publikum*. Verlag der Österreichischen Akademie der Wissenschaften, 1976. 2 vols.

Dodd, William. "Impossible Worlds: What Happens in *King Lear*, Act 1, Scene 1?" *Shakespeare Quarterly*, vol. 50, no. 4, winter 1999, pp. 477–507. *Oxford Academic*, https://doi.org/10.2307/2902281.

Dohm, Hedwig. *Werde, die Du bist*. Schottlaender, 1894.

D.V. "Über die Aufführung des dramatischen Gedichtes 'Hans Sachs' auf der Hamburger-Bühne." *Hans Sachs: Dramatisches Gedicht in vier Acten*, by Johann Ludwig Deinhardstein, Armbrusters Verlagsbuchhandlung, 1829, pp. 127–40.

Ehlert, Klaus. "Realismus und Gründerzeit." Beutin et al., *Deutsche Literaturgeschichte*, pp. 295–343.

Engländer, Siegmund. "Die Aufführung der Maria Magdalena von Hebbel auf dem Burgtheater zu Wien im Mai 1848." *Jahrbücher für dramatische Kunst und Literatur*. Edited by H.Th. Rötscher, vol. 2, Trowitzsch, 1848, pp. 195–9.

Fiddler, Allyson. "Jelinek, *Burgtheater*." *Landmarks in German Comedy*, edited by Peter Hutchinson, Peter Lang, 2006, pp. 227–42.

Foucault, Michel. *Discipline and Punish: The Birth of the Prison*. Translated by Alan Sheridan, Vintage, 1995.

Franul von Weißenthurn, Johanna. Das letzte Mittel: Lustspiel in vier Aufzügen. Kühling, 1850. Austrian National Library, https://digital.onb.ac.at/OnbViewer/viewer.faces?doc=ABO_%2BZ251380201.

– Das letzte Mittel: Lustspiel in vier Aufzügen. (Aufgeführt auf dem k.k. Hoftheather.) Wallishausser, 1826. Austrian National Library, https://digital.onb.ac.at/OnbViewer/viewer.faces?doc=ABO_%2BZ251151704.

Frederiksen, Elke. *Die Frauenfrage in Deutschland 1865–1915*. Philipp Reclam, 1981.

Freytag, Gustav. *Bilder aus der deutschen Vergangenheit*. Vol. 1, S. Hirzel, 1859.

– *Doktor Luther: Eine Schilderung*. S. Hirzel, 1883.

– *Soll und Haben: Roman in sechs Büchern*. Manuscriptum, 2002.

– *Die Technik des Dramas*. S. Hirzel, 1863.

Fundulus, Katharina, editor. *Burgtheater 1967–2009: Aufführungen und Besetzungen*. Böhlau, 2012.

F.W. "K.K. Hoftheater nächst der Burg." *Wiener-Moden-Zeitung und Zeitschrift für Kunst, schöne Literatur und Theater*, vol. 33, 16 Feb. 1843, pp. 261–3.

Goodlad, J.S.R. *A Sociology of Popular Drama*. Heinemann, 1971.

Griffiths, Elystan. *The Shepherd, the Volk, and the Middle Class: Transformations of Pastoral in German-Language Writing, 1750–1850*. Camden House, 2020.

Grillparzer, Franz. *Dramen, 1817–1828*, edited by Helmut Bachmaier, Deutscher Klassiker Verlag, 1986.

– *Selbstbiographie 1791–1836*. J.G. Cotta, 1872. Vol. 10 of Sämtliche Werke.

– *Ein treuer Diener seines Herrn: Trauerspiel in fünf Aufzügen*. Wallishausser, 1830.

Großegger, Elisabeth. "Theater als Medium der Utopie: Lieto fine und Wiener Schluss." *Mythos – Paradies – Translation: Kulturwissenschaftliche Perspektiven*, edited by Daniel Graziadei et al., Transcript Verlag, 2018, pp. 227–37.

Gutzkow, Karl. *Reiseeindrücke aus Deutschland, der Schweiz, Holland und Italien (1832–1873)*. Hermann Costenoble, 1873.

Haass, Günther. "Theater am großherzoglichen Hof in Karlsruhe 1806–1846." *Karlsruher Theatergeschichte: Vom Hoftheater zum Staatstheater*, edited by Günther Haass et al, Springer-Verlag, 1982, pp. 28–43.

Hadamowsky, Franz. *Wien, Theatergeschichte*: Von den Anfängen bis zum Ende des Ersten Weltkriegs. Dachs Verlag, 1994.

Halm, Friedrich. *Der Fechter von Ravenna: Trauerspiel in fünf Akten*. Carl Gerold's Sohn, 1857.

– *Griselda: A Dramatic Poem in Five Acts*. Translated by Ralph A. Anstruther, Black and Armstrong, 1840.

– *Werke*. Carl Gerold's Sohn, 1856–1877. 12 vols.

Hauch, Gabriella. *Frau Biedermeier auf den Barrikaden: Frauenleben in der Wiener Revolution 1848*. Verlag für Gesellschaftskritik, 1990.

Heady, Katy. *Literature and Censorship in Restoration Germany: Repression and Rhetoric*. Camden House, 2009.

Hebbel, Friedrich. "Das Versprechen hinterm Herd im Burgtheater." *Sämtliche Werke. Elfter Band: Charakteristiken, Kritiken*, Hoffmann und Campe, 1867.

Hegel, Georg Wilhelm Friedrich. *Lectures on the Philosophy of World History. Introduction: Reason in History*. Translated by H.B. Nisbet, Cambridge UP, 1980.

Heindl, Waltraud. *Gehorsame Rebellen: Bürokratie und Beamte in Österreich. Band 1, 1780–1848*. 2nd ed., Böhlau, 2013.

Hellbach, Rafael. *Die Kunst Schauspieler zu werden*. Hartleben, 1869.

Hes, Else. *Charlotte Birch-Pfeiffer als Dramatikerin: Ein Beitrag zur Theatergeschichte des 19. Jahrhunderts*. Metzler, 1914.

Hess, Jonathan M., "Shylock's Daughters: Philosemitism, Popular Culture, and the Liberal Imagination." *Transversal: Journal for Jewish Studies*, vol. 13, no. 1, 2015, pp. 28–43.

Hettner, Hermann. *Das moderne Drama: Aesthetische Untersuchungen*. Friedrich Vieweg und Sohn, 1852.

Holland, Peter, and Michael Patterson. "Eighteenth-Century Theatre." Brown, *Oxford Illustrated History*, pp. 255–98.

Holzapfel, Otto. "Anmerkungen zur Raindinger Handschrift." *Lied und populäre Kultur / Song and Popular Culture*, vol. 45, 2000, pp. 155–65. *JSTOR*, https://doi.org/10.2307/849579.

Horner, Emil. *Bauernfeld*. E.A. Seemann, 1900.

Jackson, S.E. *The Problem of the Actress in Modern German Theater and Thought*. Camden House, 2021.

"Jahresauswahl." *ANNO: Historische österreichische Zeitungen und Zeitschriften*. Austrian National Library, 2022, https://anno.onb.ac.at/cgi-content/anno?aid=wtz.

Jelinek, Elfriede. *Burgtheater: Posse mit Gesang. Theaterstück*. Rowohlt Taschenbuch, 1992.

"Die Jubiläumsfeier der Charlotte Birch-Pfeiffer in Berlin." *Der Sammler*, no. 70, 1863, p. 280.

Judson, Pieter M. *Exclusive Revolutionaries: Liberal Politics, Social Experience, and National Identity in the Austrian Empire, 1848–1914*. U of Michigan P, 1996.

– *The Habsburg Empire: A New History*. Harvard UP, 2016.

Kahn, Lothar. "Moritz Gottlieb Saphir." *The Leo Baeck Institute Year Book*, vol. 20, no. 1, Jan. 1975, pp. 247–57. *Oxford Academic*, https://doi.org/10.1093/leobaeck/20.1.247.

Kann, Robert A. *A History of the Habsburg Empire, 1526–1918*. U of California P, 1980.

Keller, Gottfried. *Der grüne Heinrich: Zweite Fassung*. Diogenes, 1993.

Kind, Roswitha. "Die Luftschifferin." *Cyanen: Taschenbuch für 1839*. Pautsch, 1839, pp. 183–6.

Kindermann, Heinz. *Das Burgtheater: Erbe und Sendung eines Nationaltheaters*. 2nd ed., Wiener Verlag, 1944.

– *Der Lebensraum des Burgtheaters*. Adolf Luser, 1939.

– "Notwendigkeit und Aufgaben der Spielplanforschung." *Maske und Kothurn*, vol. 1, nos. 1–2, June 1955, pp. 156–66. *V&R eLibrary*, https://doi.org/10.7767/muk.1955.1.12.156.

Kleinwort, Malte. "Ohnmächtige in Adalbert Stiftlers 'Der Condor.'" *Gespenster des Wissens*, edited by Ute Holl et al., Diaphanes, 2017, pp. 163–70.

Klingenberg, Gerhard. *Das gefesselte Burgtheater: 1776 bis in unsere Tage*. Molden, 2003.

Koll, Alfred. "Wiener Theatererfolge im Vormärz." *Wiener Theater des Biedermeier und Vormärz: Ausstellungs-Katalog*, edited by Josef Mayerhöfer, Österreichisches Theatermuseum, 1978, pp. 40–58.

"Komparatistik Wien Zensurdatenbank." *Zensur Online*. Universität Wien, https://zensur.univie.ac.at/. Accessed 4 Mar. 2023.

König, Peter. "Der poetische Charakter des Rechts: *Das Majorat* von E.T.A. Hoffmann." *Internationales Archiv für Sozialgeschichte der deutschen Literatur*, vol. 31, no. 2, Dec. 2006, pp. 203–17. *De Gruyter*, https://doi.org/10.1515/IASL.2006.2.203.

Kord, Susanne. *Ein Blick hinter die Kulissen: Deutschsprachige Dramatikerinnen im 18. und 19. Jahrhundert*. Metzler, 1992.

– "The Curtain Never Rises: Femininity and Theater Censorship in Eighteenth- and Nineteenth-Century Germany." *The German Quarterly*, vol. 70, no. 4, autumn 1997, pp. 358–75. *JSTOR*, https://doi.org/10.2307/408069.

– *Sich einen Namen machen: Anonymität und weibliche Autorschaft, 1700–1900*. Metzler, 1996.

Koschorke, Albrecht. *Wahrheit und Erfindung: Grundzüge einer allgemeinen Erzähltheorie*. S. Fischer, 2012.

Koselleck, Reinhart. *Kritik und Krise: Eine Studie zur Pathogenese der bürgerlichen Welt*. Suhrkamp, 1973.

Koser, Julie. *Armed Ambiguity: Women Warriors in German Literature and Culture in the Age of Goethe*. Northwestern UP, 2016.

Kwan, Jonathan. *Liberalism and the Habsburg Monarchy, 1861–1895*. Palgrave Macmillan, 2013.

Lasher-Schlitt, Dorothy. "Josef Schreyvogel, Grillparzer's 'väterlicher Freund.'" *The Germanic Review: Literature, Culture, Theory*, vol. 21, no. 4, 1946, pp. 268–305. *Taylor & Francis Online*, https://doi.org/10.1080/19306962.1946.11786290.

Laube, Heinrich. *Das Burgtheater: Ein Beitrag zur Deutschen Theater-Geschichte*. Verlagsbuchhandlung von J.J. Weber, 1868.

– *Das norddeutsche Theater: Ein neuer Beitrag zur deutschen Theatergeschichte*. J.J. Weber, 1872.

Lembert, J.W. *Der Ehrgeiz in der Küche: Posse in einem Aufzug nach Scribe und Mazeres*. Reclam, 1874.

Lewinsky, Josef. *Gedenkrede auf Betty Paoli*. Verein der Schriftstellerinnen und Künstlerinnen in Wien, 1895.

Link, Dorothea. *The National Court Theatre in Mozart's Vienna: Sources and Documents 1783–1792*. Oxford UP, 1998.

Lorenz, Dagmar C.G. *Grillparzer, Dichter des sozialen Konflikts*. Böhlau, 1986.

Lothar, Rudolph. *Das Wiener Burgtheater*. E.A. Seemann, 1899.

McCarthy Rechowicz, Matthew. *Franz Grillparzer's Dramatic Heroines: Theatre and Women's Emancipation in Nineteenth-Century Austria*. Legenda, 2018.

Meierdreeß, Viviane Jasmin. "Frauenfiguren und Weiblichkeit im Spannungsfeld zwischen Restauration und Vormärz in Charlotte Birch-Pfeiffers *Elisabeth von England*." Agazzi et al., *The Queen's Two Bodies*, pp. 101–12.

Mosenthal, Samuel Hermann. *Deborah: Volks-Schauspiel in vier Akten*. 2nd ed., Gustav Heckenast, 1850.

– "Eine Skizze meines Lebens: Teil 2." *Die Gegenwart*, vol. 6, no. 35, 29 Aug. 1874, pp. 134–6.

Mouffe, Chantal. "The Role of Theatre in the Struggle against Neoliberal Hegemony." *Why Theatre?*, edited by Kaatje de Geest, Carmen Hornbostel, and Milo Rau, Verbrecher Verlag, 2020, pp. 192–4.

Österreichisches Biographisches Lexikon, edited by Ernst Bruckmüller and Christine Gruber, Verlag der Österreichischen Akademie der Wissenschaften, 2009–. https://www.biographien.ac.at.

Pailer, Gaby. "Variations of 'Elizabeth' from French Classicism to Hollywood Cinema." Agazzi et al., *The Queen's Two Bodies*, pp. 81–100.

Paoli, Betty. *Grillparzer und seine Werke*. J.G. Cotta, 1875.

– *Julie Rettich: Ein Lebens- und Charakterbild*. Leopold Sommer, 1866.

Patten, Alan. *Hegel's Idea of Freedom*. Oxford UP, 1999.

Peter, Birgit. "Mythos Burgtheaterdeutsch: Die Konstruktion einer Sprache, einer Nation, eines Nationaltheaters." *Maske und Kothurn*, vol. 50, no. 2, June 2004, pp. 15–27. https://doi.org/10.7767/muk.2004.50.2.15.

Petrarch. "A Fable of Wifely Obedience and Devotion." *A Chaucer Handbook*, edited by Robert Dudley French, 2nd ed., Widener, 1947, pp. 291–311.

Pfister, Manfred. *Das Drama: Theorie und Analyse*. 11th ed., Wilhelm Fink, 2001.

Pilger, Andreas. "Nationalsozialistische Steuerung und 'Irritationen' der Literaturwissenschaft." *Literaturwissenschaft und Nationalsozialismus*, edited by Holger Dainat and Lutz Danneberg, Max Niemeyer, 2003, pp. 107–26.

"Premierenübersicht der Saison 2020/21." Burgtheater, https://www.burgtheater.at/en/premieren202021. Accessed 4 Mar. 2023.

Pritchett, Rinske van Stipriaan. *The Art of Comedy and Social Critique in Nineteenth-Century Germany: Charlotte Birch-Pfeiffer (1800–1868)*. Peter Lang, 2005.

Prutti, Brigitte. "Funny Games: Semiotischer Sündenfall und ästhetische Restauration in Grillparzers Trauerspiel *Ein treuer Diener seines Herrn*." *Deutsche Vierteljahresschrift für Literaturwissenschaft und Geistesgeschichte*, vol. 81, no. 3, Sept. 2007, pp. 369–404. *Springer Link*, https://doi.org/10.1007/BF03374636.

Rady, Martyn C. *The Habsburgs: To Rule the World*. Basic Books, 2020.

Rancière, Jacques. *The Politics of Aesthetics: The Distribution of the Sensible*. Translated by Gabriel Rockhill, Continuum, 2004.

Raupach, Ernst. *Der Müller und sein Kind: Volksdrama in fünf Aufzügen*. Hoffmann und Campe, 1835.

Rdtz [?], L. "K.K. Hofburgtheater." *Der Humorist*, vol. 9, no. 100, 26 Apr. 1845, p. 398.

Registres de la Comédie-Française. Comédie-Française, NYU, MIT, Université Paris Nanterre, Université de Rouen, Sorbonne Université, University of Victoria, https://www.cfregisters.org/. Accessed 4 Mar. 2023.

Reichert, Herbert W. "The Characterization of Bancbanus in Grillparzer's *Ein treuer Diener seines Herrn*." *Studies in Philology*, vol. 46, no. 1, Jan. 1949, pp. 70–8.

Reitani, Luigi. "Griseldis am Artus-Hof. Friedrich Halm: *Griseldis: Ein dramatisches Gedicht* (1835/37)." *Die deutsche Griselda: Transformationen einer literarischen Figuration von Boccaccio bis zur Moderne*, edited by Achim Aurnhammer and Hans-Jochen Schiewer, De Gruyter, 2010, pp. 223–8.

Robanus, Adrian. "*Der Goldne Spiegel*: Zoopolitik und 'gehorsame Handlungsmacht' im Staatsroman." *Seminar: A Journal of Germanic Studies*, vol. 56, no. 2, Apr. 2020, pp. 92–108. https://doi.org/10.3138/seminar.56.2.1.

Robertson, Ritchie. "The Complexities of Caroline Pichler: Conflicting Role Models, Patriotic Commitment, and *The Swedes in Prague* (1827)." *Women in*

German Yearbook, vol. 23, 2007, pp. 34–48. https://doi.org/10.1353/wgy.2008.0004.

Roe, Ian F. *Franz Grillparzer: A Century of Criticism*. Camden House, 1995.

Rub, Otto. *Das Burgtheater: Statistischer Rückblick auf die Tätigkeit und die Personalverhältnisse während der Zeit vom 8. April 1776 bis 1. Januar 1913*. Paul Knepler, 1913.

Sachsen, Amalie von. "Der Majoratserbe: Lustspiel." *Original-Beiträge zur deutschen Schaubühne*, vol. 4, Arnoldische Buchhandlung, 1839, pp. 1–140.

Sand, George. *Fadette*. Translated by Jane Minot Sedgwick, Little Brown, 1895.

– *Die Grille oder die kleine Fadette*. Translated by August Schrader, Schrag, 1863.

– *Die kleine Fadette*. Translated by G.F.W. Rödiger, Hartleben's Verlags-Expedition, 1849.

– *La petite Fadette*. Translated and with an introduction by Gretchen van Slyke, Pennsylvania State UP, 2017.

Sangmeister, Dirk, and Martin Mulsow, editors. *Subversive Literatur: Erfurter Autoren und Verlage im Zeitaler der Französischen Revolution (1780–1806)*. Wallstein, 2014.

Schachinger, Rudolf, editor. *Briefwechsel zwischen Michael Enk von der Burg und Eligius Freih. von Münch-Bellinghausen (Friedrich Halm)*. In Commission bei Alfred Hölder, 1890.

Schiller, Friedrich. "Was kann eine gute stehende Schaubühne eigentlich wirken." *Sämtliche Werke in 5 Bänden*. Edited by Wolfgang Riedel, vol. 5, Deutscher Taschenbuch Verlag, 2004, pp. 818–31.

Schmid, Hermann von. *Der Tatzelwurm oder Das Glöckl' vom Birkenstein*. Hoffmann, 1873.

Schmidt, Thomas. *Die Regeln des Spiels: Programm und Spielplan-Gestaltung im Theater*. Springer, 2019.

Schreyvogel, Joseph. *Tagebücher, 1810–1823*. Edited by Karl Glossy, vol. 2, Gesellschaft für Theatergeschichte, 1903.

Scribe, Eugène, and Edouard Joseph Mazères. *Vatel, ou, Le petit fils d'un grand homme*. J.-B. Dupon, 1827.

Shakespeare, William. *The History of King Lear*. Edited by Stanley Wells and Gary Taylor, Oxford UP, 2001.

– *König Lear: Trauerspiel in fünf Aufzügen*. Translated by C.A. West [=Joseph Schreyvogel], J.B. Wallishausser, 1841.

Siemann, Wolfram. *Metternich: Strategist and Visionary*. Translated by Daniel Steuer, Harvard UP, 2019.

Skrine, Peter. "Friedrich Halm and the Comic Muse." *The Austrian Comic Tradition: Studies in Honor of W.E. Yates*, edited by John R.P. McKenzie et al., Edinburgh UP, 1998, pp. 145–59.

Stauss, Annemarie. *Schauspiel und Nationale Frage: Kostümstil und Aufführungspraxis im Burgtheater der Schreyvogel- und Laubezeit*. Narr Francke Attempto, 2011.

Stein, Peter. "Vormärz." Beutin et al., *Deutsche Literaturgeschichte*, pp. 241–94.

Steiner, Carl. "Eduard von Bauernfeld." *Major Figures of Nineteenth-Century Austrian Literature*, edited by Donald G. Daviau, Ariadne Press, 1998, pp. 160–86.

Stifter, Adalbert. *Studien*. Gustav Heckenast, 1867.

– *Der Nachsommer: Eine Erzählung*. Edited by Benedikt Jeßing, Philipp Reclam, 2005.

"Sudermanns neueste Dramen." *Die Grenzboten*, vol. 55, 1896, pp. 35–44.

Szondi, Peter. *Versuch über das Tragische*. Insel Verlag, 1961.

Taillandier, Saint-René. "La Poésie dramatique à Vienne." *Revue des deux Mondes*, vol. 16, Oct. 1846, pp. 170–86.

Theater und Musik in Weimar 1754–1990. Hochschule für Musik Franz Liszt Weimar / Friedrich-Schiller-Universität Jena / Thüringer Universitäts- und Landesbibliothek Jena / Landesarchiv Thüringen – Hauptstaatsarchiv Weimar / Deutsches Nationaltheater Weimar / Herzogin Anna Amalia Bibliothek Weimar, 2009–14, 2017–21, https://theaterzettel-weimar.de.

"Theaterzettel der beiden k.k. Hoftheater und des k.k. priv. Theaters an der Wien und ihrer Nachfolgerinstitutionen (tit. fic.)." Wallishausser, 1787–1898. *ANNO: Historische österreichische Zeitungen und Zeitschriften*, Austrian National Library, https://anno.onb.ac.at/info/wtz_info.htm.

"Theaterzettel der beiden k.k. Hoftheater und des k.k. priv. Theaters an der Wien und ihrer Nachfolgerinstitutionen (tit. fict.), 1. September 1851." *ANNO: Historische österreichische Zeitungen und Zeitschriften*, Austrian National Library, https://anno.onb.ac.at/cgi-content/anno?aid=wtz&datum=18510901&zoom=33.

Thurnberg, Marie von. *Gedanken einer Frau über die angeborenen Rechte des Frauengeschlechtes*. Verlag der Universitätsbuchhandlung von Anton Doll's Enkel, 1846.

Thurner, Christina. "Verlorene Paradiese? Theater-Autorinnen und ihre Dramen." *Forum Modernes Theater*, vol. 25, no. 2, 2010, pp. 17–25. *Project MUSE*, https://doi.org/10.1353/fmt.2010.0014.

Twellmann, Margrit. *Die deutsche Frauenbewegung: Ihre Anfänge und erste Entwicklung 1843–1889*. Anton Hain, 1972.

van Slyke, Gretchen. Introduction. *La Petite Fadette*. Translated by Gretchen van Slyke, Pennsylvania State UP, 2017, pp. 1–31.

Wagner, Martin. "Ad fontes? Eligius von Münch-Bellinghausen und die Kritik der Quellenforschung in der zweiten Hälfte des neunzehnten Jahrhunderts." *Germanistische Mitteilungen*, vol. 45, nos. 1–2, 2019, pp. 73–88.

– "Defoe, Foucault, and the Politics of the Plague." *Studies in English Literature 1500–1900*, vol. 57, no. 3, summer 2017, pp. 501–19. *Project MUSE*, https://doi.org/10.1353/sel.2017.0021.

– "Navigating and Owning Obedience: Reassessing Friedrich Halm's *Griseldis*." *German Studies Review*, vol. 43, no. 2, May 2020, pp. 233–49. *Project MUSE*, https://doi.org/10.1353/gsr.2020.0042.

– "Zur Gehorsamskritik im Burgtheater des Vormärz: Friedrich Halm, Eduard von Bauernfeld und der österreichische Liberalismus um 1848." *German Quarterly*, vol. 93, no. 3, summer 2020, pp. 343–58. *Wiley Online Library*, https://doi.org/10.1111/gequ.12144.

Wagner, Martin, and Elystan Griffiths. "The Drama of Obedience: Introduction." *The Drama of Obedience*, special issue of *Oxford German Studies*, edited by Martin Wagner and Elystan Griffiths, vol. 50, no. 3, 2021, pp. 269–84. *Taylor & Francis Online*, https://doi.org/10.1080/00787191.2021.1958567.

Wagner, Martin, and Richard Slipp. "Wer war Friedrich Halm? Zum Pseudonym von Eligius von Münch-Bellinghausen." *Zeitschrift für deutsche Philologie*, vol. 139, no. 2, 2020, pp. 339–46. *ESV [Erich Schmidt Verlag]*, https://doi.org/10.37307/j.1868-7806.2020.02.11.

Wagner, Richard. *Die Kunst und die Revolution*. Otto Wigand, 1850.

Watt, Ian. *The Rise of the Novel: Studies in Defoe, Richardson, and Fielding*. With a new afterword by W.B. Carnochan, U of California P, 2001.

Weiershausen, Romana. *Zeitenwandel als Familiendrama: Genre und Politik im deutschsprachigen Theater des 18. Jahrhunderts*. Aisthesis, 2018.

Wellek, René. "Bakhtin's View of Dostoevsky: 'Polyphony' and 'Carnivalesque.'" *Dostoevsky Studies*, vol. 1, 1980, pp. 31–9.

"Wiener Wochenbericht. Burgtheater." *Recensionen und Mittheilungen über Theater und Musik*, vol. 7, no. 14, 7 Apr. 1861, p. 220.

"Wiens poetische Federn und Schwingen." *Die Grenzboten*, vol. 5, no. 4, 1846, pp. 177–90.

Williams, Simon. "Shakespeare at the Burgtheater: From Heinrich Anschütz to Josef Kainz." *Shakespeare Survey*, vol. 35, 1982, pp. 21–30. *Cambridge Core*, https://doi.org/10.1017/CCOL0521247527.003.

– *Shakespeare on the German Stage*. Cambridge UP, 1990.

Wlassack, Eduard. *Chronik des k.k. Hofburgtheaters: Zu dessen Säkular-Feier im Februar 1876*. L. Rosner, 1876.

Wozonig, Karin S. "Freundschaft und Politik in bewegten Zeiten: Betty Paoli und Adalbert Stifter." *Journal of Austrian Studies*, vol. 52, no. 3, fall 2019, pp. 1–18. *Project MUSE*, https://doi.org/10.1353/oas.2019.0037.

– "Moral, Leidenschaft und Brotberuf: Betty Paoli und die Wandlungen der Frauenfrage." *Ariadne: Forum für Frauen- und Geschlechtergeschichte*, vol. 65, May 2014, pp. 8–15.

Yates, W.E. "Dialect Satire and High Culture: Nestroy on Science and Scholarship." *Austrian Studies*, vol. 15, 2007, pp. 41–52. *JSTOR*, https://www.jstor.org/stable/27944841.

– *Theatre in Vienna: A Critical History, 1776–1995*. Cambridge UP, 1996.

Zangl, Veronika. "Austria's Post-89: Staging Suppressed Memory in Elfriede Jelinek's and Thomas Bernhard's Plays *Burgtheater* and *Heldenplatz.*" *European Studies*, vol. 30, 2013, pp. 271–99.

Zanucchi, Mario. "Stoische Philosophin – christliche Dulderin – brave Gattin. Die europäischen Metamorphosen von Boccaccios Griselda." *700 Jahre Boccaccio: Traditionslinien vom Trecento bis in die Moderne*, edited by Christa Bertelsmeier-Kierst and Rainer Stillers, Peter Lang, 2015, pp. 193–220.

Zhongwen, Qian. "Problems of Bakhtin's Theory about 'Polyphony.'" *New Literary History*, vol. 28, no. 4, autumn 1997, pp. 779–90. *Project MUSE*, https://doi.org/10.1353/nlh.1997.0059.

Index

GERMAN AND EUROPEAN STUDIES

General Editor: Jennifer L. Jenkins

1 Emanuel Adler, Beverly Crawford, Federica Bicchi, and Rafaella Del Sarto, *The Convergence of Civilizations: Constructing a Mediterranean Region*
2 James Retallack, *The German Right, 1860–1920: Political Limits of the Authoritarian Imagination*
3 Silvija Jestrovic, *Theatre of Estrangement: Theory, Practice, Ideology*
4 Susan Gross Solomon, ed., *Doing Medicine Together: Germany and Russia between the Wars*
5 Laurence McFalls, ed., *Max Weber's 'Objectivity' Revisited*
6 Robin Ostow, ed., *(Re)Visualizing National History: Museums and National Identities in Europe in the New Millennium*
7 David Blackbourn and James Retallack, eds., *Localism, Landscape, and the Ambiguities of Place: German-Speaking Central Europe, 1860–1930*
8 John Zilcosky, ed., *Writing Travel: The Poetics and Politics of the Modern Journey*
9 Angelica Fenner, *Race under Reconstruction in German Cinema: Robert Stemmle's* Toxi
10 Martina Kessel and Patrick Merziger, eds., *The Politics of Humour: Laughter, Inclusion, and Exclusion in the Twentieth Century*
11 Jeffrey K. Wilson, *The German Forest: Nature, Identity, and the Contestation of a National Symbol, 1871–1914*
12 David G. John, *Bennewitz, Goethe,* Faust: *German and Intercultural Stagings*
13 Jennifer Ruth Hosek, *Sun, Sex, and Socialism: Cuba in the German Imaginary*
14 Steven M. Schroeder, *To Forget It All and Begin Again: Reconciliation in Occupied Germany, 1944–1954*
15 Kenneth S. Calhoon, *Affecting Grace: Theatre, Subject, and the Shakespearean Paradox in German Literature from Lessing to Kleist*
16 Martina Kolb, *Nietzsche, Freud, Benn, and the Azure Spell of Liguria*
17 Hoi-eun Kim, *Doctors of Empire: Medical and Cultural Encounters between Imperial Germany and Meiji Japan*
18 J. Laurence Hare, *Excavating Nations: Archeology, Museums, and the German-Danish Borderlands*
19 Jacques Kornberg, *The Pope's Dilemma: Pius XII Faces Atrocities and Genocide in the Second World War*
20 Patrick O'Neill, *Transforming Kafka: Translation Effects*
21 John K. Noyes, *Herder: Aesthetics against Imperialism*

22 James Retallack, *Germany's Second Reich: Portraits and Pathways*
23 Laurie Marhoefer, *Sex and the Weimar Republic: German Homosexual Emancipation and the Rise of the Nazis*
24 Bettina Brandt and Daniel L. Purdy, eds., *China in the German Enlightenment*
25 Michael Hau, *Performance Anxiety: Sport and Work in Germany from the Empire to Nazism*
26 Celia Applegate, *The Necessity of Music: Variations on a German Theme*
27 Richard J. Golsan and Sarah M. Misemer, eds., *The Trial That Never Ends: Hannah Arendt's* Eichmann in Jerusalem *in Retrospect*
28 Lynne Taylor, *In the Children's Best Interests: Unaccompanied Children in American-Occupied Germany, 1945–1952*
29 Jennifer A. Miller, *Turkish Guest Workers in Germany: Hidden Lives and Contested Borders, 1960s to 1980s*
30 Amy Carney, *Marriage and Fatherhood in the Nazi SS*
31 Michael E. O'Sullivan, *Disruptive Power: Catholic Women, Miracles, and Politics in Modern Germany, 1918–1965*
32 Gabriel N. Finder and Alexander V. Prusin, *Justice behind the Iron Curtain: Nazis on Trial in Communist Poland*
33 Parker Daly Everett, *Urban Transformations: From Liberalism to Corporatism in Greater Berlin, 1871–1933*
34 Melissa Kravetz, *Women Doctors in Weimar and Nazi Germany: Maternalism, Eugenics, and Professional Identity*
35 Javier Samper Vendrell, *The Seduction of Youth: Print Culture and Homosexual Rights in the Weimar Republic*
36 Sebastian Voigt, ed., *Since the Boom: Continuity and Change in the Western Industrialized World after 1970*
37 Olivia Landry, *Theatre of Anger: Radical Transnational Performance in Contemporary Berlin*
38 Jeremy Best, *Heavenly Fatherland: German Missionary Culture and Globalization in the Age of Empire*
39 Svenja Bethke, *Dance on the Razor's Edge: Crime and Punishment in the Nazi Ghettos*
40 Kenneth S. Calhoon, *The Long Century's Long Shadow: Weimar Cinema and the Romantic Modern*
41 Randall Hansen, Achim Saupe, Andreas Wirsching, and Daqing Yang, eds., *Authenticity and Victimhood after the Second World War: Narratives from Europe and East Asia*
42 Rebecca Wittmann, ed., *The Eichmann Trial Reconsidered*
43 Sebastian Huebel, *Fighter, Worker, and Family Man: German-Jewish Men and Their Gendered Experiences in Nazi Germany, 1933–1941*

44 Samuel Clowes Huneke, *States of Liberation: Gay Men between Dictatorship and Democracy in Cold War Germany*
45 Tuska Benes, *The Rebirth of Revelation: German Theology in an Age of Reason and History, 1750–1850*
46 Skye Doney, *The Persistence of the Sacred: German Catholic Pilgrimage, 1832–1937*
47 Matthew Unangst, *Colonial Geography: Race and Space in German East Africa, 1884–1905*
48 Deborah Barton, *Writing and Rewriting the Reich: Women Journalists in the Nazi and Post-War Press*
49 Martin Wagner, *A Stage for Debate: The Political Significance of Vienna's Burgtheater, 1814–1867*

www.ingramcontent.com/pod-product-compliance
Lightning Source LLC
LaVergne TN
LVHW041113090826
844660LV00061B/857/J

* 9 7 8 1 4 8 7 5 0 9 5 5 2 *